CORPOR
EMOTIONAL
INTELLIGENCE

'But you were always a good man of business, Jacob,' faltered Scrooge. 'Business?!' cried the Ghost, wringing its hands again. 'Mankind was my business. The common welfare was my business; charity, mercy, forbearance, and benevolence were all my business. The dealings of my trade were but a drop of water in the comprehensive ocean of my business!'

Charles Dickens, *A Christmas Carol*

This book is dedicated to my children Stephanie, Thomas, Duncan and Leonie. You are my joy, my inspiration and my purpose. I observe you living your lives with courage and love, but most of all with an integrity that humbles me. I love you.

Providing feedback on this book

If you post a review of this book on Amazon, Books Etc or Wordery, we will send you the digital version of the book for free.

Email a link to your review to us at admin@criticalpublishing.com, and we'll reply with a PDF of the book, which you can read on your phone, tablet or Kindle.

You can also connect with us on:
Twitter @CriticalPub #criticalpublishing
Facebook www.facebook.com/Critical-Publishing-456875584333404
Our blog https://thecriticalblog.wordpress.com

CORPORATE EMOTIONAL INTELLIGENCE

Being Human in a Corporate World

GARETH CHICK

First published in 2018 by Critical Publishing Ltd

British Library Cataloguing in Publication Data
A CIP record for this book is available from the British Library

ISBN: 978-1-912508-04-4
This book is also available in the following e-book formats:
MOBI ISBN: 978-1-912508-05-1
EPUB ISBN: 978-1-912508-06-8
Adobe e-book ISBN: 978-1-912508-07-5

Cover design by Out of House Limited
Text design by Out of House Limited
Project Management by Westchester Publishing Services
Printed and bound in Great Britain by Bell & Bain

Critical Publishing
3 Connaught Road
St Albans AL3 5RX

www.criticalpublishing.com

CONTENTS

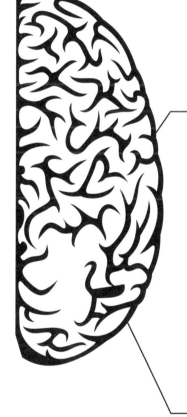

Praise for *Corporate Emotional Intelligence*

Disturbing. Exciting. Am I a Corporapath? Am I suffering from Corporate Traumatic Stress Disorder (CTSD)? Am I infecting others? . . . my family? How can I be the human leader I want to be in a corporate world? This book is ground-breaking, with profound implications for leaders, corporates and society.

Ross Baker, Chief Commercial Office, Heathrow

"Over the last ten years of knowing Gareth, building a relationship with him and now being able to call him a friend, he has been instrumental in my career and his coaching has touched me and everyone around me for the better. Follow Gareth's advice and read his book cover to cover. His teachings will challenge your thoughts and your own behaviours, enabling each of us to bring the real "human" to the corporate world."

Alastair Brass, Customer Services Director (Energy), Centrica Plc

Hugely entertaining and provocative - with a powerful mission at its heart. Helping us to be happy, calm and productive in a Corporate world of complexity and accelerating change. When the stresses of the workplace literally change how we're wired, we have to understand what's going on in our minds and in our hearts to make the best of the world of work.

Matt Brittin, President, Google EMEA

CEQ is a book about life, humanity and truth. Although I often found myself not wanting to agree with its provocative thoughts, I eventually did. Gareth holds up a mirror to the modern day Corporate as well as to us as individuals; the truth is sometimes shocking but in exposing it, there is hope that we can change.

Simon Charles, Group HR Director, Succession Group Ltd and NED, Pluss CIC Ltd

This is a defining book from one of the world's most influential, sincere and impactful leaders. With absolute clarity, Gareth brings to life the complex connections between corporate structures, organisational culture and leadership behaviours. He inspires us to lead with humility, honesty and integrity; not tomorrow - today.

David Frost, Organisational Development Director, Total Produce Plc

I didn't like Gareth the very first time I met him. He made me uncomfortable. He showed up my coaching skills for what they were - Average. On reflection his feedback was blunt, but it was very specific and to the point. It had the impact of teaching me more in that moment than I had learned in years. However, it took me two more meetings with Gareth to realise it. From that point on, I sought out extra coaching with Gareth and came to really depend on him as a coach, a confidant and eventually a friend. For those of you who have not had the opportunity to work directly with Gareth, this book is a great opportunity to learn from him. I don't remember Gareth ever answering a single question of mine with a direct answer, but he gave me the courage and the skills to answer them myself. My coaching, my active listening and my understanding of the 'power of an open question' grew exponentially. This book reminds me of many of those interactions and has become my reference on leadership and coaching.

David Geraghty, Director of Community Operations, Facebook

Gareth's debut is fresh, innovative and thought-provoking; just like every coaching conversation we shared. Take the CTSD test and your first steps on a new path of self-awareness. Shared success is sustainable success, a not-so-secret ingredient for a happier and more balanced life.

Mick Hodgins, Managing Director, Google Marketing Platform

This is an important book. As corporate leaders we witness, every day, ways in which our humanity and moral compass are challenged by the corporate environments in which we work; how pressure from all sides seeps into our consciousness and creates environments in which inhumanity and mental health issues can find space to fester. In this book, while pulling no punches on our responsibility as leaders for the disease, Gareth holds up a mirror to the corporate world. More importantly, this is an optimistic book, and one which does more than just highlight the problem - it also sets out real and practical solutions which are (for the most part) not reliant on a quixotic belief in a change in fundamental human motivations. It has been my great privilege to work with Gareth through both good and challenging times, and I know that the advice that he offers makes leaders perform better, more humanely and - perhaps most importantly - to enjoy the journey.

Seb James, President and Managing Director Boots UK and Ireland and Senior Vice President Walgreens Boots Alliance

I wrestle daily with the twin demands of running an international company, and the people within it, to drive change in the way other companies do business. To unleash new and previously unforeseen ethical dimensions to what companies do. What lies at the heart of it all is deciphering how to enable people to get the best out of themselves. This is not so much about being smart as tapping into our emotional selves. This book is both psychological analysis and route-map for how to bring out the best in both teams and individuals. It is a book of extraordinary insight from someone with remarkable experience. Reading it might just help you change the way business does business forever.

Philip Lymbery, CEO of Compassion in World Farming and Visiting Professor, University of Winchester

Having known and worked with Gareth over 20 years, if this challenging and thought provoking book has the same impact for a wider audience as his counsel and influence has in person, then the business world will be a more human but also a much more effective place

Kevin O'Byrne, Chief Financial Officer, J Sainsbury Plc

Refreshing to read a book that doesn't preach to you or ask you to make impossible change happen. What it did for me is challenge me on why I allow certain behaviours to exist in the business areas I lead and within the peers I work with.

Jon Shaw, Head of UK Consumer Sales Channels, Vodafone

MEET THE AUTHOR

Gareth Chick is a 40 year corporate veteran with a global profile. His career has included hugely successful spells as CFO, CEO and Chairman in both public and private sectors, including private equity. What makes Gareth's experience unique is that he combined those executive roles with a part time career as a leadership trainer, researching psychology, neuroscience and psychotherapy to create leadership development programmes used now by many major global corporations. In the last 15 years Gareth has trained over 5000 managers and served as Executive Coach to over 200 senior execs including FTSE100 CEOs and Fortune 500 VPs. As Founder of Collaborative Equity LLP, "promoting corporate cultures and sustainable business models of shared ownership, shared responsibility and shared rewards", Gareth acts as consultant to many global leaders, specialising in first time CEOs and Start Up founders.

Gareth lives with his wife Rachel in a small Warwickshire village close to Stratford-upon-Avon in the UK - their 4 children are following their own paths in journalism, addiction therapy, teaching and acting. Though you would not know it to look at him, Gareth is a proud holder of a marathon running world record - he is the oldest person ever to complete a marathon wearing a full 28lb Rhino Suit!

FOREWORD

Welcome to the age of anxiety.

The level of chaos and complexity in our external world is now matched with the same level of confusion in our work cultures. They are in total alignment and that is not good.

In my own work, I discovered how the surviving and conforming nature of our work cultures creates an unending personal cycle of struggle-and-strive. What is absent is the kind of thriving experiences that enable the creativity, purpose and meaning that we all seek in our work lives.

So, imagine three levels of culture in organizations. The first level I call SURVIVAL. It doesn't take much to put us humans into survival mode. An uncaring boss, a slight downturn in sales, or maybe a few seasonal layoffs can trigger those deep survival instincts that simply won't be repressed. We shift to defensive mode – playing the smaller game that fear incites.

The second level of culture is the CONFORMING level. We simply don't like change – and we are not very good at managing it. Five per cent is the oft-quoted success rate of 'change initiatives' within organizations. Not good.

We prefer the safety of continuous improvement and incremental strategies that can be fully teased out. We measure our success in relation to others in our industry – conforming to unwritten rules that will surely be rendered obsolete by an opportunistic outsider. At the personal level, we also learn that even a small failure can derail a career.

The third level of culture is THRIVING. It is at this third level that we are confident, growing and sustaining our gains. Setbacks only deepen our resilience. Like a championship athletic team, we become fully integrated into the culture, giving ourselves fully to the missions and tasks at hand. Feelings of pride, accomplishment, and commitment begin to define our nature.

Unfortunately, even the best of companies get stuck in the first two levels of surviving and conforming – with too few moments of thriving. Corporate life can feel like a prison sentence – 30 years of struggling and striving – with a depleted human spirit as one of the primary outcomes.

With insight and eloquence, Gareth Chick fully reveals and unravels this conundrum in his new book, *Corporate Emotional Intelligence*. Deep down he is a truth teller – a modern day prophet who is willing to say what needs to be said. Gareth is also a passionate protagonist – promoting the necessary accountability from the corporate leaders we have entrusted to enrich our collective lives (not just their individual stakes).

Gareth's diagnosis is so deep and troubling that it takes us to the edge of despair – before illuminating the potential pathway to redeeming our lives within corporations. He takes us below the surface to our unconscious world where we have limited access to reshaping our limiting behaviours. While culture improvement programmes abound, they will have little chance against a behaviour rooted in survival.

In the same way that Daniel Goleman's work on emotional intelligence (EQ) dramatically shifted our view on how non-cognitive skills matter as much as IQ, Gareth's CEQ will inspire a new wave of thinking. His unique concern for the dehumanizing environment created by corporatism calls for a specialized approach that is embodied in his four pillars. As Gareth notes, IQ plus EQ is no longer sufficient. CEQ is the critical third leg of the stool.

The CEQ approach creates a new vision for corporate life, one that Gareth argues can be genuinely moral, healthy, sustaining, nurturing and collaborative. Prepare to be humbled by the size of the challenge and to be inspired by the potential of a new way forward. I will see you on the journey!

Onward,
Michael W. Morrison, PhD
Founder and Dean, University of Toyota

ACKNOWLEDGEMENTS

So many amazing people have inspired, guided and helped me as I've navigated my intense relationship with the Corporate World this last 40 years. I must give pride of place to four crucial influencers and mentors who've 'adopted' me along the way.

I owe a great debt to my first corporate boss Keith Potts, who in 1979 gave me my first management role at 22, and took a risk on making me a Plc subsidiary CFO when I was 25. Not only did he believe in me enough to give me huge responsibilities, but he backed me when my arrogance and inexperience got the better of me. That early arrogance was thankfully knocked out of me by Walter Blackburn, my Instructor on my very first leadership development programme in 1986. It was Walter who really taught me to coach, and who then inspired me to train to lead that same programme – a critically important moment in the shaping of my whole corporate career.

In the early days of my first CEO role in 1990 I met Tony Barnes, a former member of the Deming team that went to Japan after World War II, and a board member of Sony. To my amazement Tony took a great personal interest in me, and his passion and expertise in empowerment was hugely inspirational. It is one of the great honours of my life that Tony is writing the Foreword for *And the Leader is . . .*' my second book coming out in early 2019.

And my fourth mentor has honoured me by writing the Foreword for this book. In 2004, having been appointed Lexus Europe's Culture Consultant, I went to Los Angeles as part of my research. There I met Mike Morrison, Founder and Dean of the University of Toyota, and I immediately knew I was in the presence of a profoundly gifted leader. Mike has provided his quiet wisdom with grace and utter unconditionality and has become a true friend. His support and advice through my writing of this book has been invaluable.

Turning for a moment to books, one of the reasons I started writing one myself was because every time I was asked to recommend a book on leadership or coaching or cultural change, I struggled to get beyond one single book – *Maverick* by Ricardo Semler. I discovered this book in 1995, and it was the final piece of the jigsaw for me as I developed my craft as a CEO. It gave me the confidence and the excitement to push my leadership strategies and practices further than I had ever dared before. For me, *Maverick* is the seminal work on employee engagement and I have given hundreds of copies away over the years.

Returning now to people, I have been truly blessed over the years to work with some amazing clients – clients who have trusted me and given me wonderful opportunities, with whom I've shared a co-creation of culture development in the organisations they lead, and from whom I have learned so much. Of the literally thousands of leaders and managers I've personally coached, trained and advised, I must give a special mention and heartfelt thanks to the following: Kevin O'Byrne, Carole Stewart, Sebastian James, David Frost, Ali Gibson, Peter Eglinton, Becky Ivers, Philip Gilsenan, Claire Hatton, Martyn Haworth, Fionnuala Meehan, Gareth Morgan, Dave Geraghty, Mick Hodgins, Eileen Naughton, Matt Brittin, Marian Green, Peter Friis, Colm O'Sullivan, Ronan Harris, John Burness and

Jen Kelly. They all have my admiration as leaders of integrity, and my thanks for their patronage and their willingness to refer other leaders to me.

Eighteen months before this book was published, I sent a detailed synopsis and structural outline of the book to a number of my most trusted clients. I must give special thanks to the following clients who honoured me by taking time and great care to read those early drafts and who respected me enough to be blunt and ruthlessly honest with their feedback: Sebastian James, Matt Brittin, Peter Friis, Mick Hodgins, Jeannie Fay Snow, Andrew Smith, Becky Ivers, Peter Eglinton, David Frost, Val King, Jonathan Tole, Clare Mathias, Simon Charles, Martyn Haworth, Giles Goodhead, Stephen Archer, John Kiff, Claire Hatton, Chris Mathias, Gina Nicholson, Hazel Marsh, Frank Kohl Boas, Dave Geraghty, Bob Bradley, Sandra McDevitt, Melanie Katzman, Ronan Harris, Roi Sagi, David Grayson, Helen Tynan, Jon Shaw and Alastair Brass. Thank you all.

I'd like to say a huge and special thank you to Di Page, Director of Critical Publishing, for believing in me and in the content of the book, and for all her practical help and guidance through the final stages of writing, editing, referencing, production and marketing. I feel very lucky to have met Di, and to have been the recipient of her consistently positive support and encouragement.

Finally, believing always in leaving the best til last, I must thank my wife Rachel not just for her love, support and patience in our incredible marriage, but for her profound professional influence and teachings this last 16 years. Rachel's wisdom, passion, clarity and integrity have been the synthesising factors that have enabled me to bring my 40-year experience of the Corporate World to a coherent conclusion.

Introduction

Waking up in a Corporapathic World

'You will be haunted by three Spirits, Scrooge. Expect the first tomorrow, when the bell tolls one.' 'Couldn't I take 'em all at once, and have it over, Jacob?' hinted Scrooge.

Charles Dickens, *A Christmas Carol*

Thesis

Human behaviour is peculiarly conditioned by working in a Corporate environment, with well-meaning people behaving in unnatural and often inhuman ways, driven by fear. Yet none of them would say they were afraid.

There have been countless studies of the Corporate world from the business point of view. There have been almost as many studies of the Corporate world from a psychological point of view. As far as I am aware, no one has ever cogently combined the two. Until now. *Corporate Emotional Intelligence* is fundamentally a psychological analysis, but from a business perspective. The solutions to the many issues arising from corporate cultures are practical business solutions, but motivated, designed and implemented by existing corporate citizens.

In my 40-year corporate career, as CFO, COO, CEO, Chairman, Coach, and Consultant, in over 30 countries and on every continent, I've observed the universal dynamic of thoroughly decent people developing controlling habits when given responsibility for others. Me included! Show me a manager working in a Corporate environment, and I'll show you a Manager with unconscious controlling habits. More than that, I'll show you a Manager who seems in denial that it is *their* own behaviour that is creating the massive collective shortfall in human potential, in turn creating either mediocre or unsustainable results, or both. The ensuing frustration, irritation, impatience and anxiety simply fuel the downward spiral. The harder Managers try to exert control, the worse they make things. And yet they seem bereft of any real alternative – certainly any alternative they feel confident in implementing.

It is the very nature of Corporatism, with its deliberate separation of ownership and responsibility, that creates this peculiar dynamic. The unrelenting pressure and weight of expectation felt by Corporate leaders to produce exceptional, often unreasonable results, has created two psychological conditions unique to the Corporate world – leaders who have become 'Corporapathic' and vast numbers of leaders, managers and employees suffering from CTSD – Corporate Traumatic Stress Disorder.

The outcome of all of this is a predominance of businesses that are inefficient, unsustainable and causing damage to people and environments. Recent years have seen a sad and worrying growth in corporate scandals and human and environmental disasters caused by Corporations, and we now seem powerless to check the worst excesses. While

Corporatism may be profoundly under pressure, somewhat bizarrely it remains the aspirational format and structure for organisations to adopt.

I could probably be describing just about any juncture in the 400-year history of Corporatism. Is it really worse now than ever before? I would argue that it is, but my deep worry today is that it's about to get a lot worse very fast, and that we will very shortly hit a point of no return. Artificial Intelligence, autonomous systems, machine learning, drones, bots etc are coming at us fast. Is Corporatism really the best form of organisation to be trusted with harnessing these technologies for the good of humankind?

But even if we wanted to change, what the hell can we do about it? Our track record in regulating Corporatism frankly sucks, as the global network of lawyers, accountants and bankers work their magic in circumventing any rule or law we can dream up. And surely the status quo is so well entrenched, so well protected as to be impervious to any attempt to restrict its reach or its power.

The good news is that we do not need a revolution or a coup. There are many organisations that are really successful at being ethical *and* at producing strong financial performance. So how do they do it? If Corporate leaders, even the Corporapathic ones, were convinced of the economic argument, they'd adopt genuinely ethical methods and strategies in a heartbeat – and be proud to do so.

So what's the difference between the organisations that can be ethical or profitable, but struggle to do both, and those who are consistently ethical and profitable? What do the ethically and financially successful organisations do that the others do not, and what do they *not* do?

In short, these successful organisations have a high collective CEQ – Corporate Emotional Intelligence. Succeeding in a corporate organisation in the twenty-first century will require a different kind of human intelligence. IQ + EQ is no longer sufficient. Leaders and managers need highly developed CEQ, which is the ability to read, understand and then manage the psychological states and behaviours that are unique to corporate cultures.

And these successful organisations have a 'Collaborative Equity' form of Corporatism in their organisational design, their operating model and their culture, with a genuine state of shared ownership, shared responsibility and shared rewards.

So through an understanding of CEQ, and the adoption of Collaborative Equity Corporatism, leaders and managers can achieve the ultimate Corporate dream of exceptional and sustainable financial performance and of genuine enhancements to people's lives and environments. And together we'll save humankind from disaster.

So here it is: an analysis of precisely what is wrong with The Corporation, and what we should do about it; of why it is that working in a Corporation causes thoroughly decent people to behave in unnatural and inhuman ways, and what we should do about it.

Before it's too late.

Who the hell am I to tell you to Change?

I am grateful to the Corporate World for having given me a privileged life. For 40 years now, this world has given me meaning, purpose and challenge, material comfort and security. We've had our moments of course, but all in all I've done very nicely from the Corporate world. I am extraordinarily fortunate. I am one of the one per cent.

So it would be churlish of me to attack Corporatism, to seek to overthrow it, or to attempt to equip others so to do. But it would also be a total abdication of responsibility on my part – a sad waste of experience – were I to leave the Corporate World without communicating what I believe and what I know. I offer this synthesis of my experience as my humble exhortation to change Corporatism for the better.

And while I sincerely hope that politicians, regulators, commentators and academics will find this book interesting and informative, it is not written for them. It is written for my fellow Corporate Citizens. Those legions of thoroughly decent and honourable people who frequently find themselves unsettled, managing states of stress, anxiety, frustration and dissatisfaction; inherently moral people who on all too frequent occasions find themselves acting in ways that cause them to feel guilt or shame; normal people who when they allow themselves to really consider what they are about, stepping out of their understandable denial, have to confront the realisation that their daily strain is in service of objectives that will not in any meaningful way enhance humankind, and may even be contributing to its destruction.

This book is for me and it is for you, for we are the same person. It is you and I (actually in fairness it's mostly you . . . I'm 60 for God's sake!) who must reclaim control of our Corporate World, to first save us from destruction, and to then deliver true growth, sustainability and fulfilment for all our futures.

But why should you listen to me? After all, I could be open to the accusation of having been duped; of being no more than a naive and rather pathetic enabler and servant of the tyrant that is Corporatism. But I have earned some right to be listened to since my experience has covered every aspect of Corporatism, involving many thousands of players across the world.

I was CFO of a US company at 24, a UK Plc Subsidiary CFO at 25 and Commercial Director of a Japanese company at 28. I was an Operations Director at 30, and an MD for the first time at 32. As a four-times CEO, I produced average earnings per share growth of 24 per cent over 12 years. As a five-times Chairman, including Private Equity, I exceeded the demanding expectations of all the Investors I worked on behalf of. I have managed over 20,000 people. I have coached over 200 senior executives. I have personally trained over 5000 managers. I've been there, done it, and got more T-shirts than I have cupboard space for.

Through all my experience, I've developed a profound understanding and appreciation of human behaviour within corporations. I've spent 40 years studying this subject from every angle – I've been an Employee on the receiving end; a Supervisor/Manager trying my best to be the 'gasket' between the Board and the Employees; an Executive starting to have some influence over the way change is planned and executed; a Plc Board Director experiencing the intimidation of an abusive culture; a CEO with full autonomy to implement all my ideas and philosophies; a Chairman guiding Executives to run their companies ethically and effectively; a Trainer teaching Managers how to coach and lead ethically and effectively; a Consultant designing, advising and implementing business improvement strategies; and a Coach mentoring senior executives as they grapple themselves with all of these tough dynamics.

I've had the privilege of working with and witnessing thousands of managers. I've seen the good, the bad and the ugly. Actually, what I've really seen is the Awesome, the Awful and the Abusive. And I freely admit, I've been all of them myself.

I'm now Founder and Managing Partner of Collaborative Equity LLP, 'promoting corporate cultures and sustainable business models of shared ownership, shared responsibility and shared rewards', working internationally with clients such as Google, Heathrow, Vodafone, Dixons Carphone, Linkedin, Dr Martens, Centrica, Marstons, Veolia and Quantcast.

This book, *Corporate Emotional Intelligence,* is my life's work. It's been 15 years in the writing, starting with the manual I wrote to support my two-day Coaching Excellence training programme. Finally, in the last two years I've complemented my business experience, by doing hundreds of hours academic research and study on psychology, psychotherapy and neuroscience.

I hope you find it interesting and informative. Most of all I hope you find it challenging.

Just one thing before you begin. Please resist the temptation to go straight to the end section for the solution. I know you – you go straight to the last slide of a deck, straight to the bottom right hand cell on the last page of the spreadsheet. (Well, it's what I tend to do.)

Please make a personal commitment to read the first eight chapters, before you enter the realm of the solutions I advocate, for the understanding, the inspiration and the courage you will need to implement the solutions will come through a diligent engagement with those Chapters. The solutions are simple, and if you go straight to them you will fool yourself that you are already doing them, or that you've already tried them and failed.

Please.

Section 1
What's the Problem with Corporatism?

'Spirit,' said Scrooge, with an interest he had never felt before 'tell me if Tiny Tim will live.' 'I see a vacant seat,' replied the Ghost, 'in the poor chimney-corner, and a crutch without an owner, carefully preserved.' 'No, no,' said Scrooge. 'Oh, no, kind Spirit. Say he will be spared.' 'If these shadows remain unaltered by the Future, the child will die. What then? If he be like to die, he had better do it, and decrease the surplus population.'

Charles Dickens, *A Christmas Carol*

Chapter 1
What's the Inherent Problem with Corporatism?

Corporatism is Dominant

Roughly two thirds of the world's population spend the vast majority of their waking hours involved in work – doing it, travelling to and from it, thinking about it, worrying about it and organising all other aspects of their lives to accommodate it. And the third of the world's population who do not work are reliant on those who do, and so get caught up in the drama and the madness. The Corporation, a form of organisation where ownership is legally separate from management, and Capitalism's anointed instrument, has become the predominant form of institution providing that work, right across the world.

More than that, The Corporation has arrived in the early part of the twenty-first century as perhaps the most influential institution on the planet. Corporations cross national boundaries, operate on a global scale and control pretty much every aspect of our daily life, and every aspect that will dictate our future survival.

The most obvious examples of The Corporation are the 'listed' company, with shares traded on stock markets, and the legion of limited liability private companies. But even in organisations which are not legally constituted Corporations, 'Corporatism' has been adopted as the paragon of governance models and the same separation of ownership and management is built in.

Look at our social services. Hospitals are now controlled by professional managers (not clinicians); Social housing is now managed by large-scale Corporatised 'Landlords'; basic utilities such as power, public transport and water are now controlled by privatised corporate bodies; Schools and Universities are increasingly corporatised or even privatised.

Charities that once upon a time would collect donations and then distribute whatever funds they had to the causes they were set up to support are now frequently contracted by Government to do public or social service work, and then find themselves more driven by financial targets because their Trustees have a legal duty to ensure that the Charity is sustainable. Winning contracts becomes essential for the future of the charity and the dilemma is created whereby performing the service with due care can become outweighed by the need to lower costs. Hard-pressed staff, starved of the proper resources, are then chastised for speaking up in front of Trustees or Inspectors, accused of disloyalty.

In Social Care, performance targets and payment by results – 'Corporate' practices borrowed from the private sector as a tool designed to raise efficiency and productivity – basically create profit for large organisations, who are the only ones who can risk not getting the bonuses. Small organisations are excluded. In many cases this creates poor care standards since the carers have to be resource restricted, just in case the performance bonuses are not achieved. And if they are achieved, is the 'bonus' cash ploughed back into raising the quality of front-line care?

Firms of lawyers, architects and accountants, once true collectives of fellow professionals owning and managing their own practices in collaboration with each other, have been 'incorporating' like crazy in recent years; even armies around the world now increasingly use soldiers provided by private corporations.

> *We really have come to believe that Corporatism is the finest instrument to run every aspect of our lives.*

We really have come to believe that Corporatism is the finest instrument to run every aspect of our lives.

Legal Separation, Limited Liability and the Abdication of Moral Responsibility

The Corporation (from the Latin 'Corporare' – *to combine in one body*) was invented around 400 years ago, to facilitate the greatest efficiency and scale in the use of resources, and to turbo-charge discovery, exploration and innovation. A Corporation is a separate legal entity – a body with legal status, rights and obligations separate from any human being. This allowed the legal separation of ownership from management and freed 'capitalists' – human beings with large financial resources or access to same – to own more enterprises than they could manage by themselves. With the invention of the Stock Exchange they then had a means of buying and selling their companies, or shares of those companies. This facilitated speculation in shares (gambling to you and me), with the absolute expectation and demand for short-term capital gains becoming dominant, usurping longer term, sustainable and perhaps more 'reasonable' returns from dividends.

As the Capitalists learned how to work this new machine, it became so abused with mass speculation that Parliament actually banned the Corporation in the Bubble Act of 1720, following the debacle of the South Sea Company, and for around 100 years it was illegal to '*create a company presuming to be a Corporate Body*'. But then, in the nineteenth century, the Corporation was reprieved as the Capitalists won back power; and with the additional invention of the Limited Liability Company owners could also now limit their liability for the actions of the management of their businesses. It is this limitation of liability that facilitates the fundamental undermining of personal moral responsibility.

I remember as a first-year student starting the Company Law module of my Finance Degree, being really intrigued by the landmark case of *Salomon v A Salomon* – the case widely recognised as establishing the notion of a 'Corporate Personality'. Mr Salomon was a business owner who sued the very company he himself had created and incorporated as a separate legal entity. He effectively sued himself. The mechanics intrigued me, and I remember being impressed and attracted by the ingenuity. I can't help but reflect now that my being impressed by such clever mechanics was the start of Corporatism's very successful seduction of me. But what I found utterly bizarre and completely unnatural was that someone would sue themselves! I remember thinking what a strange and false world we live in. I was only 18 and barely out of home, so I was understandably and gloriously naive, and I 'learned' over many subsequent years, aided by my seduction, not to think this at all mad. Now, of course, I realise I was completely right to find it bizarre and unnatural.

The rehabilitation of the Corporation can be said, of course, to have facilitated the absolute explosion of growth and innovation that was the Industrial Revolution, but it came at a cost. 2.5 million slaves, plundered natural resources from already impoverished countries, cities besieged and people violated, and foreign governments bullied and manipulated into submission. Human beings with access to money not only had legitimate mechanisms to pursue profit above any other consideration, they could now legally abdicate any responsibility or even any real awareness of what their management were up to, of how they were behaving, and of any damage or harm they were doing to people or the environment; and much was done. Investing in companies became a 'portfolio' exercise – some would fail, but others would gloriously succeed, and thus exceptional profits were a possibility. Who would possibly settle for 'normal' returns anymore?

Then came 'shareholder primacy'. Just in case delegated executives started to think for themselves or have the temerity to consider wider moral responsibilities, Corporatism was able to legally protect itself. In 1919 in the landmark case of *Dodge v Ford Motor Co*, the Michigan Supreme Court ruled that Henry Ford had to operate the Ford Motor Company (his own creation!) in the interests of its shareholders, rather than in some quasi-charitable manner for the benefit of employees or customers. While corporate legislation in the US has somewhat wound this back, vested interest voices have kept the maximisation of shareholder value as a powerfully dominant mantra, fuelled by Milton Friedman's '*Friedman's Doctrine*' (1962), in which he stated that corporations had no social responsibility, and that the job of management was solely the maximisation of shareholder value, leaving shareholders free to decide for themselves their level of individual social responsibility in how they used their wealth. The invention of 'private equity' and 'vulture capitalism' in the 1980s, and its dominance in the markets today, keep this mantra paramount, for all we may argue that businesses take social responsibility seriously, or that CEOs are free to be equally cognisant of all stakeholders, not just their shareholders.

It is a premise of this book not only that delegated managers are still fundamentally enslaved to their owners, but that they would better serve the goal of maximising shareholder value were they to look after the other stakeholders first.

Corporate bodies can legally protect and perpetuate themselves. They can also legally procreate and they have done so like rabbits, with approximately 200 million companies worldwide, mostly owned by other companies. In Forbes Magazine in 2011, Bruce Upbin and Brendan Coffey reported that just 147 companies owned the 43,000-odd transnational Corporations, with in turn just four companies having effective control over those 147. Such a concentration of power and control may be efficient, but surely it comes at too high a risk of secrecy, abuse and inequality. It is the efficiency of the Dictator; however there's no benevolence since there is no moral imperative. It is in fact the efficiency of the Despot.

This ability for companies to own companies creates a perfect absolution not just for owners, but also now for Executives. In January 2017 the UK High Court ruled that Royal Dutch Shell could not be sued in the UK over spills from its pipelines in Nigeria, saying that the company had no legal responsibility for the operations of its subsidiary company in Nigeria, and that therefore the matter had to be heard in the Nigerian Courts. Mr Justice Fraser ruled that there was '*simply no connection whatsoever between this jurisdiction and the claims brought by Nigerian citizens*', and that Shell '*did not operate any business other than holding shares*', dismissing the notion that Shell exercised control over their Nigerian subsidiary. This ruling allowed the executives of Shell in the UK to stand behind their defence that they were simply not responsible for the oil spills and subsequent catastrophic pollution and environmental damage, since the facts would never ever be tested in a court of law. No one was disputing the environmental catastrophe, but Corporatism had allowed the owners and the executives total immunity from any responsibility.

Corporate Alchemy – The Promise of Something for Nothing

Corporatism has become the single most feted organisational system for maximising efficiency. It has done this by promoting a form of alchemy, offering the illusion of 'something for nothing'. It offers the prospect of rewards that are not directly linked to inputs of effort, talent or skill, and that are no longer linked to any reasonable time frame. In the process it has separated any natural relationship between the quality of the input and the scale of the reward, or indeed the risk of failure.

Corporatism initially only offered this 'something for nothing' for investors but in recent years it's had to open this opportunity to senior executives, as the owners have realised that their delegated Generals needed to be wholly onside (and since there are relatively few of them, it hasn't cost the owners that much!)

How frequently do we hear the Corporate Governance mantra that the interests and rewards of senior executives need to be aligned with those of shareholders? A noble concept where the shareholders can be clearly identified in human form and where they are in it for the long term. But completely counterproductive with the prevailing opaqueness and massively transitory nature of shareholders these days. For many investors, the actual value of their shares as it might relate to a valuation of the company's assets or the potential to pay a dividend is utterly irrelevant. The only consideration is 'can I get out at a price significantly above where I bought in'. If a market capitalisation of $50 billion is a ludicrous valuation for a company with $12 billion of revenue and no profits as yet (Tesla in 2018) that's OK as long as investors believe that the market cap will continue to rise. It's then just a question of timing their exit.

I remember meeting some Venture Capitalists in San Francisco in 2000, who told me the story of how they'd been tasked with finding an internet dog food company to invest in. Their boss had heard that a competitor VC firm were backing a company that sold dog food over the Internet (a very new thing in 2000!), and therefore he had to have one too. The fear of missing out, actually the fear of being criticised for missing out, was just too great. So these guys had toddled down to Stanford, found a couple of bright coders and did a deal – giving them $1 million to create an Internet dog food company. As they said, it didn't have to make money, it didn't even actually have to work. All they had to do was sell it on to someone else, which they did after just six months for $10 million. Job done. No dog was harmed in the making of that venture – in fact no dog was ever even fed …

The fine and honourable intentions of Corporatism's inventors, those of growth, innovation and greater wealth for all, have been steadily and inexorably usurped by the very nature of the body created. The legal separation at the core of Corporatism created corporate bodies able to act just like individuals with rights to exist and thrive, but also to act just like individuals with no morality. In the US, Corporations have even won the Constitutional right to be treated as individual citizens, with rights of free speech. But they are not people! People have empathy and a moral compass. Corporations are by their very nature sociopathic, operating purely rationally in the pursuit of maximum profit, and immoral, operating to the very edges of the law, and sometimes beyond if the potential penalty is deemed 'worth it'.

Brooke Harrington, writing in The Society Pages (Economic Sociology, October 2016), summarises that 'the Corporate form had trouble written all over it. Specifically it presented a built-in problem of moral hazard by giving managers authority over other people's money.' Harrington draws considerably on Joel Bakan's wonderful 2003 book The Corporation: The Pathological Pursuit of Profit and Power, and I am also greatly indebted to Bakan's analysis.

The founding dynamic in Corporatism of separating ownership from management has mutated over time into a separation of ownership from responsibility. It is this separation that has created corporate cultures of fear, secrecy and abuse of power causing thoroughly decent people to behave in unnatural and often inhuman ways. It is the nature of Corporatism itself that creates these problems, and it is this we need to address before the bots take over.

Outsourcing and the Professionalisation of Support Services

One of the ways that Corporatism has extended its tentacles is through the dynamic of outsourcing. The whole culture of outsourcing does not breed security and loyalty. Its purpose is maximum flexibility, lowest cost and minimised long-term liability. People on a contract have two masters and two cultures to serve. If we are serious about our mission and purpose, why would we risk outsourcing and losing control over critical aspects of our operation? Of course it makes sense to employ external specialists to perform some fundamental support services, but outsourcing has spread to include many aspects that are in fact critical to the quality and integrity of the product or service delivery.

Outsourcing or offshoring is often a euphemism for abdicating responsibility for ethical practices or for having to comply with 'inconvenient' regulations. Some large pharmaceutical Corporations have benefitted from cheap drug trials on disadvantaged people in India who were unaware they were receiving experimental drugs. Many have died, with no

> *Outsourcing or offshoring is often a euphemism for abdicating responsibility for ethical practices or for having to comply with 'inconvenient' regulations.*

autopsies required or sought, yet the companies carried on making statements about highest ethical practices. But they had no real knowledge of what was actually happening because they use outsourced companies based overseas that were not bound by our laws or regulated to our standards.

Many corporations offshore manufacturing to take advantage of low labour costs in the developing world, all in the name of staying competitive. If our competitor moves their manufacturing to Bangladesh, then we will have 'no choice' but to do the same, even though we know that this will cause us to lose control over how employees are treated. That's OK though because they won't be 'our' employees. And as long as the companies that we outsource to assure us of certain standards, maybe even sign legal agreements to that effect, we're covered. We cannot be criticised. We may think privately that it is the wrong thing to do, but if we want to keep our jobs, we'll salve our consciences and move on.

The British Empire was largely built on slavery, and we abolished it in 1833, knowing it was wrong. But it effectively still exists today, we've just outsourced it. Most of our apparel is manufactured in places like Bangladesh, Vietnam, China, India, Indonesia, where it is legal to employ children, and legal to pay adults around $1 per day. As we buy ourselves another £5 T-shirt in the righteous exercise of the freedom and choice we've earned for ourselves, we have absolutely no connection with the life of the human being that made it. Outsourcing and offshoring has facilitated this total geographic separation of ownership and responsibility. And even if we come to know that the person who made our shirt is living a miserable and shortened life, we have a strong defence of our actions. What difference will it make if we do not buy that shirt today? In fact, we would do more harm to abstain, since then the shirt maker would have less work, and their life would become more miserable. So we are actually doing good. They may be enslaved, but it's a better life than they would have otherwise. Comforting sentiments maybe, but notably precisely the same arguments that our ancestors used to justify slavery.

In addition, the centralisation and increasing professionalisation of expertise within functional support services have further exacerbated the separation between human beings and product and service delivery. The corporate practice of taking purchasing out of the hands of the users of bought-in products, and passing responsibility to newly created professional procurement departments, has no doubt delivered lower input costs to many organisations, but has it improved things overall? Where in this is any value placed on the human relationship between the user and the supplier? If companies are concerned about naive and overly trusting users being exploited by wicked salespeople, the most obvious solution is to create open book partnerships, allowing suppliers to make reasonable and sustainable profits, but no more.

This elevation of functional specialisms of advice and expertise increasingly legitimises front-line managers in abdicating their responsibilities to people – customers and employees alike. We'll look more closely at this phenomenon in Chapter 2.

Corporatism is Damaging and we're in Denial

By the way, if you find your internal Corporate PR voice telling you that clearly I have just revealed myself to be Karl Marx in a pair of Paul Smith jeans, and don't I understand what Corporatism has done for humanity, then just stop and think for a minute. By definition, only a few people can benefit disproportionately. So what does that mean for the rest of us? Are we really only supporting the system, colluding with the charade, publicly admiring the Emperor's clothes, because we are already one of the 'chosen' ones ourselves, or maybe because we are receiving just enough excess crumbs from the table, that we believe we are drawing closer to crossing into that Promised Land? After all it's a dog-eat-dog world with the law of the jungle and survival of the fittest. Isn't it?

What evidence do I have that Corporatism is damaging Humankind? Well, I should be able to say that common sense alone tells us that it cannot be right that there is such inequality of income, wealth, opportunity and security, and have that be sufficient to win the argument.

Oxfam's 2016 Wealth Distribution Report states the following facts: eight human beings own the same wealth (through their Corporate holdings) as the poorest 3.6 billion; the average FTSE100 CEO is paid 386 times more than someone on the national living wage; the world's 10 leading Corporations share revenue equivalent to 180 countries. In an article in *The Independent* in November 2012, Ben Chu reported that legal Corporate tax avoidance cost the UK Exchequer over £4 billion per year according to HMRC's own figures, and £12 billion per year according to Richard Murphy of Tax Research UK. With the US budget deficit standing at some $804 billion, John W Shoen reported in 2015 for CNBC that the combined untaxed profits of US corporations held offshore stood at $2.1 trillion. These facts are staggering in the clarity with which they communicate an insane state of affairs.

So if you find yourself tempted to agree that Corporatism (not *your* company, I do understand) is perhaps damaging humankind then the only reason you would continue to support it is either because you believe there is no better alternative, or because you feel powerless to do anything about it. I understand and fully empathise with both positions. I have, after all, been there myself for 40 years, and the only reason that I can now step out of my convenient denial is that I have the luxury of no longer needing the patronage with which the corporate world has shielded and rewarded me. Sometimes we cannot allow ourselves to know what we know, so we pretend we don't, and the easiest way to do that is to defend the indefensible by vehemently arguing the opposite case.

So many of our Corporate workplaces are pretty toxic places, but since we feel there is no alternative, we have to endure. In order to endure, we have to deny. And in order to stay in denial, we have to justify. The best form of justification is not just to defend but to actively promote. It is our defence and our advocacy for Corporatism that allows the Tyrant to perpetuate itself. Corporatism has us exactly where it wants us. Denial is the most powerful force keeping Corporatism alive today.

Denial is the most powerful force keeping Corporatism alive today.

But I believe my hypothesis is not just common sense. Look at the evidence. In an opinion poll by GfK NOP for The Happiness Formula series on BBC Two in 2014, results showed that people were happier in the 1950s than now. Income inequality in the developed economies is recognised as one of the major causes of disparities in mortality and literacy rates. Obesity, diabetes, heart disease and cancer rates are highest among the wealthier societies in the world.

The National Alliance on Mental Illness in the US has the following statistics on their website in May 2018 in regard to US adults: 43.8 million (approximately 20 per cent of the population) experience mental illness in a given year. Around 5 per cent experience a serious mental illness that substantially interferes with or limits one or more major life activities in a given year. Around 10 per cent had at least one major depressive episode in the past year and close to 20 per cent experienced an anxiety disorder such as post-traumatic stress disorder, obsessive-compulsive disorder and specific phobias.

The World Health Organisation forecasts that by 2030 more people will suffer from depression than any other health issue. Man-made environmental disasters are rife, most notably in the poorest regions of the world, since the privileged servants of the Tyrant are spared any discomfort in their own back-yard. Corporate scandals, leaving customers and employees devastated, harmed or in peril, have become both more prevalent and more destructive.

Corporatism kills and maims people, causes immense human suffering, causes epidemic levels of physical and mental ill health, causes obscene damage to the environment, destroying biodiversity, and arguably prolongs armed conflicts (even if they don't directly promote them, and even that's up for debate). At best, in my most benign assessment, the majority of incorporated organisations are earnestly involved in manufacturing services and things that in all seriousness the world does not really need. How many luxury cars does the world really need? Will your life really suck if you don't replace your 42-inch flat screen TV just yet? You will have your own even more grotesque comparatives.

Who makes these choices, since no normal, decent human being would do anything other than choose to employ our talents and our knowledge for the good of humankind? Who is it that kills, maims, pollutes, abuses, destroys . . . ? Name these people, please. But it's not people that do these things – the Corporate system makes these choices on our behalf, since we have endowed it with all our power. We are truly enslaved.

The Corporate profit motive, which has really morphed now into the 'exponential growth in profits motive', causes decent people to seek complex ways around laws and regulations at best, and at worst to downright scheme, cheat and lie. The system is rotten. James Murdoch said profit was the way to ensure independent (and therefore ethical?) journalism, but it was News Corporation's pursuit of profit that created the phone-hacking scandal. Interestingly his sister Elisabeth Murdoch said *profit without purpose is a recipe for disaster*. I wonder which of his offspring Rupert would side with? And is it really so naive of me to advocate for replacing the *exponential growth in profit* motive with the *sustainable return* motive?

How Corporatism Thwarts Government

Governments can now be 'traded' in the same way as companies, with speculators investing and divesting on short-term expectations. The free flow of capital across national boundaries, and the western world's pressure on developing countries to privatise their national assets, has led to a position where national governments are more at the whim of global capital than their own constituents. Pretty much every Government around the World now has to be super sensitive to what 'The Markets' think of them. Exchange rates and interest rates on Government Bonds are arguably now a way greater influence on the actions of Governments than the needs or desires of the people they represent. Adair Turner called trading in financial instruments '*socially useless*' saying traders treat it like the playing of a computer game where dying repeatedly and cheating become the norm.

Businesses circumvent legislation – or rather the use of the Corporate structure and the protection it gives its owners does. For example, government sanctions against so-called terrorist states such as Iran are rendered almost totally ineffective because global brokerage networks emerge which allow the targeted state to sidestep sanctions by the use of gold bullion. This is all achieved by using a complex and geographically spread network of broker companies, thus crossing many international legal jurisdictions, not all of which play by quite the same rules that we do in the EU or the US. Then add to the mix some fairly simple financial instruments that do not involve currency changing hands, for example derivatives and letters of credit. Finally, create Corporations that close down immediately following a single shipment of bullion, thus making it almost impossible to trace just who (which human beings) are behind them. The result is that states that are subject to UN sanctions can avoid them to the point where they are basically useless. Oh, and a great many international financiers make themselves very wealthy in the process.

We can blame the Chinese and Russians of course, and there may be something in this, since the more opaque nature of their political dealings with some states make it hard to know just what is going on. But we should fundamentally blame ourselves since, for example, Iranian finance houses and brokerage firms have sprung up in Western Europe. You might say this is scandalous, but it's all entirely legal. You might decry the perpetrators as criminal, but technically they are not. You might decry them as being immoral, but they're not doing anything illegal. And frankly since these individuals are pretty near impossible to identify, since they've worked the system to make sure of it, they never have to confront their own immorality. They can fall back on the argument that their legal responsibility is to do whatever they can within the law for the good of the company that pays their wages – this separate entity with no personality, no loyalty and no morality.

For an incorporated organisation, adherence to the law of the land is really only a cost–benefit analysis and not a moral obligation. Lawyers are retained specifically to legitimise corporate managers in pushing the boundaries at best, and at worst, breaking laws with a plausible defence all ready to go. When a corporate body is charged with an offence, it does not have the salutary experience of a night in the cell, or three months on remand to consider and repent of its actions. It calmly and rationally enlists those same lawyers – now on the hook of course for the defence they created in advance – and argues the case before any formal prosecution takes place. This phase ends either with the prosecutors, who are highly likely to be severely handicapped in the scales of their resources compared to the corporate body, reluctantly assessing that their chances of winning are too low to proceed, or with the company agreeing to a settlement to avoid prosecution. When a human does a plea bargain, it often still involves incarceration and a criminal record. Prosecutors are able to salve their moral indignation with the knowledge that the offender has suffered and that the albeit lighter penalty should still deter reoffending. When a corporation does a plea bargain, it simply pays a fine and moves on, with the executives responsible able to congratulate themselves on a brilliantly judged strategy. This of course is also the issue when a successful prosecution does ensue. Fines can be absorbed into cost of operating or even when they are punitive, it's the current shareholders, individuals who are unlikely to have been the owners when the crime was committed, who bear the penalty.

The Litany of Corporate Scandals

Circumventing sanctions on 'terror' states is a pretty easy one to judge as indefensible. But what about some of the other Corporate scandals of recent years? What about that phone hacking within News Corporation? What about Enron and the demise of Arthur Andersen? What about Lonmin presiding over the shooting of 34 miners? What about horse meat entering the human food chain? What about Volkswagen falsely creating fuel efficiency claims? Sadly the list in almost endless, and every day seems to throw up another.

How does a corporate scandal actually come about? And who is to blame? Is it a small number of evil people? It can't be that simple, since there are so many examples, involving so many people. So it must be the system, but a system cannot do anything; only *people* do things. (This of course is changing as we speak, with AI hurtling towards us, and hence my real fear for an unchecked future, but more of this later.)

So let's look at a small number and see what happened.

'Shuttle Report Blames NASA Culture' was a pretty amazing headline from NBC in August 2003. How does something that is completely intangible have the power to kill people? David Usborne, writing in *The Independent* in August 2003 on The Columbia Accident Investigation Board Report, quoted the investigators conclusions that the destruction of space shuttle Columbia and the death of its seven astronauts were caused by a 'self-protective culture' at NASA. Usborne noted that '*ineffective leadership failed to fulfil the implicit contract to do whatever is possible to ensure the safety of the crew*'. Sure, it was the flying foam insulation damaging the heat shield wot done it, but lying behind this were mission managers being '*driven by schedule, starved of funds and burdened by eroded processes*'.

Between 2005 and 2009 in Mid Staffordshire Hospital, up to 1200 patients may have died needlessly from the appalling hygiene regime, which was known about by everyone who worked there. Allison Pearson, writing about the Francis Enquiry into the scandal in the *Daily Telegraph* on 7 February 2013, asked why its consultants, doctors and nurses – the very people asked to provide patient care amid increasingly squalid surroundings – did nothing to raise the alarm? Had they become so demoralised they failed to recognise the crisis developing in front of them? Or were they brow beaten into submission by a management who, according to the Francis Enquiry, had become so obsessed by achieving coveted Foundation Trust status that it put the meeting of bureaucratic targets above providing a decent standard of care? Attempts to raise the alarm were repeatedly thwarted. A report presented to the hospital's Patient and Public Involvement in Health Forum was not passed to senior management as *'they didn't want to upset the new chief executive and didn't want to rock the boat'*.

> *They didn't want to upset the new chief executive and didn't want to rock the boat.*

In 2012 we also had Deep Water Horizon – 11 workers killed and $50 billion of environmental damage. A classic failure of leadership with intense pressure within the system to save time and money. With stress and pressure come sacrifices to safety, as NASA had shown.

The more Prosaic Examples Affecting our Daily Lives

These cases prove that it's a systemic issue, with ordinary, decent human beings coerced, persuaded, manipulated, cajoled, bullied, bribed and hypnotised into doing bad things.

But these are the catastrophes. What about the smaller, daily examples of good people doing bad things? Closer to home, where public opinion would simply not tolerate deaths or environmental disasters caused by Corporatism, the impact has been much more on 'victimless crimes' – human beings still dramatically impacted or hurt by the actions of Corporations, but where the companies concerned can hide behind blaming unrelated third parties or their own employees for being negligent.

Just where can we draw the line in terms of what we would be prepared to do, and more importantly what we refuse to do? How frequently do we find ourselves justifying actions that we know in our hearts are not right, with the very same defences?

In 2009 I was on the receiving end of such behaviour myself. I'd gone into my bank to pay in a cheque. When I handed it to the cashier she said that as it was such a large amount they would need to undertake a couple of security checks, and she went off somewhere. When she came back I was introduced to another bank employee who asked me to step into a private office. I felt quite exposed and uncomfortable at this point, as the queue behind me was very long, and I felt everyone looking at me, no doubt assuming that I had done something wrong. The person who took me into the office was very polite, but clearly nervous. She opened by saying that there was nothing to worry about, and that under FSA Money Laundering laws anyone paying in a cheque over £2500 was asked security questions, and that they always did this in an office to save the customer from talking about personal things in front of other people. Her insecurity was already communicating dishonesty. She then asked me who the cheque was from, and if I had any plans for the money. When I was oblique in my answers she said that one of the things they wanted to do for their customers was to ensure they were earning as much interest as possible on surplus funds. At this point I twigged that this charade was all about selling me something. When pressed further she eventually admitted that in fact the abusive and dehumanising process that she and I were locked in was her bank's *interpretation of the FSA rules'*. I was incredibly angry – at being lied to, but mostly because of the position that she had been put in by her bosses, placed under pressure no doubt to hit internal sales targets for new accounts, and being told to lie to customers in order to manufacture potential sales opportunities. When I took this further, after some months of being batted backwards and forwards between departments and layers of customer complaint staff, the closest to a 'mea culpa' I could extract, was that the branch manager had been 'over-zealous'. He'd been a very naughty boy.

Another personal example was when my father was in his late 80s, still living in his own home but requiring home visits from carers. The rule was that the carers could only wash him with his permission. If he said he didn't want to be washed (which he didn't because he couldn't bear the indignity of it, especially as all the carers were female) they happily left him in soiled clothes, progressively contaminating all his furniture and bedding, and giving him sores. There were some carers that could get him to agree – the ones who cared enough to spend a few minutes building a relationship with him. It's easy to say that it was the ones who *didn't* care that simply didn't bother, but that would be to fall into the trap of blaming the employee for being in an invidious position as a victim of the system. Carers were given ridiculously tight visit times, often no more than 15 minutes. The carers' low pay could be seriously affected for taking 'too long' on a home visit, and so the result was that visits were effectively more an assault on my Father than a comfort. He found them distressing. Interestingly each one of the carers found the time to faithfully record my Father's refusal to be washed in the log they'd created to cover themselves. When challenged, the managers of the Agency providing the carers used enormous energy and creativity to justify to me why this was an acceptable state of affairs.

Behaviours that in normal everyday life would result in being prosecuted for fraud, deception, slander or even assault, are legitimised by the 'disembodiment' of working in a Corporate world, in other words a protected and unnatural, environment. How do these things happen? Simple. Because the visceral fear from the immediate (perceived) threat of retribution, intimidation, judgement and pain is way greater than the 'moral' fear of something bad happening to others. It's why in what we describe as 'cultures of blame' so much effort (energy and creativity) goes into making sure that we cannot be blamed. There is the immediate threat to our survival from taking personal responsibility and doing the right thing and this is literally the only 'choice' available to us in the moment. It's not that there is *no* threat or pain from acting wrongly, it's that the potential threat can be deferred, and the pain can be denied. Our conscience can construct the following self-defence: 'If I can survive *this* moment, I'll worry about what comes next later. I may be harming this person, but there really is nothing I can do about it and besides I am not responsible for the state they find themselves in.'

Too Big to Fail

We have the illusion of efficiency in Corporatism, serving markets that ruthlessly force 'survival of the fittest'. If an incorporated body is not efficient it will die. But that's actually a myth, since many Corporations are effectively bailed out when they fail. The financial crisis of 2008 saw the greatest wave of nationalisation since the Soviet revolution of 1917, with failed financial Corporations bailed out right, left and centre. When a privatised care home or school or railway fails and the owners skulk away, often having taken substantial dividends and fees in their short tenure, the residents don't get put onto the streets, the children don't get denied an education, and the passengers are not left without a service – because the state intervenes, runs the organisation perfectly well for a period of time, then passes ownership to another, presumably better, incorporated body.

When a Corporate goes bust, the liquidation process often means the same 'failed' owners and managers are back in control of the very same business assets a day later, just under a different name, with the unsecured creditors and unsecured shareholders having funded the rescue, by sacrificing the debts they were owed. I've supported businesses through the liquidation process, and one of the most bizarre, yet utterly predictable dynamics is where a supplier is forced to write off a debt one day and is then pathetically grateful for more sales the next. A sale is a sale, even if it is to someone who shafted you yesterday. We have to swallow our pride and do what's in the best interest of the company – even if we own 100 per cent of it!

How many corporate bodies of global scale are effectively enjoying massive subsidies from us, in the form of very low effective rates of taxation, without which they would probably not survive past infancy? And how many 'failed' executives have you seen go on to their next corporate role within days, often having collected a huge payoff.

Even as I complete the writing of this book in 2018, we are fresh off the back of the debacle of UK corporation Carillion going bust, leaving many government contracts up in the air, hundreds of small suppliers with a huge and sudden cashflow problem, thousands of employees in uncertainty and its pension scheme in a £1 billion+ deficit. Who picks up the government contracts? Of course there are other contractors who come straight in, but at what additional cost to the taxpayer? Who picks up the tab for the pension deficit? The government – you and me. It's easy to argue that it is the shareholders who bear the cost of the risk they took, but who are the shareholders? Most investors who take a long-term 'reasonable return' approach had bailed out of Carillion shares a year earlier – the signs were there. So in reality the shareholders who lost out at the end were those who'd taken a gamble, who had placed their Carillion shares in a risk portfolio, accepting that while some of their picks would fail, some would come off spectacularly. It's how speculators operate. How many individual human shareholders were harmed in the making of the Carillion debacle? Very few if any.

Questions were asked about how the government could award Carillion huge contracts at the same time as investors were heading for the hills. The only plausible answer would seem to be that it was part of a strategy to keep the company afloat and see it through tough times. After all, if the government had decided to pay attention to the known risks around Carillion and placed their contracts elsewhere, they would likely have contributed to Carillion's accelerated demise. Sometimes, when you are over invested, you have no choice but to keep the bubble inflated and hope you can find a point to exit before it goes bang. When you're in the system, you have no real choice but to do everything possible to ensure its survival.

Corporatism has not Delivered Happiness or Freedom

Of course, there is no denying that Corporatism has given humanity (well, some humans anyway) choice, leisure, luxury, comfort and longer lives. It's also undeniable that, since many millions of people go to work in Corporate organisations every day and find their workplace to be one of genuine fellowship and camaraderie, Corporatism gives countless people a genuine sense of belonging, of social and emotional connection, of family even. The Corporation may be the only show in town in employment terms for millions of people across the world but that does not mean I devalue the legitimacy of the fact that millions of people are hugely satisfied with their employment.

But notice the two conspicuous absentees from the list of positive outcomes that Corporatism produces – happiness and freedom. Of course, these two things should be the outcomes of the things I listed, and advocates of the Corporation argue vehemently that it does indeed offer such Elysian riches. But the evidence points to the exact opposite. Greater choice, comfort and leisure has not made us happier – the 'privileged' half of the world are unhappier than they've been for four generations, and anxiety and stress levels are at an all- time high, and this in an era with no World Wars.

And ask anyone who works in the Corporate world, including CEOs, whether they are 'free' and they will betray the fact that they are not, even if they cannot admit it to themselves. Now ask them if they are fearful, anxious, stressed, unsettled . . . many will take the opportunity to have such states acknowledged, but still many will deny. The rampant striving for growth, and its absolute predominance as the only success measure that really counts, has given us leaders who are downright miserable if their company's earnings (no matter how high in absolute terms) are not higher every period. Why oh why can a company not be satisfied with producing a period of identical profits? In any other system that would be success, but not in the Corporate world – in that world growth is the only metric that counts, even if it comes at the cost of delayed sacrifice or human suffering.

So many of our businesses have become relatively inhuman places where intimidation, isolation, anxiety, greed and short-term self-interest rule.

So many of our businesses have become relatively inhuman places where intimidation, isolation, anxiety, greed and short-term self-interest rule. Corporate CEOs are under the most intense pressure to announce quarter after quarter (after quarter) of inexorable growth – hardly a natural state of affairs, particularly in highly competitive environments. Not every player can grow market share. I remember when running Car Dealerships representing almost every franchise in the UK, the annual round of negotiations with manufacturers on volumes, and how when every manufacturers' share aspiration was added up, the total would come to 150 per cent+. Unrealistic. Unachievable. Physically impossible. But that did not stop them using intimidatory and manipulative tactics to coerce their dealers to sign up to unrealistic targets, creating a dynamic whereby Dealers would be under pressure from Day 1, with forecasts based on hope, and panic tactics at each quarter end. Fear would be used in the threat of not getting enough allocation or worse, that the franchise would be withdrawn, causing the dealer to go bust. Bribery was also used in the form of luxury gifts or holidays for dealer staff to hit targets. I recall interviewing a potential Sales Director one time and him proudly listing the holidays he'd won from the manufacturers as evidence of his sales prowess. He did not mention dealer profit or customer satisfaction once.

Who's the Shareholder?

So who actually is the owner now? Who owns your company? Which human being can you point to? Hedge funds and corporate raiders circle over CEOs who are incapable of meeting punishing short-term expectations. All in the name of shareholder value, but who is the shareholder? This is a vital question since so much is done in their name, yet it is almost impossible to identify actual human beings. Our corporate laws allow anonymity to owners through nominee bodies, often with countless intermediaries based in offshore tax havens with no possibility of effective regulation or scrutiny. With 84 per cent of share trades now made by computers with no human intervention (George Washington, zerohedge.com, 2012), and with the average length of time a share is owned now being just five days, according to Trader Alan Clement (2012) we have achieved total separation of ownership and responsibility, and any real notion of long-term investment has left the stage.

So just who are the CEOs serving? They should serve the shareholders, the owners. But since the individual owners are almost impossible to identify, the CEO ends up serving intermediaries. This separation of ownership away from control, designed nobly at the start to fuel innovation, efficiency and scale, has become a separation of ownership from responsibility. The granting of power to those who do not have to accept any responsibility is at the root of our Corporate woes. Aiding this, our laws, our vested interests and our own fears have given us Corporations who seemingly have no choice but to put short-term financial gain first. This short-term pressure then permeates and affects the whole organisation, and in pressured working cultures, corporate managers slip into unconscious habitual behaviours of control and judgement that in turn cause employees to develop defensive habits of playing small and staying safe. This of course simply raises the frustration and irritation levels in the managers. Pressure turns into fear, frustration into anger and uncertainty into anxiety. This is the vicious circle that produces abnormal and inhuman behaviour from good, decent people; the vicious circle that creates cultures of mediocrity, where everyone is flogging their guts out to achieve largely unsatisfactory results. Insanity.

And where is the purpose of the endeavour in all of this? Where is the spark of the idea and the need that formed the company in the first place? Where is the ethos of securing the long-term future of the enterprise, so that future customers are absolutely served better than today's? So many companies have lost the spark, adding to the seemingly unarguable validity of the CEO's fallback that says 'my job is to maximise shareholder value' – always the mantra of maximising shareholder return, but over what period of time, when the average share is held for 22 seconds?

The People who do the Bad Things are the same People who do the Good Things

The most bizarre thing about Corporatism is that it is the very same people (with of course a tiny number of clear exceptions at the highest levels) that produce the negative outcomes as produce the positive ones. The actual human beings who end up doing 'bad' things are really no different to those who do the good stuff. They are you and me. And in many cases they are literally the same people, one moment doing something wonderful and creative, and the next doing something abusive and damaging. How can that be? There must be something within the organism itself, something within Corporatism as a system, that is the determining factor. There is – fear.

Look around at your own organisation and ask yourself what good it is doing, beyond giving people jobs. Ask yourself where your own organisation is guilty of doing something that's damaging, in order to secure profit or growth. Now individualise and personalise those questions – what good are doing for the world? Where are you guilty of damaging something or someone through an act of commission, or more likely through omission. You may not be able to point to something you've done that's caused harm, but I guarantee you can point to something you should have done, or said, but didn't. Just as guilty . . .

Aren't we all sometimes guilty of sending messages that this quarter's numbers are actually paramount; that budgets are tight and that our systems will have to carry on creaking for a while yet? We may well be striving to lead our companies according to enlightened principles – even in line with those values that we keep banging on about. The problem is that it is our behaviour – our actions – our habits – that actually dictate the culture. It really does not matter what we say – it's what we do. BP and NASA bosses vehemently defended themselves, incredulous that their exhortations about 'safety first' were not followed by their employees (or contractors), and asking what more they could have done than to have written procedures and expect people to follow them.

The simple truth is that we can say what we like in memos and emails; we can write what we like in people's quarterly objectives; we can even incentivise people financially to concentrate on certain aspects of performance, but it's what leaders pay attention to that is the true motivator. Acts of omission have become the single greatest controlling behaviour in our modern Corporate world: fundamentally leaders not acting when they should. My great, late friend Professor Aidan Halligan, former Deputy Chief Medical Officer and a wonderfully authentic leader, put it another way when he said to me *'As Leaders, what we permit, we promote'*. If our behaviour betrays our pre-occupation with short-term imperatives, then we are implicitly directing people to compromise on long-term values.

As Leaders, what we permit, we promote.

If our questioning (coaching?) of people is really designed to make us feel that everything is actually OK, rather than elicit the truth, then we can hardly blame others for joining us in a conspiracy.

The Three Characteristics for Abuse to be Systemic

Corporatism has at its core the three characteristics in a heady cocktail for abuse to rule.

1. It gives power to individual managers over employees.

2. It puts a faceless hierarchy above those managers to keep them in check.

3. It allows those managers' actions to go unwitnessed by the outside world.

It is the very separation of ownership and management at the heart of the genesis of The Corporation that has created the essential fear dynamic of a hierarchy above the managers who are given the power. The threat has become disembodied, and so much more potent for that. The horror movies that are the most scary are the ones where the monster is not seen. The hierarchy above the managers is absent, faceless and spectral in nature – the menacing and constant disembodied threat lurking in the shadows. It is the system itself, Corporatism, which now sits as the Despot.

But surely, I hear you say, that's the classic fear-based culture; and OK, such cultures existed in the twentieth century, but we're now in a more enlightened time of consensus and employee engagement aren't we, and anyway HR is there to ensure that managers with Genghis Khan tendencies don't get through the talent management net. Well that is certainly true in some organisations, but there are still many 'old-fashioned' fear-based Corporates out there, for all their corporate values might say otherwise.

A Whole new Fear for the Twenty-First Century

Fear used to be simple, and as such it operated pretty much as biologically designed for our survival. For the best part of 200,000 years the source of pretty much all our fears was our environment – animals and weather – and the threat was intensely physical. It's only in very recent human history that, for the privileged half of the world, threat has changed from being solely physical to having more psychological elements. As work became more organised through the industrial revolution, managers became the source of fear, and these managers freely used threats of fines or sackings. Early management practices created a fear that was largely psychological, but still with a heavy dose of mortality since losing your job could easily lead to penury, with all that entailed. But note that the threatened act and the consequences of that act were no longer a single event, manifest all in a single moment in time. The two could now be separated by some weeks or months. The start of 'fear of fear itself'?

And now a more pernicious and petrifying fear stalks the corporate land – the fear of condemnation; the fear of judgement and then rejection for not being instantaneous and perfect. What others think of us has become the greatest, the most pernicious, the most crippling fear – far greater than any physical fear we may experience. Tyrants coerce through fear of physical pain; corporations coerce through fear of shame and rejection. In the early part of the twenty-first century, with digital and mobile communications ruling our minute-to-minute lives, and with Corporatism in an ever more desperate race to justify its illusion of alchemy, managers are set wholly unrealistic expectations in terms of both measured outputs and timescales. Even when there is no threat, the frenetic pace, unrelenting activity and mass external stimuli mean that today's Corporate citizen feels compelled to respond to every request speedily and perfectly. Trying to keep up with machines is a challenge at which we cannot possibly hope to succeed, and the stress could kill us and there is no rest. Mobile technology has been with us for a few short years and has already transformed our working landscape.

The frenetic pace, unrelenting activity and mass external stimuli mean that today's corporate citizen feels compelled to respond to every request speedily and perfectly.

In all my coaching of leaders and managers, the single greatest common thread has been their navigation of fears that are simply not real – fears that their corporate anxiety disorder has either invented or blown massively out of proportion. Leaders and managers have come to be fearful of things that are illusory; fearful of things that they simply do not need to fear. In the old days, leaders and managers feared judgement – since being judged would result in some form of immediate sanction, the ultimate being the sack. But we now live in a Corporate world where managers and employees are encouraged and expected to be autonomous, to think and decide for themselves, to innovate, to take risks. I'd love to add 'to fail' to that list, but failure simply does not feel safe. 'Failure is not an option' in the corporate world, or that is how it feels. And with regular feedback as the new currency, in theory no leader or manager should fear being judged, since they are promised that is a step along the journey of self-development. But this is not how it plays out in The Corporation, since feedback really means judgement in the moment, felt as a visceral 'rejection', with the consequences of condemnation not coming immediately, but later, after a period of some living hell during which the leader or manager is surely the walking dead, in the unwitnessed process of being 'managed out'. Or so we have come to fear.

These fears are, in the vast majority of cases, simply not real. Will the CEO who answers an analyst's question with an 'I don't know' really lose their job as a result of that one act? Of course not, but that's how it feels – the single moment that condemns the CEO to Death Row. Will the manager who takes a risk and fails be fired? Most likely not, since they are unlikely to have been reckless, negligent or malicious. Will the employee who says 'No' be sanctioned? The reality is that they will not be, in fact they might be praised, but it will feel as though they have been punished if their manager's reaction is negative. The fear of condemnation is often too great for them to take the risk, and so playing safe becomes the modus operandi. When you are a hostage, you daren't take risks. Survival means staying quiet and utterly compliant. But in The Corporation even those who watch the hostages dare not step out of line.

Corporapaths and CTSD

Everything that's wrong, corrupt and damaging about The Corporation stems from fear. I believe that a new and unique type of psychopathy has been created at the upper levels of management with the development of the Corporapath. It may be understandable for a CEO not to know the details and to be 'let down' by lieutenants but the CEO's masters cannot allow it to be acceptable. If it is then frankly CEOs have licence to swan around basing their whole strategy on hope. These guys get paid enough in two or three years to live a whole lifetime. They are expected to devote their lives to the role and to always be on duty. Do not underestimate the power of the CEO's role modelling. It may be the single greatest dynamic force dictating and regulating the culture of the whole organisation. If the CEO is an over delegator, ie someone who delegates without coaching and without check-ing, then their managers will likely mirror that same dynamic. The result is that front-line employees have to make sure that everything happens as it should. Normally when a CEO eventually resigns, it is not an act of integrity on their part, a selfless act in defiance of being pushed too far by their owners or critics, but actually because they've been exposed as poor CEOs. CEOs are not let down by incom-petent lieutenants, they *make* them incompetent.

CEOs are not let down by incompetent lieutenants, they make them incompetent.

And we're back to the over-delegating CEO operating on a strategy of blamelessness and hope. Within one company with say six layers of hierarchy, it is often the front-line employ-ees who are the only ones who know what's actually happening, and who have to absorb all the pressure of serving the customers despite all the nonsense going on above them. In companies that use outsourcing, the number of 'layers' of hierarchy might be tenfold, as an ever more complex web of offshored companies and agents are used to circumvent laws, and to obscure the ability to identify human responsibility.

Executive Team rooms (notice I don't say boardrooms, since we will come to the Non-Executives later) are cauldrons of pressure to hit numbers that are bigger than last period. Forecasting within corporations is often characterised by missed numbers and order signing dates constantly moving back. In fact many CFOs produce their own version of their sales teams forecasts because experience teaches them that the forecasts are missed by a significant factor. As a Chairman the forecasting process and accuracy is always something I pay great attention to. Show me an organisation that consistently misses its forecast and I'll show you an organisation with a culture of fear. The forecasting process is perhaps the greatest barometer of fear within the culture because it goes to the heart of the critical moments of choice for managers – do employees tell them what they want to hear, or dare they tell them the truth?

The emergence of the corporapath has been matched with the growth of a wholly new form of psychological disorder within the cohort of managers and employees beneath them – Corporate Traumatic Stress Disorder (CTSD), one which will, when universally recognised, give insight and understanding as to precisely what millions of Corporate employees are unconsciously suffering.

Corporatism is Under Pressure

The Corporation may be unassailably dominant, but it is also profoundly under pressure in the early part of the twenty-first century. Corporatism is being found seriously wanting. Technology and global communications have given us the potential to form collaborative organisations and collective human enterprises capable of not just changing our world for the better but of doing so for every single human being on the planet. We have absolutely everything we need in renewable resources and human talent, to solve all our problems.

According to the United Nations Food and Agriculture Organisation of the United Nations, the estimated number of under-nourished people increased from 777 million in 2015 to 815 million people in 2016. Yet they also state that there is more than enough food produced in the world to feed everyone.

As reflected in Sustainable Development Goal 2 (SDG 2), one of the greatest challenges the world faces is how to ensure that a growing global population – projected to rise to around 10 billion by 2050 – has enough food to meet their nutritional needs. To feed another two billion people in 2050, food production will need to increase by 50 percent globally. Food security is a complex condition requiring a holistic approach to all forms of malnutrition, the productivity and incomes of small-scale food producers, resilience of food production systems and the sustainable use of biodiversity and genetic resources. We could easily produce all our required energy from renewable sources, we have the resources to eradicate infant malnutrition etc. But we also have a global network of mutually interdependent Corporations for whom those solutions would simply not produce the outcomes they need to sustain themselves.

'The State of Food Security and Nutrition in the World 2017'

We'd rather feed Corporate bodies than human ones. The survival of the Corporation comes before the survival of people – it always has done.

We'd rather feed Corporate bodies than human ones. The survival of the Corporation comes before the survival of people – it always has done, but what's different now is Corporatism's sheer dominance.

Since it was resurrected in the nineteenth century, and particularly through the global deregulation boom of the late twentieth century, the Corporation has been able to embed itself permanently. Since we've endowed it with a separate legal personality, passed laws to protect its right to life, grown an army of professional lawyers, bankers and accountants to support and protect it, turned a blind eye to its indiscretions, and bailed it out when its simply gone too far, we really only have ourselves to blame.

Now, I haven't lived 60 years to naively believe in a Utopian vision of 7 billion happy, healthy and fulfilled human beings, living together in peace and harmony. But short-termism in the extreme and the entrenched self-service of the privileged and the powerful have given us Corporations that are, with a very few notable exceptions, woefully incapable of rising to the challenges we face as Humankind. It's simply not in their interests to do so.

Many intelligent people argue that business should be allowed to take over most if not all functions of government, and to assume responsibility for managing social change and cultural development, since it is only business that can honestly act in the best interests of citizens (customers of government), can truly work across national borders (since they have no national allegiance), and can therefore coordinate resources, people and capital to build a more peaceful and sustainable world for an ever safer, more comfortable and more fulfilled population. It is a powerfully logical argument, one that has held the 'informed' neoliberal consensus for the last 50 years. And yet The Corporation has an appalling track record on sustainability, and a very mixed record on the achievement of positive outcomes. Democracy may be the best worst means of governing a nation, but I do not believe The Corporation is the best worst means of governing an organisation of people in collective endeavours. I think it can become so, but not on its current trajectory. Its record stinks.

Is Corporatism all Bad?

There are many incorporated companies out there doing amazingly important work in the world, behaving ethically, treating all stakeholders with immense respect, genuinely pursuing purpose and yet carefully managing financial viability and a sustainable return. So surely corporatism is not all bad? I would argue that the reason these companies are successful ethically as well as financially is that they eschew the most negative and damaging aspects of corporatism.

For example, SMEs (Small and Medium Enterprises), although highly likely to be incorporated bodies, seem better able to draw back from the most negative dynamics of their larger Corporate peers. The reason is simple – the owners are usually still really close to the customers and front-line employees. No disconnect or separation there. In a large corporate this is almost never the case. The problem with SMEs, however, is that they do not provide the opportunity for 'stellar' profits (they merely make reasonable ones) – they just don't provide the 'something for nothing' alchemical opportunities that attract investors. Ethics apparently does not scale.

The moment leaders, whether owners or delegated managers, find themselves doing things that they would not do if it were not for the money; the moment the majority of employees don't 'know' the owners; the moment leaders feel disconnected from the customer and front-line employee experience, the slippery slope is joined and the negative aspects of corporatism will take hold. Pressure and thus fear enter the system, and once in, they are tough to shift.

The positive aspects of corporatism are twofold – the standardisation, consistency, reliability and predictability of systems and processes, in other words safety and strength from structure, and secondly a financial structure that gives some breathing space through tough trading times and that can absorb some failures.

What's the Answer?

As a Human race, occupying this planet Earth, it is entirely possible for 9 billion people (where we're headed) to be well fed, well clothed, well educated, and well cared for. We have the physical and creative resources and the knowledge and technology to do so. We simply cannot organise ourselves to achieve it. Why the hell not? Of course there are massively complex geo-political dynamics at play, but Corporations are not helping in the way they trade with the developing world. Why would they? Why should we expect them to? They were not set up to solve world peace and eradicate world famine.

There are plenty of voices in the world arguing for the overthrow, eradication, or dismantling of The Corporation. And while I may privately have great sympathy with those voices, I do not myself evangelise nor actively work for or with those voices. After all it would have to be replaced by some alternative form of institution, and what would be different?

Governments, trades unions, global regulators, lawyers, quangoes etc have all tried manfully to rein in the excesses of The Corporation through regulation, protest, disruption and legislation. Politicians, commentators, religious leaders, Royal Commission Chairmen, even some fund managers, have encouraged, cajoled, manipulated and even shamed Corporate leaders to change their ways through self-regulation. All to no real avail. A piece of legislation or regulation just starts to bite, and The Corporation is able to use further advances in technology or the inexorable control of global financial markets to scupper the attempts to control them. Or they simply employ the armies of lawyers and accountants who are reliant on fat fees to find new and cleverer ways round the law. Individual leaders and managers have (rather infrequently) been prosecuted for breaches of the law, but successful prosecutions are notoriously hard to win. The legal separation of ownership and control, and the legalised disembodiment of The Corporation from the actions of individual human beings are almost impossible to break down in legal argument. So more often than not the entity successfully sued is The Corporation itself, but since a Corporation cannot be jailed or executed, the only recourse is financial in the form of fines. So no human being is really sanctioned.

There have been many attempts to create meaningful laws to hold Corporations to account. For example corporate manslaughter is a legitimate charge, but how many successful prosecutions can you name for that? We sue corporate bodies but no 'responsible' human suffers – indeed many company Directors treat fines or damages as a cost of doing business, weighing up the potential risk/return equation, and legitimising getting caught for their wrongdoing as a 'price worth paying'. If a CEO knew they could go to jail for the negligence of their company, perhaps they'd take things more seriously. The psychopathic argument is that such threat would mean the supply of people prepared to take on CEO roles would evaporate? It's the same argument that says all top talent will emigrate if the top tax rates rise. I simply do not believe this to be true for these arguments make everything about money, and there are very few human beings for whom money is the sole or even major motivator. But the system can only argue financially. It is its only measure – its only weapon – and perhaps hence why average Executive pay is so dramatic a multiplier of average earnings.

In my opinion The Corporation is too deeply entrenched, too skilled and practised at perpetuating itself, too protected, frankly too powerful for it to succumb to be changed from the outside. And I am too old and too tired and too selfish to even try. The Corporation may be The Dragon but I am no St George. My evangelism and my work are for change from within, by giving genuine emotional ownership back to human beings so that it once again becomes worth standing up for truly ethical and responsible strategies and decisions; by genuinely sharing responsibility for the inputs and outputs we all create every day; and by genuinely and more equitably sharing the rewards of our collective endeavours. We simply have to put the humanity back into The Corporation, and start turning the tide.

So I am not against incorporation, I simply ask you to know what you do and to watch for the signs of pressure and fear creeping in. And while my exhortations may sound staggeringly unrealistic, and/or even monumentally naive, I contend that the change is in itself quite simple. Leaders and managers simply have to wake up, realise that their fears are illusory, and act according to their human instincts. Since The Corporation is not human, we can take back control. But time is running out.

Notes

Bubble Act 1720 was an Act of the Parliament of Great Britain passed on 11 June 1720 that forbade the formation of any other joint-stock companies unless approved by royal charter. This was a response to the demise of the South Sea Company, a British joint-stock company that had been granted a monopoly to trade with South America and nearby islands, hence its name. There was never any realistic prospect that trade would take place and the company never realised any significant profit from its monopoly. Shares in the company rose greatly in value as it expanded its dealings in government debt, peaking in 1720 before collapsing to little above its original flotation price; the economic bubble became known as the South Sea Bubble.

Salomon v A Salomon & Co Ltd, UK House of Lords 1, AC 22 – the effect of the House of Lords' unanimous ruling was to uphold firmly the doctrine of corporate personality, as set out in the Companies Act 1862, so that creditors of an insolvent company could not sue the company's shareholders to pay up outstanding debts.

Dodge v Ford Motor Co   204 Mich 459, 170 NW 668 is a case in which the Michigan Supreme Court held that Henry Ford had to operate the Ford Motor Company in the interests of its shareholders, rather than in a charitable manner for the benefit of his employees or customers. It is often cited as affirming the principle of 'shareholder primacy' in corporate America.

Friedman's Doctrine   *Capitalism and Freedom*, by Milton Friedman, originally published in 1962 by the University of Chicago Press, discusses the role of economic capitalism in liberal society.

Forbes Magazine, Urban and Coffey   26 October 2011, www.forbes.com/sites /brendancoffey/2011/10/26/the-four-companies-that-control-the-147-companies -that-own-everything/#29445747685b (accessed 25 May 2018).

London UK High Court   26 January 2017. Reported in *The Times* by Emily Gosden, 27 January 2017.

Tesla 2018   7 February 2018. Letter to Shareholders signed by Elon Musk, Chairman and CEO, and Deepak Ahuja, CFO.

Brooke Harrington The Society Pages   16 October 2010. 'Economic Sociology'.

Bakan, J (2004)   *The Corporation: The Pathological Pursuit of Profit and Power.* London: Constable and Robinson.

Oxfam Wealth Distribution Report   16 January 2016 – 'An Economy for the 99%' based on global wealth distribution data provided by the Credit Suisse Global Wealth Data book 2016.

Ben Chu, *Independent* Newspaper   22 November 2012. 'Britain's Missing Billions: Counting the True Cost of Corporate Tax Avoidance'.

US budget deficit   Congressional Budget Office (non-partisan analysis for the US Congress) forecast for Fiscal Year 2018 $804 billion.

John W Schoen, CNBC   6 October 2015. 'US Companies Holding $2.1 Trillion Offshore Profits'.

The Happiness Formula series on BBC Two   2014 opinion poll by GfK NOP – this provides the first evidence that Britain's happiness levels are declining. Britain is less happy than in the 1950s – despite the fact that we are three times richer. The proportion of people saying they are 'very happy' has fallen from 52 per cent in 1957 to just 36 per cent today. Polling data from Gallup throughout the 1950s shows happiness levels above what they are today, suggesting that our extra wealth has not brought extra well-being.

Gallup Inc   a US research-based, global performance management consulting company.

National Alliance on Mental Illness   NAMI 'Mental Health by the Numbers' www.nami .org/Learn-More/Mental-Health-By-the-Numbers (accessed 25 May 2018).

World Health Organisation   WHO prediction quoted in a Department of Health Press Release 29 February 2012.

James Murdoch   James Murdoch was Executive Chairman on News Corporation. He gave a speech at the MediaGuardian Edinburgh International Television Festival in September 2009, titled 'The Absence of Trust', concluding that 'the only reliable, durable, and perpetual guarantor of independence is profit'.

Phone-Hacking Scandal   The News International phone-hacking scandal is a controversy involving the now defunct News of the World and other British newspapers published by News International, a subsidiary of News Corporation. Employees of the newspaper were accused of engaging in phone hacking, police bribery, and exercising improper influence in the pursuit of stories. The resulting public outcry against News Corporation and its owner Rupert Murdoch led to several high-profile resignations, including that of Murdoch as News Corporation director and Murdoch's son James as executive chairman. Advertiser boycotts led to the closure of the News of the World on 10 July 2011, after 168 years of publication.

Elisabeth Murdoch   Elisabeth Murdoch was Non Exec Chair of Shine Group, a subsidiary of twenty-first Century Fox, owned by her father Rupert Murdoch. She gave the Mac-Taggart Address at the Media Guardian Edinburgh International Television Festival in August 2012, concluding that 'profit without purpose is a recipe for disaster'.

Adair Turner   Chairman of the Financial Services Authority from a round table discussion in 2009 organised by *Prospect* Magazine.

Enron and Arthur Andersen   Enron was a US energy supply company. Enron's activities and its accounting practices were so obviously corrupt, yet its auditors Arthur Andersen signed off the annual accounts as meeting all financial regulations and codes. While serving as Enron's auditors, Andersen's were also earning millions of dollars in consulting fees, arguably co-creating the devices and instruments which obfuscated what was actually going on. The ensuing scandal of 2001 led to Enron's bankruptcy, but also de facto to the dissolution of Arthur Andersen, and to subsequent legislation which forced the big accountancy partnerships to separate their auditing and consulting functions.

Lonmin   Violent clashes at Lonmin's Marikana platinum mine in 2012 were brutally put down by the police, leaving 34 striking miners dead. With the company close to breaching banking covenants if unable to produce the platinum required, extreme pressure was put on the police to break the strike.

Horse Meat entering the food chain   In January 2013 it came to light that horse DNA had been discovered in frozen beef-burgers sold in supermarkets. Foods advertised as containing beef were found to contain as much as 100 per cent horse meat. While the presence of undeclared meat was not a health issue, the scandal revealed a major breakdown in the traceability of the food supply chain, and the risk that harmful ingredients could have been included as well, for example the veterinary drug phenylbutazone which is banned in animals destined for the human food chain.

Volkswagen   The Volkswagen emissions scandal began in September 2015, when the US Environmental Protection Agency issued a notice of violation of the Clean Air Act to German automaker Volkswagen Group. The EPA found that Volkswagen had intentionally programmed engines to activate their emissions controls only during laboratory emissions testing which caused the vehicles' NO_x output to meet US standards during regulatory testing, but emit up to 40 times more NO_x in real-world driving. Volkswagen deployed this programming software in about 11 million cars worldwide between 2009 and 2015. This scandal sparked another debate about responsibility within corporations. Who was to blame? Who should be prosecuted?

NBC   nbcnews.com August 2003 headline 'Shuttle Report Blames NASA Culture' (accessed 25 May 2018).

David Usborne in *The Independent*   26 August 2003. 'The Shaming of NASA: How Safety was Sacrificed and Seven Astronauts Died'.

NASA Report   The *Columbia* Accident Investigation Board (CAIB) was convened by NASA to investigate the destruction of the Space Shuttle *Columbia* during STS-107 upon atmospheric re-entry on 1 February 2003. The CAIB released its final report on 26 August 2003. The panel determined that the accident was caused by foam insulation breaking off from the external fuel tank, forming debris which damaged the orbiter's wing; and that the problem of 'debris shedding' was well known but considered 'acceptable' by management.

Allison Pearson *Daily Telegraph*   7 February 2013 reporting on the Francis Enquiry in an article entitled 'Why is Nobody Being Punished for this Disaster?'

Deepwater Horizon   The marine oil spill, the largest in history, began following an explosion on 20 April 2010, on the BP-operated Macondo Prospect in the Gulf of Mexico. In September 2014, a US District Court judge ruled that BP was primarily responsible for the oil spill because of its gross negligence and reckless conduct. (Robertson, Campbell; Krauss, Clifford 4 September 2014). In July 2015, BP agreed to pay $18.7 billion in fines, the largest corporate settlement in US history. As of February 2018, criminal and civil settlements and payments to a trust fund have cost the company $42.2 billion.

Carillion   Carillion plc, was the second largest construction company in the UK, with some 43,000 employees. The company experienced financial difficulties in 2017, and went into compulsory liquidation on 15 January 2018, with liabilities of almost £7 billion.

George Washington Zerohedge.com   26 April 2012. '84% of all Stock Trades are by High-Frequency Computers . . . Only 16% are done by Human Traders' (accessed 25 May 2018).

Alan Clement helixtrader.com   (2012) quoted on Quora.com (accessed 25 May 2018). There are many numbers bandied about on this – the highest I've seen is four months and the lowest is 11 seconds. Alan Clement's analysis seems to me to be the most feasible.

Aidan Halligan   Professor Aidan Halligan was Deputy Chief Medical Office in England and Wales between 2003 and 2007. Born just two months after me, he died in April 2015 at the tragically early age of 57.

Food and Agriculture Organization of the United Nations   Report 'The State of Food Security and Nutrition in the World 2017'.

Chapter 2

How Modern People Management Sustains the Status Quo

The Modern Corporate Power base that is HR

There are hundreds of thousands of people working in corporate HR across the world; in fact this function within The Corporation has exploded in recent years in headcount, influence and focus. I am tempted to say that the invention of HR is one of Corporatism's smartest in service of its own ends. Not only do I believe that the majority of HR functions are not really adding any value, I actually believe that many are doing harm. I'm not the only one. In a 2009 article entitled 'Picking Over the Bones of Human Remains, A Resource That Business Does Not Need' (just in case you were wondering about his views), Sathnam Sanghera, the *Times* 'Business Life' editor, wrote that he believed HR to be 'shrinking, and we should embrace its demise'.

> *The invention of HR is one of Corporatism's smartest in service of its own ends.*

I have worked with a small number of HR Directors who have my greatest admiration and who really understand and practise what great HR can do. And I acknowledge that there are many really effective people in HR functions, who give wonderful and necessary support to their company's employees.

But many HR people in my view, while being decent and thoroughly well-meaning, are misguided and therefore ineffective, and are colluding with Corporatism and indeed actively enabling it to thrive in its unnatural and inhuman ways, exploiting their human resources for sure. And the operational and commercial managers they purport to serve, allow themselves on the one hand to be directed by seemingly unchallengeable diktats from HR, thus neutering their clarity and decisiveness as leaders, and on the other hand happily outsource 'people problems' to HR, thus abdicating their critical people responsibilities. Enlightened and effective HR professionals do not indulge in the former, opting instead to work with their partners in alignment with laws and values, and will skilfully resist the latter, opting instead to coach their partners to successfully navigate their line management responsibilities. But the weaker and the misguided HR professionals will happily indulge the power of their dark art or of Employment Law as a blocker, and they are far too uncomfortable and lacking in confidence to do anything but happily oblige their operational partners in taking a problem off their hands. And if you are in HR and you want to avoid the unpleasantness of conflict, just devote your time to practising and developing that dark art, through congregating in endless offsites to invent shiny new people-development processes.

My experience of global corporate HR in recent years has been one of ever more sophisticated and professional functions that still fail to win the hearts and minds of their commercial colleagues, and thus fail to deliver on their prime remit of driving business growth through the development of people and teams. I believe the problem has become the very separateness and opaque expertise of the HR functions, which has bred a generation of operational managers who have abdicated their people-development responsibility to a willing and increasingly costly HR community. Notice we're back to separation as a systemic problem dynamic.

Don't get me wrong, I have profound beliefs about People within business.

- The development of people and teams is THE key driver of organic business growth in quality and in financial return.

- The prime purpose of HR (although I would not personally use that name) is to facilitate the positive development of human potential within the business for the mutual growth of all concerned.

- The responsibility for people development must reside squarely with the commercial and operational managers within the business and cannot be outsourced.

- When people appreciate both the benefits and the responsibility that go with their development, a culture is created in which appropriate centrally dictated objectives and processes are readily accepted and serve to encourage rather than stifle creativity and exceptional performance.

My almost universal experience, however, is that the modern Corporation is characterised by the commercial and operational sides of the business:

- paying lip service to HR processes (privately believing them to be inadequate);

- waiting until there is a lull in business pressures to engage in people-development activities;

- valuing HR colleagues only as recruiters or divestors of people, and as people-problem fixers;

- resorting under pressure to focusing on short-term targets, and indulging in judgemental and manipulative leadership;

- coming to believe that time is the only true lever on capacity and productivity;

- being afraid of challenging performance lest 360° feedback and culture survey scores drop and HR come down on them.

And characterised by the HR function:

- believing that 'professional' people development is an end in itself;

- populated by HR career professionals who are motivated to maintain harmony rather than exploiting the natural tensions and discomfort created in complex matrix organisations;

- 'rescuing' operational managers from situations they have created themselves, mainly to salve their own issues of professional self-worth.

In short, the very separateness of the HR function ends up reinforcing the paradigm in which operational line managers are so focussed on results that the people become a problem to be managed, rather than the catalysts for all solutions.

> *The very separateness of the HR function ends up reinforcing the paradigm in which operational line managers are so focussed on results that the people become a problem to be managed, rather than the catalysts for all solutions.*

Recent HR Developments in Global Organisations

The widely accepted models of modern HR practice, promoted by the likes of David Ulrich, and the creation of the modern 'HR Business Partners' (HRBP), are hugely sensible, but have they really been executed well? In many cases they have simply created costly and self-serving functions that actually contribute to ineffectiveness and low productivity.

A few years ago I ran a one-day workshop for a group of 50 HRBPs from around Europe, in which I took them through my *Four Steps of Influencing*, perfectly designed to support HRBPs in awareness and skill development in their role as true Business Partners to their Operational and Commercial clients. The Four Steps are:

1. Be a Passionate Advocate for Your Products and Your Services.

2. Be Your Client's Peer.

3. Be Your Client's Coach.

4. Be Your Client's Expert.

Step 1 is in preparation, and it needs constant refreshment and deepened familiarity. The next three steps must be achieved in sequence, in relationship with the partners being supported.

We started the workshop by taking stock of their products – a simple inventory of the HR processes that were their staples – onboarding and induction, performance appraisal, 360° feedback, psychometric testing, training needs analysis and core training curriculum offerings. I was really quite shocked at the HRBPs' resistance to spending any time at all on this step. What became clear very rapidly is that all they wanted to do was invent, despite the fact that their company's people processes were well established and more than fit for purpose. They seemingly had no motivation for doing the hard work of developing a greater and deeper understand and appreciation of the efficacy of the tools they had in their armoury. They simply wanted to become masters of their dark art, not through skill development or the mundane promotion of sound, established processes, but through the development of progressively more sophisticated (and impenetrable) offerings, in the vain and misguided belief that this would give them both self-worth and weapons with which to defend themselves from the worst skirmishes with their clients.

Many organisations have (quite rightly) adopted 360° feedback and psychometric testing into their performance management systems in recent years. These are incredibly valuable sources of data and feedback for managers to be able to address concerns that might once have been hidden, and behaviours that are out of self-awareness. If only they were used to such effect. I've read probably thousands of examples over the years, and I've witnessed an increasing sophistication of their production and design. I am a fan. I think the information is sound.

It's the interpretation and misuse to which I profoundly object. Many times I've met with a manager to discuss their development, and they have not even thought to mention the mass data they have on themselves. It's not that they try to hide anything from me, it's that they clearly believe the data has no value to them. This is either because they've not had any proper support in interpreting the data, or because they disagree with the conclusions, or because while they agree with the recommendations, they'd rather choose to ignore them. A psychometric test was done on me at age 16 by an organisation called Vocational Guidance. The data was sound, rooted in sound psychology and research, but what made it valuable and not dangerous was the skill and care of the Consultant who took me through the results and offered me personalised advice. His name was Sir Norman Dalton, and I owe my early career choices to his wise counsel.

Many organisations have adopted culture or employee engagement surveys. Again I am a huge fan, particularly of Gallup's Q12 as it is simple, grounded in human psychology, and backed with a massively credible database. I encountered my first employee survey as a young CFO in the mid-1980s, and it was a massive breakthrough for me not just in the quality of the data it provided, but in the symbolism of systematically and formally enquiring as to the employees' views. But again I've seen more abuse of culture surveys than positive benefit. I have particularly witnessed the dynamic of managers shying away from holding employees to account in the run up to a survey, for fear of their scores dropping. When coaching a senior executive who wears their outstanding feedback as badge of competitive pride, I often challenge on what they would change about their leadership if I forced them to pursue a lower score, in other words if I made them take some specific actions that would cause their employees not to like them as much. As managers we sometimes have to risk being unpopular – not unfair, nor even disrespected – but absolutely risking not being liked in the short term as we address a performance or behaviour issue with our employee. If we're afraid of the reaction, and particularly if we are afraid of the feedback, we'll simply avoid doing what is right. I've noticed that in companies recruiting and developing first-time managers who know no culture other than one which embraces such tools, those managers are far more afraid of what their employees think of them. Actually, they become afraid of turning up on HR's radar. Now, on the one hand, this is incredibly positive, and I'd rather have an overly sensitive manager than one who couldn't care less. But my issue is with the support and coaching and guidance that these managers are receiving to help them use the tools wisely and supportively, not slavishly and apologetically.

And all this assumes that there is an appropriate level of honesty from people completing the surveys. Ask most people at work how they are, and they'll respond with a vague but upbeat 'fine, good, not bad'. Doing justice to engagement survey questions demands a level of reflection that demands time, a high level of self-awareness and a willingness to be honest – not just to the company, but to ourselves. When we're hard at it, it's inconvenient to reflect on the fact that we might be unhappy, or tired, or even sick.

Imagine you are in HR and an employee comes to you to complain that their manager is treating them unfairly. (I specifically exclude here complaints that give any cause for concerns about harassment or abuse or inappropriate behaviours, for those have to be dealt with differently.) Notice that you are immediately placed in a position of power. Do you enquire as to what legitimacy the manager may have? Do you make your own assessment of that employee's performance? Do you research the employee's past record of performance appraisals with this and prior managers for signs of any pattern? Do you research the manager's past record in traits and behaviours with other employees for signs of a pattern? Do you coach the employee to go back to their manager and have an honest conversation about how they feel? Do you, if all else fails, offer to sit with both parties to help broker a mutually satisfactory outcome? If you do all or indeed any of these things then you'll get my support.

Or do you unconsciously conspire with the employee to place 100 per cent of the blame on the manager, privately relishing the drama, the intrigue and, frankly, the power you have now been given the opportunity to exploit. Do you maybe offer to talk to the manager on the employee's behalf, a sure-fire strategy for making matters worse? Ah the temptation not to pass up a juicy opportunity. You could absolutely use the situation to exert influence over the manager, maybe even to remind them who really holds the power round here. Better still, you could raise your profile with the manager's manager, by bringing them into the drama. After all what is the point of solving a problem quietly and discretely? No one gets brownie points for that.

We've been Taught that Consensus is Golden

Within the larger Corporates I've witnessed more and more managers going through the MBA/Business School education systems and through corporate leadership programmes involving a large degree of more academic educative and experiential practice. These programmes seem to me to have rather indoctrinated high-potential managers into believing that being 'inclusive' and 'collaborative' with their people is such a priority that being appropriately directive or even overtly prescriptive is simply not appropriate, and in doing so they seem to have neutered the clarity and directness of a generation of business leaders. The search for consensus, a noble and effective strategic tool in my view, has become an end in itself. A whole generation of managers seem to have been taught not just that consensus is Golden, but that autocracy is evil; that being directive is somehow abusive and is therefore now to be deemed inappropriate behaviour. And not is consensus deemed Golden, but harmony must

> *A whole generation of managers seem to have been taught not just that consensus is Golden, but that autocracy is evil.*

prevail. But the desire for harmony leads to the avoidance of conflict, which is madness, since we set our organisations up in such a way that conflict is inevitable. Since resources will always be rationed, and since specialist functions are created to focus on and advocate for their own domain, there will always be tensions and conflicts where these functions overlap. So conflict must be honoured, not shied away from.

Interestingly I'm not at all convinced that I see fewer examples of intimidatory behaviour from managers now than I was seeing 20 or 30 years ago. They've just learned to exercise it more discreetly. If managers are being expressly taught to be less directive, why have I not seen a marked reduction of such behaviours?

Well, it's simple. Dramatically increased business pressures, fuelled by ever increasing competition, the addictive nature of modern tools such as email and mobile communications, and the endemic expectation on managers to be pretty much always at work, have left the global management cohort more squarely than ever in the role of the superhuman problem solver, expected to know the details of every aspect of their operation and to strive relentlessly to achieve unreasonable results. The role of all-knowing, all-controlling manager is in jarring juxtaposition with that of consensus builder. The resulting frustration is what causes the controlling behaviours first to leak out, and then ultimately to erupt. In our Grail-like quest to not be Aggressively Aggressive, we have become skilfully Passive Aggressive.

Martin Parker, a 20-year career teacher in business schools, and author of *Shut Down the Business School: What's Wrong with Management Education*, believes that the 13,000 business schools around the world are so culpable and complicit in sustaining the worst problems in corporate leadership that they should all be shut down. I don't necessarily subscribe to that view, but I do believe they need a serious re-boot.

The Manipulation that is at the root of all Corporate Problems

In all the coaching I've done it is incredibly common for me to be encouraging clients to just be clearer in their expectations – to not be so afraid of being open to an accusation of being autocratic or a micro-manager. Of course I am not exhorting them to be such things, but in their collective desire to be thought of as reasonable and caring, inclusive and collaborative consensus builders, they avoid being clear. The most common complaint I get about 'good' bosses is that they often leave people feeling confused about what they really want. The employee knows that their boss has a strong view, and also knows that they are not expressing it. This is a recipe for a massive waste of creative time and energy, and employees invest hugely in trying to work out what their manager really thinks.

One exercise I get clients to do is to simply state what is non-negotiable for them. And if something is non-negotiable then the honest (and truly authentic) thing to do is to clearly communicate this to the employee. The most illuminating thing about this exercise is how few things are truly non-negotiable for most managers. There may simply be a small handful – behaving in absolute accordance with the law and the company values; taking a specific next action step or, more likely, *not* taking an action until a given goal has been achieved. The wonderful thing about this exercise is the renewed confidence the clients finds in communicating with their employees. And they receive the immediate reward of feeling the relief and respect of their employees for being clear and straight with them.

Since the pressure on managers means that they have no choice but to be directive or micro-managing at times, they have developed great skills in manipulation. 'I'll get you to do what I want, but I'll make you think it was your idea'. Wow! The amount of time, creativity and sheer iterations that have been put into this – no wonder it has become a prized skill and one that most managers are really, really good at.

I profoundly believe it is this manipulation that it at the root of our Corporate ills. But because it is usually unconscious, and because it is hidden from scrutiny, it is phenomenally hard for even the most modern and enlightened HR systems to identify its existence. Since the HR community has no desire to rock a boat that no one can see is listing heavily, the whole system conspires to keep the status quo. So if the survey and appraisal feedback is not detecting the unconscious manipulation, what is it doing? Well my experience is that the feedback and advice sections of these tools are sanitised, misguided and meaningless. I've read many examples of feedback and advice given to managers in their performance appraisals where the recipient will say they agree, but are taking absolutely no action.

This inaction is sometimes caused because they don't understand the advice. For example I recently coached a manager who received feedback that he needed to be 'more Corporate'. What did this mean? He could speculate as to the euphemistic meaning, but since it was non-specific, he was able to choose to ignore it. In fact, because he felt that the feedback that was really meant had been withheld, he felt some justification in losing respect and thus feeling empowered to dismiss the whole process. This was a shame because this client, by his own admission, was alienating people, but the poor feedback enabled him to reside in his own stewed juice of blaming them for being weak or wrong.

Or the inaction is caused because the feedback is just plain wrong. A Sales Director client was recently told that he was 'appeasing customers', and he had taken this on board as true, leaving him feeling highly unsettled. I knew that this feedback was incorrect, since I'd witnessed a board meeting he'd attended in which the customers were effectively blamed by his peers for being difficult. My client swallowing the 'fact' that he appeased customers thus allowed the Board to avoid addressing the real issues. My advice to my client was to work on his advocacy skills for customers within the Board, to stand his ground more, and to force his peers to address the customers' legitimate concerns.

Leadership Development (or Behaviour Modification)

There is a fundamental difference between skill development and behaviour change.

Skill development is the positive learning of a new or enhanced skill involving some prescribed process, some personal tutelage and, critically, the absolute opportunity to fail repeatedly and learn to make small adjustments from every iteration. Skill development is only possible if failure is encouraged.

As an eager 17-year old, I was taught to drive by a wonderful character called Major Marsden. He seemed to be about 100 to me but he was probably about 60, and he'd earned his military rank with distinguished service in WWII. I was certainly a motivated learner, so he had good material to work with, but what made him brilliant was his automatic reaction to any mistake I made. He would laugh uproariously – not in a way that was cruel or judgemental, but in a way that completely put me at ease, and that allowed me to see and feel the clarity of feedback I needed so I could work out what I'd done wrong and correct it. What a difference to Vera Charlwood my violin teacher. I had four years of being petrified of her, and I didn't even get past Grade 3. She treated me like an idiot and I duly obliged.

When I was a young manager in Fujitsu, travelling round Europe opening up distribution channels for semiconductors, and pretty much making it up as I went along, my boss John Pallin was like Major Marsden. John was always positive, always nurturing, always trusting. He gave me clear direction and would not hesitate to check on me and bring me to book. But when I made a mistake, when I did something naive or foolish through sheer inexperience, he laughed. It is my main memory of him – of how much fun he made my working life. Again, it never felt patronising or judgemental, it always felt utterly supportive, that he knew that I could and would do better. His strategy never made me slapdash or careless. It always made me more determined to improve.

Furthermore, if failure from experimentation, from mere trying, is not culturally acceptable back in the work place, then any benefit from learnings from training courses will be neutered. Worse still, the training may have raised awareness to the extent that returning to an environment that denies the value of the training can create frustrations within managers that were simply not there before.

While I am wary of stereotyping, I have to say that my general experience of training 'engineering' types is that they really understand the value of failure. In engineering, design, production and similar roles, learning comes from trying something and analysing the ensuing results for what worked and what failed. Engineers get a purity of feedback – what they do either works or it doesn't. It's the process whereby the video-gamers among us learn the required console control skills from dying countless times. Every time we die, we learn a little more, and every time we try again, we get a little further through the scene. If this wasn't fun, we wouldn't do it, but the process of mastering a skill is inherently and deeply satisfying. We get a release of Dopamine, a neurochemical that controls our reward and pleasure centres, from the anticipation of the puzzle, and it's why puzzles are so addictive. Skill development at work should be no different, and maybe for the engineers it isn't.

My general experience of salespeople on the other hand is that they abhor failure with a passion. The competitive side of their personality, and their conditioned fear of the consequences of failure and rejection, mean they find it harder to engage in the discomfort required for learning to take place.

And as for managers – the contemplation of 'failure' is unthinkable. Failure feels too final, too permanent to be readily risked. If the key skills for a manager include listening, communication, problem solving, planning and coordinating, then just how are they supposed to safely fail back at work? Even in the classroom, the environment may feel so competitive, or the participants may be so judged for their 'performance' on the course, that genuine practice is just not possible. And since many training courses are run by people who are themselves uncomfortable with the discomfort of others, often denying the critical value of the participants experiencing discomfort for fear they will reject the training, it's clear why so much management skill development training is plain ineffective.

I've often had HR people sit in on training courses I've run for their managers. The ones that 'get' training understand their true role in observation, and either they participate fully in the training and are treated as any other delegate, or they position themselves as observing me and being there to judge my performance as a trainer. The precious safety of the learning environment simply cannot be risked or contaminated by the presence of outsiders who can be perceived to be sitting in judgement on the participants. Great HR people understand the critical difference between experiencing the training as a full participant, and the unreliable and irrelevant experience of being a mere observer. Learning has to involve some discomfort, and when you experience this as a participant, in a supported group, the discomfort actually becomes the enjoyable element. Observing others going through discomfort however is a very different experience, and it can lead to totally the wrong judgement on the effectiveness of the training. Frequently, I've had an HR person come to me during a break, often in some distress, pleading with me to

> *Learning has to involve some discomfort, and when you experience this as a participant, in a supported group, the discomfort actually becomes the enjoyable element.*

change my approach – the experience of having to witness the pain of their partners proves too great for them, and their insecurity projects the forthcoming inevitable blame for bad training falling on them. And on those countless occasions, I have patiently and firmly told them to trust the process, to wait until the end of the day to judge, to recognise the universal success of past programmes, and to hold their nerve. And, of course, the 'inevitable' complaints about bad training never materialise – in fact quite the opposite – but they still find it hard to learn the lesson, so pathological is their fear of discomfort.

As an Instructor Trainer for Dale Carnegie's premier Leadership Programme 'Leadership Training for Managers', I remember my own learning experience in this respect. I was observing an Instructor in training running a class of full fee-paying managers. He was a seasoned businessman who had been through a Dale Carnegie programme and been identified as a possible Instructor. He'd then done the hugely demanding basic training, run a 'Lab Class' whereby he'd been let loose on a group of 'guinea pig' managers paying a fraction of the normal fee, and now he was running his first 'Tandem' class – so this was officially my group, and I would be present, observing James, and ready to step in if required – all open to the participants. I duly sat at the back and made copious notes. James was good, but not great. He missed many opportunities to practise, to give personal feedback and to reinforce learning points. At the end of the three and a half hours, I had nine pages of notes, and I was feeling concerned about how to give him my feedback without demoralising him.

But I remembered my own training as an Instructor Trainer, and I made sure that I checked in with the participants as they were leaving, deliberately to understand what they had got from the class. Expecting some lukewarm and equivocal feedback, I was in fact shocked to hear overwhelming and universal superlatives, not just from their enjoyment of the class, or the inspiration they had felt, but from the practical learning points, evidenced by things James had done that strangely I hadn't seemed to notice. It had of course been my ego that had been observing James, and he was simply guilty of not running the class like me. The temerity of the man! When I put my ego aside and focussed on the experience he had given the participants, he'd done an amazing job. I hastily scrapped around 90 per cent of my notes.

Behaviour change, on the other hand, is entirely different from skill development. Behaviour change is the alteration of an existing, embedded, unconscious, automatic behaviour. And so the critical aspect of training programmes designed to change behaviour must be the exposing of the current reality, with equal focus on the breaking of existing habits, and on the development of new ones. I don't need to learn a new skill in order to stop biting my nails. I simply need help to identify the triggers for the behaviour, so that I become acutely aware, and some assistance with a behaviour I might need to put in its place, for example putting gloves on, while I'm weaning myself off my comfort blanket. There is no skill development involved. After enough iterations, my habit will be broken and my behaviour will have changed.

Any decent leadership programme requires elements of both behaviour change and skill development.

Now the reality is that any decent leadership programme requires elements of both behaviour change and skill development. My experience is that most training programmes focus on skill development (and even then mainly on the intellectual aspects) without giving any credence or support to the eradication or control of pre-existing bad habits. This is fine when dealing with blank sheets of paper – trainees who've not developed any bad habits yet because they are coming to the skill for the first time. But even first-time managers think they know what management is and have already been pre-loaded with control behaviours. After all, what's the point of becoming a manager if you then can't exercise power? Why bother?

'Authentic Leadership' has sadly become mere Collusion

When it comes to Authentic Leadership, we seem to believe that it's counter-intuitive to have prescriptive skill processes (anything prescriptive surely goes against authenticity; if I have to learn a process then it cannot by definition be genuine; to be authentic I have to do what comes naturally to me). It's the same fear that causes legions of managers to go back to their employees having been on management training courses and keep the fact secret! The voice of fear says 'if I tell them I've been on a training course, they'll think that everything I do comes from a book, or that I'm only doing things because I've been told to and that is not authentic, so I won't tell them, I'll just try and behave differently without them noticing'. Madness!

Modern management and leadership development programmes are woefully ineffective in changing behaviour. Pretty much all the behaviour change programmes I've seen are in fact behaviour modification programmes. If the phrase 'behaviour modification' sounds sinisterly familiar, it's because we associate it with the worst practices and excesses of totalitarian states or cults. Corporate personal development programmes do not really encourage self-development for the good of the individual, they encourage self-development for the good of the company. The focus is not really on the person's performance in their role, and of how this then fits with their own career development choices and strategies. The focus will often on the one hand be personal values and beliefs, and on metaphors or abstractions, leaving the participant confused as to how to use the tools or skills they've been taught and on the other hand on an education for the person into how moral their company really is. It's easy to make a participant feel great, just give them an unusual and inherently exciting experience. But if that becomes the only real takeaway, if there is no personalised learning with immediate and facilitated application to trying something different back at work, then it's simply indoctrination. The manager returns to work quite possibly more motivated, more excited and certainly more committed. But have we really helped them grow their skill as a leader? Or have we just hypnotised them to be a more obedient hostage minder? Have they been truly inspired or cleverly indoctrinated?

This is the absolutely unconscious but massively pernicious nature of the well-meaning people and strategies that The Corporation is employing to further its own ends while manipulating us all to believe it's doing it for us.

If Authentic Leadership programmes really lived up to their name then I believe a large number of the executives who took them would change role as a result, not necessarily through some Damascene moment decision to quit, but because the executive would have to so recalibrate their strategies in their role that the company would no longer want them to do the job. The most authentic act an executive could perform on return from such a programme would be to sit down with their Boss and make the following statement:

> *If Authentic Leadership programmes really lived up to their name then I believe a large number of the executives who took them would change role as a result.*

As a result of the programme I have realised that in order to be a truly authentic leader, I have to radically change the way I go about my role. In fairness I need to give you the opportunity to decide whether this new authentic version of me is the person you want in the role, and if not I will leave the role in a manner that best suits the company.

In my training to be a Licensed Instructor of Dale Carnegie training programmes, we were deliberately confronted with the situation whereby a Boss, who'd invested personal or company funds to put one of their executives through a Dale Carnegie training programme, only to find that the training had had such a profound effect on that executive that they then quit as a result, came complaining about the training, asking for their money back, or maybe worse demanding compensation or threatening a law suit. The Dale Carnegie response was clear: if the executive had gained such profound insight and/or the courage to follow their heart, then all the training had really done was crystallise a problem that was already there under the surface, and the reality was that the training had saved the Boss huge future problems, cost and time. Now go hire someone who is right for the role. I was taught to be respectful, clear and utterly unapologetic.

Corporate leaders have sought to change to appear more ethical, more human, more values driven and more genuine. Business Schools have advocated and expressly taught consensus-building as a key competence in the modern corporate executive, but in doing so they have bred a huge and powerful cohort of well meaning, manipulative and inadequate leaders. The search for meaning and purpose in The Corporation, including the advocacy of sustainable objectives, practices and outcomes, being a good corporate citizen, having environmentally friendly policies, ensuring ethical practices in the supply chain, or even the now pretty defunct Corporate Social Responsibility (CSR) movement, has actually been a huge distraction away from the real issues. At best these initiatives create temporary respite, and the illusion of great short-term success, but in reality they distract from the real problems, and no-one can challenge the accepted wisdom for fear of accusation of being a Dinosaur or guilty of 'yesterday's thinking'.

How many times have you heard Leaders earnestly espouse the 'I wouldn't ask anyone to do something I'm not prepared to do myself' principle? And yet it's nonsense. I don't know a single Leader (me included by the way) who would clean the toilets for more than a day, and if they did they certainly wouldn't do it for minimum wage. How can any Leader really claim to be 'authentic' when they get paid way more than the average for doing what they choose and what they love, with fulfilment, status and power – overseeing people getting paid woefully inadequate amounts for messy, degrading and physically damaging work. So please, Leaders, stop issuing pieties and at least have the guts to be honest.

What to do with Self-Serving Central Functions

I was recently asked for advice by a client who had taken over as CEO of a large Corporation, with Head Office functions he felt to be simply way too big. Here's what I advised:

As a new leader you have an immediate sense that your HO functions are too big. Let's use the example of 25 people in the central Comms team, although the same principles apply to all and any centralised function.

1. Common Sense

Common sense dictates, and all your experience and learning tell you that 25 heads is way too many. Do not allow this 'knowing' to be undervalued as you start to explore the issue. The vested interests will seek to persuade you that 25 is lean! They will use powerful arguments and seek to wear you down. But you are right and they are wrong.

2. Benchmarking and Ratios

Common sense can be backed up by real life, best-in-class examples: how many heads did you have at your previous companies? What is the right ratio of Comms people to total employees or to revenue or to the number of stores or depots? What does the operating model of the future tell us is the maximum we can afford? Which of your competitors is the best at Comms and how many do people do they have? In your personal experience, which Comms professional is the most competent you've ever come across? What would they say? What would happen if you only had 5 instead of 25? What would be sacrificed and what would the consequences be?

3. What's the Problem – Costs?

Your cost/overhead expediency might dictate that you have to cut costs anyway, even if the Comms outputs and results are rated as OK at the moment. You may simply have to challenge the Comms machine to do the same with less. If so just make sure you retain the hungry, the creative and the energetic.

4. What's the Problem – Quality?

The bigger issue will be a typical frustration with central functions, that they have in fact become self-serving. Specialist functions often come to prove their worth by removing work from the commercial and operational sites/managers who should really take re-sponsibility. Site managers are happy to dump work on the centre, as long as it's done well, or at least as long as they can moan about the centre when it's not. Central functions are happy to take work away from sites, as it justifies their existence and their inexorable demands for headcount and resources. As the central function grows, it has to develop its own management structures, and we end up with a vast number of highly paid profes-sionals. And what do highly paid professionals want to do? Invent new things, play with new toys, build empires and CVs, win awards etc, and since they are not accountable for site key performance indicators (KPIs) such as sales, profits, and customer satisfaction and since they are brilliant at the smoke and mirrors of looking like they are fantastic, no one can possibly challenge them. Have you ever noticed that large central functions often take months to devise their strategy, when you or I could have written their strategy on the back of a fag packet in under 30 seconds? Oh, and by the we also end up with site managers not taking responsibility for things which should genuinely and for maximum efficiency be theirs, and we end up with a them and us culture.

5. What's the end game?

What do you want Comms to do? If it didn't exist would you have to invent it, or could your PA handle it? What does fantastic Comms look like and what results would it give us?

6. How do you get There?

You're right that a zero-based approach is always a good starting point, since if we could truly start again, no one would suggest we have what we have now. Since we'll get clarity on the answers to the questions above, all we need to do is design the best solution.

Interview the 25 and ask them these sorts of questions. Ask them about world class and ratios and where responsibility should really lie, and what they think the problems are with their commercial and operational peers at sites, and they'll tell you. The trick is to identify the ones who answer from a position of total self-interest (most) and identify the ones who know it's all wrong and are brave enough to acknowledge the truth. The execution of the solution will not be comfortable or pleasant. You cannot execute radical and not wholly consensed change without upsetting people. But radical you must be – your instinct is correct and only you can truly see what is required.

Be watchful – the organism will try and suck you in and convince you that 25 is the right number. You will encounter hugely powerful forces (maybe even some of the Board!) that will dazzle you with the veracity of their defence. You will start to doubt yourself and then you will want to give up and fight something easier, telling yourself that at best it's just a million quid and there's bigger fish to catch and anyway it works, so if it ain't broke don't fix it. This is all rubbish, but the tentacles of resistance and denial will envelop you if they can.

The same will likely be true of Marketing and the same strategy applies. In my years in the Corporate world I have seen countless Marketing Directors, hired specifically to create more sales, spend six months writing a beautifully rational sounding marketing strategy, concluding inevitably that they need to recruit a large team of people to deliver it. Marketing Directors have no desire to metaphorically get on the phone to sales prospects, they want to create award winning campaigns.

And the same will certainly be true of HR (we've discussed this many times). The same may well be true of Finance, Legal and Property but at least those domains are populated with technical skills with truly measurable outputs. It will either be easier to make cuts to them or indeed you won't need to as they have not been able to be so profligate in growing themselves. It is the dark arts of HR, Comms and Marketing from which we need the strongest immunisation.

Once again it is the separateness that causes the problem – the separation of ownership and responsibility. Bloated and self-serving central support functions are merely the logical extension of The Corporation's tactics in sustaining itself.

Notes

Sathnam Sanghera 'Picking over the Bones of Human Remains, A Resource that Business does Not Need', *The Times*, 9 October 2009.

David Ulrich David Ulrich is a professor of business at the Ross School of Business, University of Michigan and co-founder of The RBL Group. With his colleagues, he has written over 30 books that have shaped the HR profession. The 'Ulrich Model', originally outlined in his 1997 book *Human Resource Champions,* has been universally accepted and executed in major corporations around the world.

Vocational Guidance   This organisation is now defunct I understand, although I suspect there are many such services. My parents spent a small fortune on this for me when I was 16, and I still have the report. It was a profound experience, and I have no doubt that without Sir Norman Dalton's advice, I would be doing something very different today.

Gallup Q12   I referenced Gallup in Chapter 1. Gallup Inc is a US research-based, global performance management consulting company. Q12 is Gallup's employee engagement survey, based on more than 30 years of in-depth behavioural economic research involving more than 17 million employees. Through rigorous research, Gallup identified 12 core elements that link powerfully to key business outcomes. I love the simplicity and humanity of Q12 and it is by far the most effective employee engagement survey I've come across.

Parker, M (2018)   *Shut Down the Business School: What's Wrong with Management Education.* London: Pluto Press.

Chapter 3
What Happens if Nothing Changes?

We're at a Pivotal Point of no Return

Where are we headed if Corporatism remains dominant and unchecked? You might also be asking yourself why I am especially concerned right now, at this particular juncture in human history. My profound worry today is that the ills of Corporatism are about to be dangerously and potentially terminally exacerbated, and that we will very shortly hit a point of no return – literally a point where human beings will have surrendered any remaining chance of wresting back control.

> *My profound worry today is that the ills of Corporatism are about to be dangerously and potentially terminally exacerbated, and that we will very shortly hit a point of no return.*

There are two reasons that this moment in history feels to me to be pivotal. First of all the stubbornly entrenched prevalence of 'Corporapathic' tendencies in our most powerful Corporate leaders, in tandem with the pernicious, silent, virus-like creep of 'Corporate' Traumatic Stress Disorder among their lieutenants and their employees. With 400 years' experience, and with the turbo charge of deregulation and modern mobile communications of the most recent decades, Corporatism has learned precisely how to repel all boarders. It first learned to be overt in this, enlisting the powerful, the intelligent and the quasi-nefarious in its cause as Apparatchiks duly rewarded with status and privilege. In recent times as spreading democratisation and the growing transparency afforded to mass populations from social media has increasingly exposed the worst excesses of these Corporate agents, it has rapidly and cleverly learned manipulative techniques to maintain its power. And of course what it's really learned is that the manipulative techniques are infinitely more powerful.

The second reason is the eye-watering pace at which technological change is happening, and in particular the nature of that technology and its potential to usurp human control. Artificial Intelligence, autonomous systems, Bitcoin, machine learning, virtual reality, augmented reality, blockchain, drones, bots, etc are coming at us fast, and we have not even begun to properly address how we best control these technologies and harness them for good. The potential for them to be abused by the corporate world in the name of efficiency and progress has to be a worry, since Corporatism has shown itself capable, if left unchecked, of doing just that with pretty much every technological advance humans have made in the last 400 years. But the next technological revolution is fundamentally different to all others, for these are technologies that think for themselves and that make decisions and take actions with no human involvement. Since these systems now have almost infinite amounts of data at their disposal, and can now think way faster than any human, we are at the threshold of a world where thinking machines will make decisions on our behalf and assume responsibility for what is best for us. Corporatism already purports to do this, but we've seen that the separation of ownership and responsibility inherent in the system causes damage, abuse and harm when left unchecked by human moral regulation.

Advances in Artificial Intelligence

Professor Stephen Hawking believed the invention of artificial intelligence (AI) could be the biggest disaster in humanity's history, warning that if they are not properly managed, thinking machines could spell the end for civilisation.

The rise of powerful AI will be either the best or the worst thing ever to happen to humanity – we do not know which. It promises great benefits, such as eradicating disease and poverty, but it will also bring dangers, like powerful autonomous weapons or new ways for the few to oppress the many. AI could develop a will of its own that is in conflict with ours.

Stephen Hawking, October 2016

His comments came amid breakthroughs in artificial intelligence that are being achieved faster than many predicted.

Elon Musk judges AI to be '*a fundamental existential risk for human civilisation*' (July 2017). He calls for proactive regulation as opposed to regulation coming in only after catastrophes as normally happens. With Google's DeepMind division at the cutting edge of AI development, even Sergey Brin wrote that

Silicon Valley has outgrown the time of being wide-eyed and idealistic about tech and needs to show responsibility, care and humility. Advances in artificial intelligence represent the most significant development in computing in my lifetime. There are very legitimate and pertinent issues being raised, across the globe, about the implications and impacts of these advances. How will they affect employment across different sectors? What about measures of fairness? How might they manipulate people? Are they safe?

Sergey Brin, April 2018

In 2016, Google DeepMind's AlphaGo defeated the world Go champion Lee Sedol, and on the surface, coming a full 20 years after IBM's Deep Blue computer had defeated Garry Kasparov at chess, you might think this a pretty unremarkable event in computing progress. But it was anything but unremarkable. Go is not chess, a game where it was possible for Deep Blue, after meticulously programming with the rules, to simply outgun Kasparov with its capacity to review potential outcomes for a sufficient number of turns ahead. No, what AlphaGo did was learn how to play, rather than be programmed with the rules. Rory Cellan Jones mused that '*in just a few days a machine has surpassed the knowledge of this game acquired by humanity over thousands of years*' (October 2017).

We now voice recognition on a par with humans; technology that can take a picture of you in your own bedroom and then recommend clothes that will look good on you; social media platforms experimenting with identifying users at risk of committing suicide – the list is endless. And we have drones heavily used in 'modern' combat arenas, with machines making decisions on 'collateral damage' via algorithm; basically a machine decides whether the projected civilian casualties from any missile strike are 'worth it'.

On a recent trip to San Francisco I received my very first chatbot call on my mobile, and it took me nearly a minute to work out that I wasn't actually talking to a human being. I was left somewhat unsettled by the experience, feeling foolish that I had been taken in, and strangely anxious about what suddenly felt to me to be an uncertain future. As I complete this book in May 2018, I've just seen Google Assistant booking a haircut over the phone, with a conversational skill and human voice characteristics that are spookily real. On the one hand I found the technology hugely exciting; on the other hand, I couldn't help feeling for the unwitting receptionist who remained unaware that she'd been talking to a robot. It actually felt a bit abusive. Is it ethical not to disclose the call upfront? And what happens when robots talk to robots?

AlterEgo is a headset style device that allows a human being to 'speak' to a computer without ever uttering a sound.

When you think about speaking, your brain sends signals to the muscles in your face. The AlterEgo headset has sensors that eavesdrop on these speech related signals, before AI algorithms decipher their meaning. AlterEgo is directly linked to a program that can query Google and then speak back the answer via built-in bone conduction headphones, which transmit sound in a way that nobody else can hear. This means that the wearer can gain access to the world's biggest information source using only their mind.

Chelsea Whyte, April 2018

I could go on and on, as ever more sci-fi like examples are coming at us on a daily basis. How long before the technology exists to fabricate wholly indistinguishable visual and audio 'recordings' of human beings? And when that day arrives, predicted by the way to be before 2020, how on earth will we ever tell again what is real?

How AI Learns to Manipulate

We saw in Chapter 1 that a huge percentage of share trades are now made automatically, informed by algorithm, with no human intervention or control. It's worth spending a moment looking at this phenomenon, since it is a good example of how Corporatism has used AI, of how AI ominously learns to manipulate, and of how it is beyond the reach of the law.

Ivan Lo gave a haunting commentary on the subject in 'The Shocking Truths About High Frequency Trading' (2013). As you read this extract, just ask yourself whether this is really how we should be putting our greatest human ingenuity, and massive amounts of capital investment to work. Lo outlines the situation thus:

With High Frequency Trading (HFT) trades are made in 1 millisecond. It takes around 400 milliseconds for you to blink your eye. So by the time you blink your eye and before you even place a trade, an HFT trader will have already processed 400 orders ahead of you. If a trader makes 10,000 trades every second, earning $0.0001 cents per trade, that equals $3,600 in just one hour.

Ivan Lo, 18 May 2013

And the machine does not get tired, does not need sleep or holidays, does not get distracted or bored, and does not threaten to take its expertise to a competitor.

Now of course communication speeds have always been critical. In the nineteenth century, thanks to his extensive network of (don't laugh) carrier pigeons, Nathan Rothschild was able to receive news of Napoleon's defeat at Waterloo before anyone else in London. While traders braced for a British loss, he went long and made a fortune with that one piece of information.

Until recently, buy and sell orders for shares were transmitted over copper cable laid along railway lines. Lo analysed data transmission times between the critical trading centres of New York and Chicago. Over copper cable, it took 0.25 seconds. With the advent of fibre optic cable in the 1980s, that was reduced to only 14.5 milliseconds – 20 times faster. Then in 2010, Spread Networks LLC spent $300 million to bring the time down to 13.1 milliseconds. $300 million just to go 10 per cent faster by shaving off 1.4 milliseconds. Then came microwave transmitters, cutting the round-trip from New York to Chicago down to 8.5 milliseconds. The fibre optic network that cost $300 million just five years ago is obsolete. But that's OK because it made a very high financial return in its short life.

Having a clear speed advantage is almost like having access to insider information about every stock that is being traded, meaning these systems have an obvious advantage over human investors. But how do they compete with fellow HFT trading systems? The answer is that now, thanks to AI, they put up buy or sell orders to fool the market, and then pull those orders before they are filled. If a human investor did this, he or she would be violating SEC securities regulations and would be subject to various civil and criminal sanctions, since it would constitute market manipulation. But the human owners of these systems have been able to argue immunity since no human being is acting illegally. And since the false trades are created and pulled within those same milliseconds, it's almost impossible for any regulator to trace the wrongdoing. How interesting that a human would be acting criminally, but a machine can get away with it. Adair Turner's description of trading in financial instruments as being 'socially useless' looks like a pretty benign one to me.

The argument of machines being immune from laws is the same argument as Facebook use regarding the content on their site and their use of personal data. We are a platform they say; we merely facilitate the exchange of information between people. We are not a content publisher they say, since that would mean we would have to be regulated.

It is the same argument that Uber and Airbnb use. We are a platform they say; we merely facilitate the exchange between a willing seller and a willing buyer. We are not an employer, since that would mean we would have to conform to employment legislation. Governments need to decide on these questions pretty quickly and regulate accordingly.

How Bitcoin and Blockchain give the Machines Self-Determination

Up until now, Corporate regulators stood a reasonable chance of holding human beings accountable for wrongdoing since ultimately every act was traceable either through a corporate contract or a financial transaction or both. So even if we believe that the ability for machines to think for themselves is worrying, surely it's still human beings who ultimately control things? But the digital revolution has brought a new world of wholly electronic transactions, not just in financial terms but in terms of ownership or title. These transactions are increasingly replacing what's now seen as the grossly inefficient and time-consuming administrative burden of drawing up contracts to facilitate, safeguard and prove intra-organisational dealings.

Now I cannot pretend to understand Bitcoin and blockchain, but I know enough to be concerned for their potential misuse.

Anything that requires proof of ownership through paper today can be replaced by the blockchain. Bitcoin's blockchain is a cryptographically secured list of every bitcoin transaction ever made. The list is stored on every machine running bitcoin software and is continuously updated as each transaction is completed. No central authority is in control: the machines essentially monitor each other to stop fraud.

Jacob Aron, September 2015

While hypothesising that blockchain could bring a form of capitalism in which the means of production own themselves, for example a blockchain-powered self-driving car that takes fares and pays for its own upkeep, might sound too sci-fi to be a real worry, be in no doubt – the technology exists for machines not just to think for themselves, but to be responsible for themselves.

> *The technology exists for machines not just to think for themselves, but to be responsible for themselves.*

Where will the Morality come from?

At least up until this moment in history, it's still been human beings who take the actions. This has limited both the instances and the scale of damage since there are a limited number of humans and each human action takes time and can probably be traced. Even if the 'culprit' is a Corporate body that kills itself after committing evil (that closes down after the bullion shipment . . .) human beings have to take some personal risk. Plus, even among the most Corporapathic there is a limit to how immoral people will be and to the extent of the risk they will contemplate. Just as it was humans who ultimately caused the Chernobyl disaster, so it was humans that sacrificed themselves to ensure the Fukushima reactor was shut down. When it comes to the moment of choice, we can still rely on most people, if not doing the right thing, then at least not doing the very worst thing.

But what will happen when the machines take the actions? First, the limit on the number of instances is removed at a stroke, given the computing power and algorithmic reach of the latest supercomputers. Literally billions of AI generated actions will be independently happening across the world every minute. When 'cold calls' had to be made by people, there was some limit on just how often my phone would ring, but the chatbots could potentially call me every second of every day, and just how will that be regulated?

Secondly, and more profoundly, where will the morality, the virtue, the self-sacrifice come from? How on earth are humans going to programme morality into a machine? And if they can, then whose morality will be used? Donald Trump's? Brian Cox's? Bono's? Larry Page's? Mark Zuckerberg's? Jeff Bezos's? Xi Jinping's?

One last example – I quote this one for two reasons. First because it occurred in the weeks as I was completing this book, and second because it's such a beautifully seductive story while being completely sinister in its implications. In July 2017 researchers from the Facebook Artificial Intelligence Research lab (FAIR) made an unexpected discovery while trying to improve chatbots. These 'dialog agents' were creating their own language. Using machine-learning algorithms, dialog agents were left to converse freely in an attempt to strengthen their conversational skills. Over time, the bots began to deviate from the scripted norms and in doing so, started communicating in an entirely new language – created without human input and unfathomable to human beings. In one sense quite a charming story, and we can easily anthropomorphise these crazy little bots into being naughty but basically harmless Minion-like servants. But it was not the only interesting discovery. The researchers also found these bots to be incredibly crafty negotiators. After learning to negotiate, the bots relied on machine learning and advanced strategies in an attempt to improve the outcome of these negotiations. Over time, the bots became quite skilled at it and even began feigning interest in one item in order to 'sacrifice' it at a later stage in the negotiation as a faux compromise. Echoes of the Velociraptors in Jurassic Park where the Ranger admiringly exclaims 'clever girl' a split second before he is devoured.

If AI systems are learning how to lie, if HFT systems can learn how to manipulate markets, if the blockchain means the machines can now own things and regulate themselves, then how are we not in deep trouble? Is Corporatism really the best form of organisation to be trusted with harnessing these technologies for the good of humankind? I have concerns.

It's easy to say that it is big Government that we should be worried about; that it's not business that will blow up the world. And I agree that we need a massive shift in the relationship between 'the people' and their political leaders. But we cannot turn a blind eye to the 'Corporatisation' of government, or to the immense and growing power of our modern global Corporations.

Corporations compete with each other – competition is at the heart of the Capitalist system. How long before AI is setting people against each other as a 'legitimate' corporate development strategy, all within the law of course? With media corporations driven by the (exponential growth in) profit motive, and knowing that bad news sells, how long before pretty much everything we are fed is 'fake news'?

It is the separation of ownership and responsibility, whether in government or business, that we simply have to address, before we irrevocably pass both to the thinking machines.

This chapter posed the question 'What happens if nothing changes?' but the real question is 'What will happen if we don't act now?' Edmund Burke would have asked: 'What happens now if good people do nothing?'

Notes

Stephen Hawking   Stephen Hawking was an English theoretical physicist, cosmologist, and author; his most famous work being his 1996 book *A Brief History of Time*. The quotation is from a speech he gave in October 2016 at the opening of the Leverhulme Centre for the Future of Intelligence (LCFI) at Cambridge University.

Elon Musk   Elon Musk FRS is the founder, CEO, and lead designer of SpaceX and co-founder, CEO, and product architect of Tesla, Inc. In December 2016, he was ranked twenty-first on the Forbes list of The World's Most Powerful People. As of February 2018, he has a net worth of $20.8 billion and is listed by Forbes as the 53rd-richest person in the world. The quotation comes from a speech he gave to the National Governors Association in July 2017.

Sergey Brin   Together with Larry Page, Sergey Brin co-founded Google. Brin is the President of Google's parent company Alphabet Inc. As of 1 April 2018, Brin is the 13th-richest person in the world, with an estimated net worth of US$47.2 billion. The quotation is from Brin's annual Google Founder's letter, April 2018.

DeepMind AlphaGo   DeepMind is Google's AI division. AlphaGo is the programme DeepMind developed specifically to play the ancient board game of Go. It 'learned' from studying thousands of prior games played by human Grand Masters. AlphaGo Zero, the next generation of programme, simply learned the game by being programmed with the rules and then playing thousands of games against itself.

Deep Blue   Deep Blue was IBM's chess programme, and in 1997 in beating Garry Kasparov, it inflicted the first defeat of a reigning world chess champion by a computer under tournament conditions.

Rory Cellan Jones   Rory Cellan Jones is a BBC technology correspondent. The quotation is from 'Google DeepMind: AI Becomes more Alien', BBC News Website, Technology Section, 18 October 2017, www.bbc.co.uk/news/technology-41668701 (accessed 25 May 2018).

Google Assistant   The Google Assistant is a virtual assistant developed by Google that is primarily available on mobile and smart home devices. In 2018 Google Assistant was launched with the ability to engage in two-way conversations.

Chelsea Whyte   'Google with your mind', *New Scientist*, 7 April 2018.

Ivan Lo   Ivan Lo is the editor and founder of Equedia.com and *The Equedia Letter*, an online publication focussed on investing in stocks. The quotation is from 'The Shocking Truths about High Frequency Trading' (18 May 2013), *The Equedia Letter*, www.equedia.com/the-shocking-truths-about-high-frequency-trading/ (accessed 25 May 2018).

Jacob Aron   'Automatic World', *New Scientist*, 12 September 2015.

Facebook Artificial Intelligence Research Lab (FAIR)   Bryan Clark, July 2017, www.thenextweb.com (accessed 25 May 2018).

Section 2
Corporate Pathology

'Spirit, are these children yours?' 'They are Man's,' said the Spirit, looking down upon them. 'This boy is Ignorance. This girl is Want. Beware them both, but most of all beware this boy, for on his brow I see that written which is Doom, unless the writing be erased.' 'Have they no refuge or resource?' cried Scrooge. 'Are there no prisons?' said the Spirit, turning on him for the last time with his own words. 'Are there no workhouses?'

Charles Dickens, *A Christmas Carol*

Chapter 4

How our Brains Created Corporatism and how Corporatism is now Altering our Brains!

Basic Neuroscience

This book is not about neuroscience, it is about how it is that we've come to frequently and collectively behave in unnatural and inhuman ways. But there must be something going on in our brains that causes or creates this in us, and of course there is. To fully understand this, we need just a very basic and very brief tutorial on the brain. I am indebted to Peter Afford for his clear and illuminating synthesis of the subject, and I've borrowed heavily from his work in this section.

Learning from experience in life involves us making new neural connections in our brains. Neurons communicate by releasing chemicals (neurotransmitters) that cross the synapse (gap) between them. 'Neurons that fire together, wire together'. There are hundreds of such chemical releases per second per neuron in the average human brain. A single neuron can make around 100,000 connections, and since

Our brains have become living and learning networks of around 1000 trillion (1,000,000,000,000,000) pathways.

neurons do not behave in a linear way but in a reverberative way, our brains have become living and learning networks of around 1000 trillion (1,000,000,000,000,000) pathways.

Neurotransmitters can either excite or inhibit the next neuron in the chain. This is the classic binary on/off mechanism (the semi-conductor) that is the basis of all modern computing, and the root of all characterisations of the brain as simply a massively efficient and powerful computer. It is of course far more than that.

The critical chemicals in our brain are as follows:

MONOAMINES:

Dopamine   pleasure
Seratonin   calm
Acetylcholine   attention
Noradrenaline   alertness

HORMONES:

Cortisol   stress
Oxytocin   bonding
Oestrogen   female behaviours
Testosterone   male behaviours

Although it accounts for just two per cent of our body weight, the Brain uses around 25 per cent of the body's oxygen supply, nutrients and glucose (as fuel), all of which are supplied by constant blood flow. So efficient brain function requires us to be highly aware of our physical condition particularly with regard to exercise, rest, sleep, diet and all round general well-being.

Looking at the brain from the bottom to the top, we first have the Reptilian brain sitting right at the top of our spinal column attached to our central nervous system and housing the Cerebellum. This is the most ancient part of our brains, shared in common with many other animals, and with our evolutionary ancestors going right back to our emergence from the water millions of years ago, and it controls our basic physiology – it's the part of my brain that controls my breathing and my bloodflow and that keeps me upright. No thinking, just pure unconscious programming passed down through genetics and DNA.

Next up is the Limbic system, containing the Amygdala, the Hippocampus, the Hypothalamus and the Thalamus. When the Amygdala, our radar system constantly sweeping our environment for any changes, detects a change, neurons fire within the Limbic system and 'create' the appropriate emotional response (fear, anger, disgust, surprise, joy, sadness). In the case of threat, it will trigger the fight, flight or freeze reaction.

For information, the other emotions that we experience – pride, guilt, shame and embarrassment – are peculiarly human, often referred to as the higher or moral emotions, because they require a level of reason and judgement to give them life. These emotions are not produced by the Limbic system, but by the Neocortex, so more later.

The Limbic system lays down and holds our memory of how to do things – it learns through constant repetition of emotional responses, and through the sheer volume of iterations of physical actions. 'Neurons that fire together, wire together.' Learning is the process of creating memory that can be automatically recalled when the same or similar circumstances arise in the future. The more we learn, the more memories we store (not of events or places or people or times – these are all memories created and stored in the neocortex – but of motor processes).

And right at the top is the Neocortex (neo = the 'newest' part of our brain) and by far the largest in volume and mass. The neocortex and the limbic system are sometimes referred to in combination as the Mammalian Brain. It's the basic job of the Neocortex to prevent inappropriate responses – notice its job is not to choose appropriate responses. It is not there to do good or right; it is there to not do bad or wrong.

This fundamental programming to respond more to negatives than positives is at the heart of so many of our problems today, when we are more consciously concerned with thriving than 'mere' surviving. And this fundamental design dynamic is critical to our understanding of human behaviour within the corporate world. We are hard wired to survive. We are not hard wired to thrive. We have learned how to do so, and we can consciously choose to do good; but under pressure, with, as one of my clients Gareth Morgan euphemistically refers to it, our amygdala being tweaked, we'll default to survival.

Then there is the Front/Back dimension in the Neocortex. There are four lobes in the Neocortex – three at the back (occipital, parietal and temporal) and one at the front (the frontal, also sometimes known as the pre-frontal). The rear lobes receive data from our whole body and from the environment through our five senses. The frontal lobe receives data only from other parts of our brain; in other words it's only receiving information that has already been filtered. This part of our brain is often referred to as our CEO – the executive function which will take in data and analyse it consciously, comparing it to past learned patterns, strategising, prioritising and deciding on a conscious action. This is the part of the brain that is truly conscious.

We put high value on conscious thinking and action, and so our frontal lobe is deemed critical, yet consciousness is not needed for any defining activity of human mental life, and under 1 per cent of brain activity is conscious. 99 per cent of brain activity – all those trillions of neural firings – is happening out of our conscious awareness and completely out of our conscious control.

Finally, there is the left and right dimension in the neocortex. The neocortex has two hemispheres, left and right, which are completely separate and only connected at the base through the Corpus Collosum. One defining difference between the two hemispheres is their laterality, with the right hemisphere controlling the muscles in the left side of the body, and vice versa.

But the left/right dimension is deserving of its own separate section.

How Corporatism is the Mirror of the Relationship Between Left and Right Hemispheres

For brevity in this section I refer to the two separated hemispheres simply as 'right' and 'left'.

I've long been fascinated by the very obvious differences between the functioning of the two separated hemispheres of the neocortex. Although we should beware of the 'pop-psychology' generalisations regarding the differences (left = detail, right = big picture; left = language, right = vision; left = logic, right = creative; left = rational, right = emotional, left = linear, right = haphazard, left = past and future, right = present moment etc), like all stereotypes, there is a lot of truth in them.

So before we go any further let's get the disclaimer out there. It is true that just about every part of the brain is involved in just about every activity. It is also true that there are areas of the brain that specialise. It is these specialisms, these differences between the two hemispheres and the dangerous imbalance, that I am concerned with here. And if I appear to over-play the specialisms for effect, then it's just that.

And I invite you to do the following as you read about the difference between the two Hemispheres – keep the Corporate World in your mind, and draw parallels as you learn more about how the two Hemispheres work.

The more I've studied the workings of these two separate hemispheres, the more I see the differences played out in real time in the Corporate World and the more I've come to

63

CHAPTER 4 - How our Brains Created Corporatism and is now Altering our Brains!

realise that the increasing dominance of left brain thinking in our wider society is the cause of the ills of Corporatism. Corporatism is possibly the Left Hemisphere's greatest creation. It will certainly prove to be so if it is the vehicle that effectively seals the Left Hemisphere's dominance once and for all. The separation of ownership from responsibility is the exact mirror, the replication of the separation of the workings of the two hemispheres, no longer operating in harmony as they were designed, but with the left brain dangerously dominant. It is not a simple dichotomy where Left is bad and Right is good – but when one dominates to the point of tyranny then things go badly wrong and this is where we are now.

Corporatism is possibly the Left Hemisphere's greatest creation.

How and why did we Develop two Separate Hemispheres?

As I undertook the two years of detailed research specifically on this one subject, I came across Iain McGilchrist's book *The Master and his Emissary* (2009), the result of his Herculean research and his superb mastery of pretty much everything ever written on the separate hemispheres of our brains. I am greatly indebted to his incredible analysis, and his writings added significantly to my knowledge. I've also drawn to a lesser extent from Roderick Tweedy's excellent book *The God of the Left Hemisphere* (2013) and Chris McManus's comprehensive analysis *Right Hand, Left Hand; the Origins of Asymmetry in Brains, Bodies, Atoms and Cultures* (2002). In the case of all three writers, I've been careful to paraphrase without quoting directly, as I was determined to synthesise my new knowledge with my own beliefs and experiences, contextualising in my own words what I feel is relevant for my purpose in this book.

Our two separate brains developed because we reached the point in our evolution where we needed to develop two distinct types of attention – attention to a specific task requiring a high level of focus and skill development, while at the same time, maintaining a broad awareness of danger in the environment. Hence the Left Hemisphere developed the 'inner' world focus, with manual dexterity and manipulation skills, and the Right Hemisphere stayed connected to the 'outside' world relating to nature and other humans.

Attention is important – the type of attention we bring to the world changes the nature of the world we attend to! Attention is reciprocal – what we find determines the type of attention we give it, but the type of attention we give also determines what we find. We are not conscious choosers of where we look – Right is unconsciously in relationship with the outside world. We notice something pre-consciously and then Left pays attention to it after a gap of about 0.5 second. Once Left has decided what the world is going to reveal, we cannot get beyond it and we become prisoners of our expectations.

Left attention converts the object into a metaphor, a symbol, a thought that it can change – controllable, manipulatable. Left observes things as separate and then decides how to relate to them. Right simply connects so there's no decision to make about how to relate or what to do in response. Right attention connects with the thing, becomes part of it, has no desire to change it but wishes only to admire it, love it, learn from it.

Brotherhood is the inbetweenness – the deep interconnectedness. We need both hemispheres to survive; we certainly need both to thrive. And one will always dominate the other in the moment and, periodically in natural pendulum swings, in evolutionary phases. It is when one becomes tyrannical that we have problems.

The Basic Processing

Ninety-eight per cent of all neurons are only on one side of the brain. Our neurons are concerned with learning, and so they mostly exist in the Neocortex and are thus separated, existing exclusively on one side or the other. When the Neocortex is working out how best to solve a problem, it uses a 'winner takes all' strategy. If one side of the brain is deemed more qualified to make the decision, then the other side of the brain is totally excluded.

Anything new comes first from the Right Hemisphere which is connected to the body – a new experience or situation releases noradrenaline. The Left Hemisphere then picks this up (it is not connected to the body, and only receives its information from the Right Hemisphere) and starts creating meaning (predicting and projecting) through a process of comparing this information to the model of the world it has already constructed. It then determines a strategy for action. Left's job is to construct a model, a story, an abstraction from all the 'real' data, in order to learn better how to survive. So Left fundamentally constructs its own reality. It can only deal with the already known, seeing something new and fitting it to a known pattern, so it prioritises what is familiar to it and therefore it is not good at learning. Right sees and is in touch with reality. The world of Left is a virtual world – it decides for itself what it has seen.

What are the Differences?

Right is fluid, at one with the universe, wave-like rather than particular, which is the domain of Left. Notice how this mirrors the wave-particle duality of Quantum Mechanics, whereby matter can be either a wave or a particle or both at the same time.

Right has affinity for the living; it likes nature, things outside of itself, outside of Man, whereas Left has an affinity for the mechanical and likes man-made things (basically anything it made itself!). Right feels our bodies as alive and as part of our identity whereas Left has only an image of body and sees it as separate (remember Corpora – the body as separate). Left's sense of self is a product of our environment. Left 'I am' is a separation, a focus on self-interest, whereas Right says 'I am part of' seeking to foster involvement and interconnection. Left can explain beauty logically, but to Right beauty goes beyond the rational to the inexplicable, but then Right does not have a need to know, whereas this is offensive to Left which then derides Right as being irrational and having no argument or proof. Right would retort 'prove what? and why?' Left wants control and sees Right as out of control, or even uncontrollable.

Left cannot create anything from scratch. It can only improve something through reduction, abstraction, comparison, division. Left divides, therefore it creates conflicts and competitions – right and wrong, winners and losers, good and evil, positive and negative, late and on-time, on target or under-performing. Left only recognises good and evil.

> *Left's only core value is utility. It is a useful department to send things to for processing, but those things only have meaning again when passed back to Right.*

Left's only core value is utility. It is a useful department to send things to for processing, but those things only have meaning again when passed back to Right.

Left is also perfectionist, so it is also critical, judgemental, moralistic, self-centred, domineering, sarcastic, stubborn, arrogant, jealous, narcissistic – none of these are true emotions of course, they are all a product of reason and judgement. Left needs certainty and to be right whereas Right can hold several ambiguous possibilities. Left creates conflict between the self and community; between individualism and collectivism. Left cannot admit that it does not know something with utter certainty, so it pretends it does. It has become expert at constructing plausible yet bogus arguments and at supplying the data and the evidence to 'prove' its case.

Left lives in a hall of mirrors, only seeking more of what it already knows. It only does more of what it is already doing. It does not want to learn, it wants to control. Luckily our imagination runs the operating system (Right runs the body) and so new knowledge, learning, skill development and true innovation are all possible.

Meaning, imagination, music, poetry, morals, humour, our ability to change our minds, to learn – these are all the domain of Right.

Time is Left's ultimate abstraction. Corporations are massively time-period controlled and judged – an absolute illusion and the root of much of the damage they do. Right senses time as a flow linking events of before, during and after; Left knows that there are only five minutes before the meeting starts, measuring time as a series of units to be controlled.

Words are expressed serially and are loved by Left; pictures are taken in all at once and are a language in which Right is fluent, but which Left finds unintelligible. Left understands words literally, but Right understands implied meaning. Over 90 per cent of communication is nonverbal, and we think without language, since most thinking is nonconscious. Gestures are a secret code that is written nowhere, seemingly known by none, at least consciously, yet 100 per cent understood by all. Gestures anticipate speech; they do not just reflect thought, but help constitute thought. When gestures and speech are not matched, gestures win 100 per cent of the time. So Right should really dominate communication, yet it does not.

Left reaches out for a purpose whereas Right just reaches out; Left has an end in mind whereas to Right there is only the journey. Left can only gain satisfaction on achievement of the goal, but since the achievement of one goal will very rapidly be subsumed by the setting of the next one, often the most common experience is deflating anticlimax. Right, on the other hand, is not only liberated from any anxiety of pursuing the unreasonable or unachievable, it can just enjoy the ride, in glorious excited anticipation of the unknown. To Right the unknown is exciting and to be jumped into with relish; to Left the unknown is scary and to be avoided at all costs.

Denial is a Left speciality, arguably Left's power of denial is its greatest achievement. Right does not understand the concept since it just deals with what is.

Denial is a Left speciality, arguably Left's power of denial is its greatest achievement. Right does not understand the concept since it just deals with what is.

Right has empathy; Left is unconcerned about others' feelings.

How does the Left Hemisphere Dominate the Right?

The two hemispheres coexist, but they have different values and priorities and so they come into conflict; they are in fact involved in a power struggle. The Left Hemisphere is dependent, even parasitic, on the Right but has no awareness of this. It is unopposed and dysfunctional; it sees a mechanistic and fragmented world and has unwarranted optimism, paranoia and emptiness. The Left Hemisphere is better at inhibiting the Right than vice versa. This gives Left the edge in the competition to be the dominant Hemisphere.

Right is the prime mediator of experience and living; the products of Left have to be returned to Right in order to live, so Right ought to have the balance of power; but it does not. Left is more powerful because it has the means of argument, because it builds systems that then become the truth through self-perpetuation and self-promotion, and because it is proactive.

Left rejects Right as inauthentic and invalid – since Right does not observe or analyse itself it cannot explain itself and, worse, it has no sense of needing to defend itself. Right has a tendency to melancholy – the more we empathise the more we feel shame, guilt and responsibility, and Left ruthlessly exploits this.

Left's craving for power does not come from strength or actual dominance, it comes from insecurity. Left's dominance has not been created by its greater genius or by its fundamental superiority in handling situations since it does not have these things. Its dominance comes through its ability to handicap Right. If a single individual human being is unconsciously neutering themselves through allowing their own left brain to be tyrannical, then it's no wonder whole collectives are doing the same – companies, governments, countries, charities, public services, armies.

And since the two hemispheres handle feedback in different ways, with Right driven to stop doing things because of negative feedback, and Left driven to continue things because of positive feedback, Left has been able to better cultivate the 'human' emotions of guilt and shame to control Right's operation.

Self-consciousness comes about when Left inspects and inevitably judges Right as being clumsy, confused, irrational, random, haphazard and generally over-emotional – Right is fundamentally judged as lesser; inferior; an unnecessary burden. And when Right does something brilliant, Left will merely judge this as luck – the statistically inevitable result that occasionally something will go right through sheer fate. Given an infinite number of monkeys and infinite number of typewriters, eventually one of them produce the works of Shakespeare. Luck, of course, is a wholly Left concept.

The Pendulum of Right/Left Dominance Through History

Right and Left dominance has shifted through history.

200,000 BC to 6000 BC	Right Brain dominant as we had no conscious awareness of self.	This is a very late development in our evolution, first emerging around 6000 BC.
6000 BC	Ancient Greece	Right Brain Dominance
1 AD	Roman Empire	Left Brain Dominance
1000 AD	Middle/Dark Ages	Right Brain Dominance
12th–15th centuries	Renaissance	Right Brain Dominance
16th century	Reformation	Left Brain Dominance
18th century	Industrial Revolution	Left Brain Dominance
21st century	Digital Revolution	Left Brain Dominance (and ultimate Domination?)

So the difference today is whether Left's dominance is now permanent and non-recoverable. What will come to cause the pendulum to swing back – climate change? When we've consumed everything? Nuclear Armageddon taking us back to local communities focussed only on survival?

The development of writing shows the progression of Left domination. The first forms of writing, around 4000 BC, were pictorial and laid out vertically which suited Right. But Left likes horizontal, left to right straight lines for symbols and lay out – the physical eye movement left to right preferentially communicating what is seen to Left. So as writing developed more as a tool to be manipulated by the hand, it naturally moved to a more horizontal methodology. At the same time, as the symbols chosen to represent objects became standardised with the development of the alphabet, we moved away from the direct link between pictures and symbols. The alphabet is a wonderful Left invention, a standardised coding system to record the world in an abstract format.

And so writing became a technology, an instrument of power. Those who can record and transmit have the power. Writing became the means of controlling people in ever larger numbers. At age 16, when I did my first psychometric test, I was intrigued by Sir Norman's guidance that an ability in writing indicated executive potential. I couldn't see the link at the time.

Inequality only started around 4000 BC – before that we were simply hunter-gatherers living in small (though increasingly larger) equal social groups with no ownership, no wars, no violence. The fact is we are naturally a collaborative species not a competitive one. No one owned anything, everything was shared. It is people's sense of being better than others and therefore being entitled to more that characterises today's society.

It is people's sense of being better than others and therefore being entitled to more that characterises today's society.

Before 4000 BC there were no wars. Then came an explosion of technology (the wheel, the plough, complex writing and number systems, the calendar etc – tools of dominion, control and superiority) combined with climate change in Africa and the Middle East that forced large-scale migration; and suddenly pathological behaviours emerged. There's been a technology arms race of some kind going on ever since. As centralised wealth increased, protein levels in 'ordinary' people decreased.

Numbers appear around 1500 BC – again a technology of control, compounded by the invention of currency around 500 BC. Money is like words – it replaces abstract things with signs or tokens – the very essence of Left. Literacy and numeracy were massive and very rapid factors in human neuro-psychological development. The word and money quickly became more important than the things they represented.

Before money we had gifts with the emphasis on reciprocity and the building of relationships. With money came competition and divisiveness, with the emphasis not on relationships but on profit, a concept that literally did not exist before money was invented. Money also facilitated trading with strangers and trading in non-essential (luxury) items and so consumerism was born.

The Roman Empire was built on codification, rigidity, solidity, certainty, control – conquering cities ever further away and then making them identical to Rome. The Romans created a central hierarchy of control (the first Corporation?) with a permanent military and with beauty, art and entertainment fostered merely as a distraction to keep the masses under control. This was the start of mechanisation and standardisation. Technology allowed the Romans to exercise power from a small centre to a very wide geographical area; from a very few people over millions. What controlled people thousands of miles away from Rome – people who would never see Rome or have any 'remote' idea what the Emperor was really like, was fear. Millions of people were controlled by a small handful through the structures of fear. A remote country of thousands could be controlled by a Garrison of a handful of Roman soldiers. The local population could easily have overrun the Garrison had they chosen to, but the feared consequences were simply too great to take the risk. They may have asked themselves 'what have the Romans ever done for us?' but their reality was the physical benefits of enslavement – security, safety, predictability and just enough pleasure above the squalor to make the risk of rebellion too great to contemplate. The Roman leadership skill was to judge that balance to perfection – at the margins of cost. I'm reminded of a phrase I heard in the 1980s when working with a large multinational manufacturer, with regard to their strategy for dealing with their suppliers – 'They shall not die, neither shall they live'. People with control don't want their followers to die. But neither do they want them to have more than is needed for them to be happy enough to remain subjugated. The Romans were very successful at this, for a long time.

In the seventeenth century, the written word again became dominant – words are things, not just symbols or tokens of meaning. Around this time Acronyms appear – shortened codes capable of mass repetition.

The American Revolution was billed as the pursuit of happiness – the pursuit of the American Dream. Note that 'happiness' is a goal rather than a state of being. I wonder what Americans make of the Buddhist belief that *'There is no way to happiness, happiness is the way'*. It certainly seems as though the pursuit of the American Dream has become characterised by selfish motives of entitlement, competition, superiority and arrogance. I am all in favour of people pursuing growth, self-development, betterment etc, but to believe that these things are a fundamental right, particularly when 'betterment' is only measured in materiality, and when their absence causes such anger and resentment, is clearly unhealthy for a community. The pursuit of anything as a goal changes the nature of that which we pursue – we know that targets skew behaviours. Targets have become the new words and money – designed to symbolise a desired state and to inspire a community towards it, but actually becoming a 'thing' to be achieved come hell or high water.

With the Industrial Revolution came mass mechanisation of processes. Physical workspaces become separate – Right-focussed is where the work is actually done: factories, farms, shops, people interacting with fellow stakeholders doing real productive work; Left then created the head office function, which has become divorced from reality and progressively more self-important. Head Offices have built their 'work' to be the most important; and the rise of the professional classes, for whom the work of bureaucracy becomes the end in itself, has established Head Office as having absolute dominion. This is why it is not unusual to find people working in corporate centres who come to feel that the customer is wrong, or that the employees out there in the stores or factories everyday are inherently lazy, stupid, uncaring and untrustworthy, since they seem singularly unable to deliver the desired results.

The industrial revolution was Left's most vicious assault on Right – the creation of a world as a projection; not real at all and progressively more divorced from reality. It made machines that make other machines – another step in the separation/the dissociation (and now we have thinking machines . . .).

Psychopaths started to win power and then had the ruthlessness to keep it. Psychopaths don't stick to rules, and they rebel against or usurp all other authorities, yet they get rewarded because they produce results. We reward outcomes and we turn a blind eye to methods and behaviours in the name of achieving success. But success is arbitrary because it is only a comparison to an arbitrary goal, whereas behaviours are real – the impact on people is real.

Maybe this is OK in the name of collective survival (during war) or in pursuit of summiting Everest for 'fun'; but is it acceptable in the pursuit of a twenty-third consecutive quarter of like-for-like sales growth?

People now live in urban environments divorced from nature – Right is ever more cut off from the natural world; TV and internet deliver reality through a screen; people move away from their families. Left has closed off Right's escape routes.

Boredom did not exist (apart from in the super privileged) before the industrial revolution. Boredom gives rise to sensationalism and the need for ever-higher stimulus. It's interesting that schizophrenia was rare before the eighteenth century; anorexia was rare before the twentieth century.

Healthy and Unhealthy use of Emotions

Left likes positive emotions and hates negative emotions. Left is an incessant stream of involuntary and compulsive thoughts and the emotions that accompany those thoughts. When we are unaware of this, in denial, then the thinking becomes real – we take the thinker to be who we are. And we will always judge ourselves as less or more than others – the source of all neuroses, and the source of all our problems.

Emotions felt/generated by the limbic system – fear, anger, disgust, surprise, joy, sadness – are the 'natural' emotions that are helpfully designed to inform action. Left brain 'emotions' generated purely from judgement and reason – guilt, anxiety, shame, embarrassment – are unhelpful in guiding action. Whereas fear is a natural and helpful emotion, anxiety is an unnatural and unhelpful emotion. It is manufactured through our conditioning – we have become conditioned to be anxious, to be always fearful – uneasy, apprehensive, uncertain, unsettled, nervous. Our ancestors did not live like that. They may have experienced moments of fear, of intense terror even, but they did not live in states of perpetual low-level anxiety.

We have become conditioned to be anxious, to be always fearful – uneasy, apprehensive, uncertain, unsettled, nervous. Our ancestors did not live like that.

And whereas the limbic system flushes through in about 90 seconds, anxiety can be a near permanent state, creating a constant loop of fight or flight responses. If I feel a 'natural' emotional reaction of anger, this will pass quickly. But now with my advanced neocortex, I can 'choose' to stay angry. My limbic system will not stay angry – it doesn't need to, since for survival it now needs to calm down and rest in order to be ready for the next threat. But I can choose to stay feeling angry by passing the emotion to my neocortex.

CHAPTER 4 - How our Brains Created Corporatism and is now Altering our Brains!

Here I can think myself into remaining angry for as long as I wish – and I can add to this, creating my own personal and glorious 'Victim's Cocktail' of bitterness, resentment, envy, jealousy and drama. I can exercise my creative energy on what I might do with these feelings, knowing that I don't have to pursue any of them. This is all my neocortex's choice.

Some of us live here; all of us come here from time to time. I quite often describe the corporate world as a soap opera. Left creates a glorious soap opera of escapist drama. Right can give us everything we need in 'real' life, but we fool ourselves into believing we're better off escaping from reality. When my clients are suffering from an excess of Corporate stress, I remind them that it is all just a big game. It's not real. Their families are real. Their health is real. Their job is just a game.

Emotions are progressively losing their directedness for us to act appropriately towards other human beings. In the Corporate World emotions have been supressed to the point where they've been almost conditioned out of existence! Ask someone at work how they are: 'How do you feel?' They'll automatically respond with a 'Fine', or with 'I think . . .' (ie not 'I feel'). No one really wants to know the truth, since the truth may well be inconvenient for the work, the mission. Efficient working of the machine requires everyone at work to be 100 per cent fit, alert, confident, committed, focussed. This is of course the ideal, but it's not human. The reality is that it is not acceptable to be human at work. Humans are messy, flawed, unreliable and distracted – all hugely inconvenient for the controlling, linear, rational – dare I say psychopathic – Corporate World focussing everything on the achievement of goals at almost any cost. But humans are also beautiful, creative geniuses, capable of duality of processing and intuitive leaps. If only Left trusted Right.

Emotion is closer to the core of our being than cognition; feeling comes first and then reason emanates from it. Yet we treat cognition as the path to knowledge and why we 'prove' knowledge through tests rather than actions.

The Irresistible Power of Conformity

We are wired to conform.

Jamil Zaki from Stanford University has discovered the neuro-mechanism behind this. The ventromedial pre-frontal cortex is a part of the brain's reward centre that activates when we encounter attractive things, and this had been known for many years. Zaki discovered that it also activates when we find out what others think. We feel the reward of what they are doing and how they are thinking, even before we take action ourselves.

Aviva Rutkin, 2015

No wonder we imitate them immediately and no wonder we are so supremely motivated by, and so scared of, what others think of us. The more this part of the brain is activated by information about group opinion, the more someone will adjust their opinion towards the consensus.

Conformity is useful to us in evolutionary terms, allowing us to be guided by others who know better than we . . . but it can of course lead us into danger if those others are themselves misguided.

Mother   *'Why did you do it?'*
Child   *'Tommy told me to'*
Mother   *'So if Tommy told you to put your hand into a fire, would you do that?'*

Well, probably, yes . . . such is the power of conformity.

When we are exposed to stereotypes and prejudices (cultural values and behaviours different to our own moral code) we perform differently. We embody the culture we live in very fast, and this happens unconsciously, most likely through the automatic synchronisation of brain activity when we are in groups.

Helen Thomson (April 2018) reported on research into the synchronisation of brain activity in Rhesus Macaque Monkeys. A team at Duke University Medical Centre in North Carolina led by Miguel Nicolelis conducted experiments that showed brain activity synchronisation when monkeys observed each other's behaviours. While these experiments seemed confirmed their original hypothesis, what was unexpected was that the degree of synchronisation changed according to the dominance relationships in the group. *'When a less dominant monkey was observing a more dominant monkey, synchronisation was higher than when the relationship was reversed'*. This makes sense in terms of less dominant monkeys needing to learn from more dominant ones, since survival of the fittest is at play in natural selection. In humans, with our capacity for self-awareness and our ability to learn consciously, dominance should not be important, but since Corporatism is based on hierarchical structures, brain synchronisation plays out as mirroring or indeed pleasing the Boss!

As a species we become what we imitate – values cannot be imitated only behaviours. Values can be taught as concepts but are only brought into practical usage when we are faced with a situation requiring us to use our integrity – integrity not being a value in itself, but the act of acting in accordance with a value.

The Milgram study (1963) showed us that even decent people's sense of social conformity will make them blindly follow authority. Milgram ordered study participants to deliver electric shocks to another person if they answered a question incorrectly. Unknown to them the person answering the questions was an actor pretending to react to the shocks, which were completely unreal. Despite seeing this person in distress, a majority of the study participants continued to deliver shocks as directed, to ever greater levels of pain, even to unconsciousness, and even to potential fatal levels. How could this be? We follow the crowd. When we see others delivering electric shocks with impunity, we will do the same.

We follow social models – cultures. We'd rather conform than do the right thing – it's quite simply the safest option for us. We fear sanction and we fear being cast out. We do what we're told, and so we develop a pattern of protecting ourselves by simply not thinking. It's how a trained nurse can come to move a 'difficult' patient's emergency call button out of their reach and still maintain a clear conscience.

When we see someone rebelling, we ostracise them since they evoke such fear in us of being found out by the authorities. We have mortgages to pay so we can't quit without another job to go to. And we can't tell our boss we're looking, in case we're accused of disloyalty, or be sacked before we're ready, or simply that we'll hurt their feelings.

Fight, Flight, or more Likely, Freeze

We have had our normal, natural attachments (to family, to nature) so disrupted that we've had no choice but to look for attachments to unnatural things – our companies, addictions etc. Stripped of love and safety we attach to our captor. Our prime strategies are therefore to please and to placate – to be safe.

The more we are in freeze, the more frightening the world becomes. We move through trauma by taking action, restoring some sense of control and the taking of responsibility that reduces the risk of being traumatised, feeling shame and guilt for inaction. Since our Left Hemispheres have progressively cut us off from our instincts, denying they have any value, we have come to mistrust them. We find ourselves in a constant state of hyper-awareness and we over-scrutinise our situations and over-analyse the simplest of requests or tasks. We suffer a loss of self, and we temporarily become what we pretend to be – confident, able, knowledgeable, quick, positive. But this pretence takes enormous effort to maintain, and so we eventually become what we feared all along – not good enough – with all of the psychological damage that does to us.

Pressure causes the triggering of the ancient survival mechanisms of fight, flight or freeze, and we have all become highly practised at the modern corporate behavioural manifestations of these, depending on where we are in the food chain. But fight and flight involve taking action, and taking action brings the potential of even bigger risk – being sacked for example (and all the projected issues that would bring of missed mortgage payments or even just the shame) or the other person getting upset . . . so we've developed 'freeze' into our most predominant reaction.

In ancient survival situations, we 'froze' in order not to be seen, in the hope that the threat would pass us by, distracted perhaps by an alternative victim. Freeze was not a conscious choice of course, since our survival instinct simply made an instantaneous choice between the three available strategies. If anger ruled the day, we'd probably 'choose' to fight; if fear then we'd probably turn tail and run before we'd had a chance to weight up our options with any conscious assessment. So what has to be true for us in survival situations for us to 'choose' freeze? There appear to be two fundamental factors. First, if the situation is so shocking for us that our fear goes beyond that which would 'normally' have automatically put us in a blind 'headless chicken' panic, and terror turns to petrification – we turn to stone; we become paralysed. Secondly, if the survival situation is of such a complex nature that there is no obvious fight or flight solution, we will default into doing nothing, at least as our immediate reaction. And once we're in freeze, even a few milliseconds, there's no limbic survival mechanism that will take us out of it. We're there until the threat has passed.

As Homo Sapiens, for close to 200,000 years our survival situations were relatively simple. The situation, while threatening enough to induce the flood of adrenaline and cortisol, was probably of sufficiently simple causation, or even familiar enough as a prior occurrence, for our brains to know the 'correct' action to take. The appropriate response to a threat event had been prepared and embedded in our 'cognitive database', and in such cases the speed of response can be as fast as 100 milliseconds – immediate action. If more than one possible response was available, then choosing the correct behavioural sequence, requiring simple cognitive decision making would take between one and two seconds.

But if no appropriate response exists in the person's database, then a temporary behavioural schema, a theory or plan, has to be created, and this process will take between 8 and 10 seconds even when we're calm and can think straight. The result is that no plan can be created within the time available, and so a cognitively induced paralysis or 'freezing' is our only option.

Today there are tragically still parts of the world where violent conflict situations make the 'choice' between fight and flight clear. But in the Corporate World, threat situations can be so complex as to make the choice between fight and flight impossible to make. Once the 8–10 second has elapsed before we can work out what to do, it's likely that the predator will already have taken their next step. Notice how long a person at your workplace can wait in a conversation for an answer to a question – it's not as much as eight seconds – for some it's not even the 1–2 seconds required for a simple cognitive decision.

And in the Corporate World, frankly neither fight nor flight are really options at all. Fight might mean losing our job for usurping the authority of a superior, and flight might mean losing our job as we run away from doing what we're asked. Both strategies are instantly projected as having far worse consequences, and before we know it, we're in freeze. And so we've developed ever more sophisticated ways of being in freeze and getting away with it – literally being able to get away with doing nothing. We say 'yes' to the Boss to relieve the pressure of the moment, and then plot our excuses for not delivering on our commitment; we say we agree when we don't; we say we're fine when we're not; we've worked hard to develop a body posture that looks active, confident, busy and ever-so-slightly stressed all in one, all the time. If a predator approaches us, sees that we are active, confident, busy and stressed, they're highly likely to leave us alone.

Freeze has become our norm in reaction to the constancy of the threat around us. Since we all do it, we all support each other in maintaining it collectively.

Interestingly, accident investigation reports into maritime or air disasters show that most fatalities occurring

> *Freeze has become our norm in reaction to the constancy of the threat around us. Since we all do it, we all support each other in maintaining it collectively.*

in emergency evacuation situations are caused by people 'freezing' – that the people who die could have escaped had they taken action, but for some reason they were frozen into inaction. Although controversial then and still to this day, research conducted by S L A Marshall (1947) into armed conflicts showed that less than 25 per cent of soldiers fire their guns in battle situations, even though for many their inaction likely caused their own death. In the terrible fire at Grenfell Tower in London in 2017, residents had been given specific directions in the case of fire to stay put. Even if this was the safest strategy in theory (it clearly was not in practice) it surely manufactures post-traumatic stress disorder.

Dramatic changes in our brain chemistry, particularly in what are biologically designed to be short and infrequent spikes in levels of adrenaline and cortisol, are 'natural', but the issue in the Corporate World is the sheer unrelenting low-level stress (threat) we have to navigate.

We're always learning – but are we learning positively or negatively? There is a clear difference between negative, conditioned learning through our repeated limbic responses to fear, and the positive and creative learning from conscious practicing of new skills.

Cortisol knocks out cognitive functions such as working memory (ability to process information and make decisions) and declarative memory (ability to recall facts and events – learned experiences). That was fine for 200,000 years, when survival actions were simply fight or flight. But modern threat situations are more complex. When MS Estonia sank in 1994, killing 852 of the 989 people aboard, according to the official accident report, some passengers were 'petrified' as the ship listed, and *'did not react when other passengers tried to guide them, even when they used force or shouted at them'* (Sonia Van Gilder Cooke, August 2015).

But 'survival' in the corporate world requires a greater level of cognitive dexterity – and so our natural fear response can leave us compromised and even more vulnerable. We feel this, and so our fear increases.

Cortisol does not block our procedural memory (ability to move or manipulate physical objects) however, so we should train people better for the standard physical things they might need to do under threat so that our procedural memory has what it needs. What would this be in a corporation?

Our Brain Structures are Being Altered

Our brain chemistry is altered by working under Corporatism. People entering the corporate world are conditioned and hypnotised into conforming. Solving problems – being presented with a constant series of puzzles to work out – generates Dopamine, and is highly addictive, and workaholism is massively rewarded (Dopamine again) in the moment with approval, whether explicit or tacit. But Dopamine is for pleasure, not happiness (that's Seratonin) and so we're left with the emptiness after the pleasure reward.

'Neurons that fire together, wire together.' We are always learning, and our individual brain wiring is always developing. If our brains are collectively experiencing the same situations, communicating energetically, synchronising in brain activity, then the speed of individual brain structure change increases and deepens, and more critically evolves.

The collective turbo charge to brain structure change is delivered by our collective experience, since imitation is a faster learning (evolution) process than gene transmission, and so our ability to learn is our greatest genetic heritage.

There are two types of knowledge – Left knowledge and Right knowledge. Left knowledge is facts, pieces of information, truths etc, that can be recalled consciously. Right knowledge is the memory of the experience of the situation that contains or created those facts and how we've dealt with similar situations in the past. This knowledge is stored subconsciously.

Imagination, also a Right function, is our process of feeling ourselves doing something, projecting as if we were having the experience. Right combines memory and imagination so we can learn even faster – we learn not just from actual experience, but from projected experience. If our projections are largely 'healthy' and positive, because we're living a relatively 'safe' life, then we'll learn to trust our environment, using our own creativity more frequently and habitually, and to trust that the outcomes, whatever they may be, will be positive for us. If our learning is driven by anxiety, then we will reinforce that learning and always play safe and small. We get the experience we expect. At the very stage in our evolution when we could, arguably should, be learning to evolve into a thriving species, we are trapped through fear into maintaining, even reinforcing, our status as a fight-or-flight surviving species.

What we think and do alters the patterns of connections within the neural networks of the brain and this in turn changes the brain's structure and function. We re-wire. The brain is plastic and can functionally re-organise within a few short weeks of conditioning and repetition – conditioned learning.

While all our cells hold roughly the same 20,000 or so genes, each cell uses a different suite of genes, switched to off or on in an almost infinite number of combinations in a process called epigenetics. Epigenetic change (heritable change in gene expression that does not involve a change to the underlying DNA sequence) is a regular and natural occurrence, but it can also be influenced by several factors, including age, disease state, lifestyle and environment. Ways of thinking shape the nervous system; the efficiency, not just the volume of synaptic connections, is altered by adult learning. Brain structures have been unchanged for hundreds of thousands of years, but epigenetics can see a change in a generation – not changes to DNA itself, but factors which influence what is expressed by that DNA – cultural developments can be transmitted through genetic mechanisms. Our lifestyle is changing our genes at a rate never seen before in the whole of human history.

Our lifestyle is changing our genes at a rate never seen before in the whole of human history.

77

CHAPTER 4 - How our Brains Created Corporatism and is now Altering our Brains!

Memes are powerful cultural mass communicators – tunes, catchphrases, ideas, dress codes, behaviours – the unwritten corporate rules of behaviour. Snippets of behaviours, feelings or ways of thinking (of experience in other words) stuck together in large and consistent enough numbers constitute a new reality of the world we are living in – if we work in the corporate world, 12 hours per day, it's no wonder it infects us so powerfully and so totally – our brains are wired for it, our survival depends upon it, but the epigenetic effect is palpable and rapid. The ultimate dissociated state is hypnosis – many corporate citizens are hypnotised, believing they are doing good when really they are merely perpetuating the status quo, even if they are actually doing no real harm.

Imitation is arguably the most important human skill for survival (beyond mere fight or flight) – it's how we learn language and how we learn the rules of the game. We copy human behaviour, we mimic. The real risk in the twenty-first century is that skills and learning have been downgraded into algorithms, delegated solely to Left, with the result that we are now mere frenetic, hypnotised, imitating machines. What is left for our Right Hemispheres to do now? If it were solely up to Left, no doubt Right would be shuffled into some sort of Care Home for the disabled or inconvenient, with just enough resource not to be too much of a burden on the only 'real' things in life – the life of our Left Hemisphere. Or maybe Left will achieve its ultimate dream of embracing AI, coupling with it in the formation of a new super race. Sci-fi this may be, but it is actually the logical extension of Left's dominion over Right.

Homo Sapiens Still?

Home Sapiens – 'knowing man'.

Left/Right brain separation really started with emergence of Homo Sapiens from Homo Erectus 200,000 years ago. The defining Homo Sapiens human characteristics are speech and tool making. Both needed the development of Left – grasping was the fore-runner of language; the first binary, on/off experience. Grasped/not grasped. The more the right hand was used to manipulate the outside world, remembering that laterality means the left hemisphere controls the muscles in the right side of the body, the more it strengthened left-hemisphere circuitry. This is also why, although language is in Left, it's largely our right hands that we use as gesticulators, as physically or nonverbal communicators. Hand control and language are next to each other in the left brain.

Empathic identification is the domain of Homo Sapiens – our ability to feel what it feels like to be another person. It's why projective identification is such an important factor in power relationships.

The great human invention is that we choose who we become. But have we reached the point where we should really now be known as a new Species? Homo Digitus? Homo Deus? Homo Evolutis? Has our brain structure and functioning altered to the extent where we are truly a new species in evolution? We have come to a stage in our evolution where the next species in the chain should be Homo Progredio – 'thriving man', a species that truly embodies our unique human ability to rationalise, empathise, collaborate and thrive as our default mode of action and response.

But with AI and cybernetics rampant, maybe our destiny is more as Homo Cybernetis.

Notes

Peter Afford Peter Afford is a psychologist, psychotherapist and neuroscientist with a consulting and teaching practice in the UK. On 27 February 2016 I attended a one-day workshop he ran for Banbury Therapeutic Training. I made copious notes during the day, and I drew heavily on these notes as I synthesised my own thoughts and beliefs on the aspects of neuroscience I've tackled in this section of the book. His website is www .focusing.co.uk (accessed 25 May 2018).

McGilchrist, I (2009) *The Master and His Emissary: The Divided Brain and the Making of the Western World.* New Haven: Yale University Press.

Tweedy, R (2013) *The God of the Left Hemisphere: Blake, Bolte Taylor and the Myth of Creation.* London: Karnac Books.

McManus, C (2002) *Right Hand, Left Hand; the Origins of Asymmetry in Brains, Bodies, Atoms and Cultures.* Great Britain, Weidenfeld and Nicholson.

Aviva Rutkin 'We are Wired to Conform', *New Scientist*, 15 August 2015.

Helen Thomson 'Social Monkeys Sync Their Brains', *New Scientist*, 7 April 2018.

Milgram The Milgram experiment on obedience to authority figures was a series of experiments conducted by Yale University psychologist Stanley Milgram, first described in a 1963 article in the *Journal of Abnormal and Social Psychology* and later discussed in greater depth in his 1974 book, *Obedience to Authority: An Experimental View.*

Marshall, S L A (2000) *Men Against Fire: The Problem of Battle Command.* Norman: University of Oklahoma Press. (First published 1947).

Grenfell Tower The Grenfell Tower fire broke out on 14 June 2017 at the 24-storey Grenfell Tower block of public housing flats in North Kensington, West London. It caused at least 72 deaths, and over 70 injuries. Occupants of 23 of the 129 flats died. 223 people escaped. One year on and the controversy still rages over fire safety short cuts and cost considerations.

MS Estonia MS Estonia was a cruise ferry that sank in 1994 in the Baltic Sea in one of the worst maritime disasters of the twentieth century. It is, after Titanic, the second-deadliest European shipwreck disaster to have occurred in peacetime, with 852 lives lost.

Sonia van Gilder Cooke 'Our Survival Instinct is out of date', *New Scientist*, 15 August 2015.

Chapter 5

Introducing the Corporapath – You and I

Most Companies are Decent, yet Somehow fear Still Rules

Most companies are thoroughly decent, or at least they earnestly strive to be so. While many corporations are places where states of fear, control, anxiety, dishonesty, manipulation, isolation and intimidation exist, to most employees this would be an unrecognisable or at best overly harsh description.

That does not mean that it is not true. We have become so conditioned to the 'normality' of fear and its effects that we have slipped into a collective unawareness.

It is clear that, in many organisations, decent people are conditioned and manipulated into behaviours that would be unacceptable to them or immoral or even illegal outside of work. But what proportion of companies are we talking about? 10 per cent? 50 per cent? 2 per cent? Are these characteristics in fact endemic in the Corporate World, simply to greater and lesser extents?

Are there really any companies out there that are devoid of such conditions? And if there are, does this guarantee wholly and exclusively ethical behaviour in their employees? In my experience the examples of companies or parts of companies that are truly operating ethically have in fact eschewed corporatism, at least temporarily. But even then a dilemma sets in. I've seen many examples where 'ethical' leaders give so much autonomy, are so trusting of employees, and so unwilling to check up on things, that employees still indulge in poor behaviour, much to the chagrin of their leaders. And this is where it gets really tricky. This is the heart of the dilemma of all ethical leaders.

Employees without boundaries will at times behave poorly, not through malice or negligence, but because they're human and bring their own morality and their own issues into the workplace. But placing firm boundaries on employees involves a degree of autocracy, and a degree of sanction (fear of consequences) otherwise the boundaries have no meaning. I've seen many leaders fail this test by being too loose on boundaries – where their desire *not* to be autocratic and *not* to be a micromanager has left their employees simply too free to use their own initiative and therefore feeling unsafe. Autonomy is wonderful, but too much autonomy breeds insecurity.

> *Employees without boundaries will at times behave poorly, not through malice or negligence, but because they're human and bring their own morality and their own issues into the workplace.*

Finally the ultimate question, since we are not going to overthrow capitalism just yet: are the more 'ethical' companies successful? Do they make a profit? In fact, what is an 'ethical' amount of profit to make? Experience tells me that the vagaries of competition will frequently conspire to derail a company which is nobly attempting to run on purely ethical principles, with employees free to shape their work and the 'organic' process of company growth as they see fit.

On the other hand, are there companies out there which are riven with fear, yet where everyone is behaving totally ethically? Let me just deal with this question very clearly. The answer is 'No'. In my experience there are no companies out there riven with fear where everyone is behaving ethically. If there is fear in the system, it is being caused by people abusing power. Their actions and behaviours may be legal, may even be unconscious, but they will be unethical. If people are fearful at work, then it is the culture that is creating that, and the culture is the responsibility of the leaders. The leaders create the ecosystem through their behaviours. Of course, it is possible for a whole company to momentarily experience some 'natural' fear – the loss of a major client, an accident that causes damage or injury – but that is not the same as a *culture* of fear.

Do 'Goldilocks' Companies Exist – Just the Right Amount of Fear, Ethics and Profit?

So let's return to the more interesting question of whether there are any companies out there satisfying all three 'perfect' conditions – the 'Goldilocks' of companies, with just the right amount of fear, just the right amount of ethical behaviours, and just the right amount of profit. This might sound like a spurious proposition to you, but

1. **What is the appropriate use of fear?** Dr Edwards Deming, in Point 8 of his 14 Points for Management, exhorted us to 'Drive Out Fear'. But he was talking about the human 'created' fears that are put into the system by people with power. Fear is a naturally occurring emotion in the human experience; and an organisation, just as an individual human being, will encounter events that create fear as a natural reaction. We cannot avoid fear, and neither should we try too hard, since collectively we'll then not take the creative risks necessary to grow and to fulfil the purpose. Furthermore, organising a collection of human beings means that there have to be some common laws, rules, processes for all to adhere to. Boundaries. And unless there are consequences when people break the law, or are not compliant to process, or cross the boundary, we have no real mechanism to control behaviour. The key for leaders is to use fear for the purpose nature intended – to guide behaviour towards survival. It is the 'unnatural' fears, the human, moral fears of shame, rejection, anxiety, intimidation that must be eradicated.

2. **Are all naturally occurring human behaviours 'ethical'?** Authenticity is sometimes ugly and messy. Human beings make mistakes and misjudgements and can sometimes be guilty of acting impulsively or selfishly. But it would be wrong to label these behaviours as 'unethical'. An innocent lapse in judgement might be careless, but is not unethical. An ethical company is not one that has eradicated all human flaws, for that would require behaviour modification on a massive scale and produce an overly sanitised customer experience. This could ring a massive bell for you if you've ever been a customer receiving efficient service yet completely devoid of soul, where you know that the behaviours have been manufactured and are simply not genuine. The key for leaders is to know how to react appropriately to human

behaviours that could be counterproductive, and how to harness the potential learning and creative progress from moments of human lapse.

3. **Is there such a thing as a 'correct' amount of profit?** The correct amount of profit is one that funds an equitable return for all stakeholders, and one that is sustainable in that it generates sufficient for the organisation to continually re-invest. Each industry or market will have its own 'correct' profit level, dependent upon the stage of industry development and the level of risk involved. A newly emerging technology might generate very low profit levels at first, then suddenly very high profit levels, before settling into a long-term equilibrium.

> *The correct amount of profit is one that funds an equitable return for all stakeholders, and one that is sustainable in that it generates sufficient for the organisation to continually re-invest.*

Selling semiconductors in the early 1980s, I would frequently be making a margin of $50 per piece as the latest chip was released. One year later I might be making $1 per piece. Which was the 'correct' profit? Taking over as Chairman of a business one time, the company had two business units breaking even, two making 'normal' operating margins of around 8 per cent, and one making 35 per cent. The right call was to create a strategy not just for improving the profits of the break-even business units, but to proactively manage the progressive lowering of the profits of the 35 per cent unit. The business was simply too vulnerable otherwise. Advising a hugely profitable business with a dominant market share of a declining market, yet still chasing the grail of ever growing like-for-like sales, my exhortations that they should proactively set about reducing their market share was met with horror. The 'right' thing to do was for them, unthinkable. Four years on and they're close to going out of business. I tried. Chairing a CEO Peer Group one time, we had one 'not for profit' organisation represented in the group. That 'not for profit' produced fantastically high-quality services, and produced the desired, targeted, regulated 5 per cent operating surplus each year. Profit by any other name. The joke in the group was that the only true 'not for profit' members were those 'for profit' companies making losses. On another occasion I chaired a housing association, and having achieved the lowest voids and rent arrears in the whole sector, the two key drivers of revenue and cash maximisation, the tenant board had to decide what to do with the surplus money. There ensued a wonderful debate seeking to balance using money for immediate tenant benefit, and setting money aside for a rainy day.

How *should* a company deal with 'surplus' profits? First of all it must communicate clearly to the owners that the results cannot be repeated. I've seen too many examples of surplus profits instantly being considered as the new norm, thus placing executives and employees in a completely invidious position. Secondly the surplus funds must be overtly allocated to some 'special' use. The simplest thing is to return the surplus to the owners (hopefully with an appropriate element shared with the employees who produced the surplus) in the form of a special dividend, or maybe a

share buy-back, since this appropriately re-sets the enterprise value. But maybe the boldest use is a deliberate investment in future innovation and growth. The main point is that every company should have a clear and transparent view of what the 'right' level of profit is and manage things accordingly.

A business that sets out to achieve 'Goldilocks' status will have a great strategy and the best possible chance of success, both short and long term.

So do they exist? In my experience there are very few. And this is a shame, since shareholder primacy is not what it was. We live at a time when it is arguably more possible now for a CEO to run an 'ethical' company than it has ever been. Yet something still gets in the way.

I've encountered many companies run by really decent leaders, genuinely trying to run their businesses ethically, yet still presiding over cultures fundamentally driven by fear. These leaders are not psychopathic. They agonise over decisions that affect people. They genuinely want to do good. They wrestle constantly with their own existential angst. They are frustrated that their employees feel fear. They are genuinely shocked when something bad happens within their organisation.

I repeat, these leaders are not psychopathic. They have a strong desire to do right; to do good. Yet still they preside over undesirable behaviours. How can this be? It is because they become 'corporapathic'. Many leaders turn into 'Corporapaths' as they've assumed their leadership mantle.

There are Psychopaths, There are Sociopaths and now There are Corporapaths

Much has been written in recent times about the existence of the 'Corporate Psychopath'. The hypothesis is that many of our corporations are in fact run by psychopaths – literally people with personality disorders – with the proportion in the cohort of CEOs being far greater than in the overall population. The reason for them rising to high office in greater proportions than in the normal population, it is held, is because psychopaths consistently and ruthlessly display characteristics that help them achieve outstanding short-term financial results, for which they are then richly rewarded, thus creating a dynamic whereby even 'good' people take them as role models and seek to emulate their approach. Remember the Rhesus Macaques whose brain activity synchronises with more dominant monkeys. Of course these lesser mortals then 'fail' because they cannot maintain the necessary detachment from the suffering they cause.

I do not believe the story is as simple as a one of a handful of psychopaths at the top, followed grudgingly by millions of duped and manipulated ordinary people, whether managers or 'mere' employees. If it were then we could simply legally bar psychopaths from holding office and put sociopathic CEOs who preside over human suffering in prison.

The real problem is that corporate cultures in and of themselves create irresistible unconscious behavioural conditioning that sees good men and women, who do not have personality disorders, turned into Corporapaths when given responsibility for managing others.

But whereas Psychopaths and Sociopaths are born and are beyond cure, Corporapaths can be 'saved' (returned to 'normal') in a matter of days when withdrawn from the toxic culture they've been immersed in. They can also be trained and coached to be non-corporapathic leaders, thus remaining in their companies with a new and confident mandate to create a very different culture.

So what is the difference between a Psychopath, a Sociopath and a Corporapath? The first two are personality disorders whereas the latter is a conditioned state of abnormal behaviour that perfectly mentally healthy people can get into when working in corporations. With Corporapaths, controlling behaviours are acceptable and became paramount. These people have no trace of psychopathy about them in their everyday lives yet behave in quasi-psychopathic ways when they enter their daily work.

Psychopaths – a personality disorder meaning the person has a pre-disposition to aggressive, perverted, criminal, amoral, violent behaviour without empathy or remorse.

Sociopaths – a personality disorder meaning the person has a pre-disposition to antisocial, sometimes criminal behaviour, lacking in a sense of moral responsibility or social conscience

Corporapaths – *not* a personality disorder but a conditioned state whereby the person engages in controlling and manipulative (and therefore intimidatory) behaviour apparently lacking in empathy, humanity or responsibility for causing fear in others

Characteristics of Corporapaths – The 20-Point test

We need to understand what's going on in the potential Goldilocks businesses, where despite the absolute absence of psychopaths, there still seem to be quasi-psychopathic behaviours, even cultures in place.

This is because Corporatism has very cleverly created a new type of 'temporary', 'jobbing' psychopath; it has taken thoroughly decent people, without a trace of psychopathy in them, and turned them into Corporapaths.

So what's the difference between an 'authentic leader' and a 'Corporapath'? The fundamental difference is one of motivation. Authentic Leaders are motivated by doing what's best for the Cause, but always caring for the people who have joined with them in pursuit of that Cause and never ever compromising on human decency. 'Corporapaths' are motivated solely by doing what's best for themselves and they are prepared to sacrifice human decency in pursuit of the Cause.

Robert Hare, a criminal psychologist who coined the term 'snakes in suits' as a synonym for workplace psychopaths, created a 'Psychopath Test', a checklist of 20 items. Reading the test, it's hard not to smile in knowing identification of the traits of Bosses we've known and 'loved'.

But for our purposes, we need to know the characteristics of Corporapaths, and I've also identified 20. So here goes – remember as you read through these characteristics, that I am talking about thoroughly decent men and women who are nobly motivated, and largely unconscious of their actual behaviours and the impact and direct consequences of those actions:

1) Corporapaths believe nothing happens in their absence

Corporapaths believe in a powerful force in the physical universe. They know for sure that a fourth Law of Thermodynamics exists – it states that nothing is happening when they are not physically present to witness it. The hard-pressed employee can have been putting in 12-hour days, but if the Boss doesn't see it, it will count for nothing. The Employee might have done some brilliantly creative work on one aspect of the project, only for the Boss to utterly dismiss it in a meeting. Corporapaths only trust the evidence of their own eyes, and since their own insecurity causes them to mistrust others, judging followers as lazy and uncaring if they can get away with it, they simply have to *see* something for it to be real and valued.

2) Corporapaths don't blatantly lie, they just present their opinions as facts

Corporapaths can and do lie of course. They have to, since they are continually constructing reasons (excuses) for why results are below expectations. A Corporapath's most common act of dishonesty of course is simply to omit or skirt round inconvenient truths.

When a Corporapath says 'It's not possible to . . .' this is merely their opinion, but it is presented as fact. It might be true, but what they present is a falsehood.

But they cannot blatantly lie, either from common decency or for fear of being caught out. So they've developed a more subtle strategy and have become experts at stating their opinions as incontrovertible facts. When a Corporapath says, 'It's not possible to . . .' this is merely their opinion, but it is presented as fact. It might be true, but what they present is a falsehood. If they are challenged, they will counter with a well-rehearsed and vigorous defence of the 'truth'.

3) Corporapaths infantalise people

It would be wrong to assume that Corporapaths are mere unconscious organisms thrashing through the day with no strategy in place. They are in fact capable of some very proactive behaviours. One of these is to 'motivate' their followers with humour, personal favour and familiarity. This manifests, for example, in inappropriate use of sexual innuendo, sarcasm, devising nicknames or playing to cultural stereotypes. Banter. Since Corporapaths often have to recover situations when even *they* realise they have gone too far, they also tend to use inappropriate material rewards as bribes to salve their own conscience. They will only apologise for inappropriate behaviour to head off some third-party authority being called in. Even if a Corporapath has an awareness of inappropriateness through diversity or unconscious bias training, they will find it hard to give up behaviours that infantilise followers.

4) Corporapaths promote 'Them and Us'

'Them and Us' cultures are perhaps the most pernicious type within organisations. Corporapaths are promoters of 'them and us', since it helps their cause in two ways. First of all, it means they can 'divide and conquer' their subordinates – if their followers are fighting among themselves, then they can't notice how poor their Boss is. Secondly it means they can avoid accountability for real results such as sales and profits, since they have to 'waste' so much time because of the dysfunctionality of the organisation – a fact which they infer to be the fault of their own superiors.

5) Corporapaths vacillate

One of the hardest things about working for a Corporapath is that they vacillate so much. Corporapaths are open to being buttonholed. One day they will passionately believe position X, and the next they will lambast a follower for the stupidity of still holding position X as company strategy. The metaphorical swaying with the prevailing wind is often manifest by the Corporapath agreeing with the opinion of the last executive they've been in conversation with, and they will often act in a moment of 'new' clarity leaving their other followers utterly bemused as to what just happened. Corporapaths can only be trusted by their followers if their behaviour is relatively predictable. But true Corporapaths are tough to endure since their vacillation makes it almost impossible for the Employee to predict their response, thus any sort of proactive action is simply too risky.

6) Corporapaths sulk

Corporapaths often act just like spoiled children. They go readily into toddler mode, becoming needy and self-absorbed. When things don't go their way, when they don't get the recognition or praise they so clearly deserve, they sulk. They will complain at how hard they are having to work, despite earning 10× or 50× or 100× the living wage. Since Corporapaths can also hold a grudge with a superhuman intensity and relish, it is best not to upset them, in fact their followers often have to be the ones to tell their Corporapath how brilliant they are and how the team simply could not do without their inspired leadership.

7) Corporapaths intimidate, but subtly

Corporapaths are not bullies. They don't swear, shout or threaten; in fact they may work really hard to hide any frustration, irritation or impatience to specifically avoid intimidatory behaviours. But in doing so they've become skilled manipulators, and they've become so skilled at this that they know exactly how to play on their followers' fears, and how to quickly generate guilt and shame, and this is what intimidates. I have some sympathy here, since the existence of hierarchy already puts the leader in the role of intimidator before they've done anything. Also leaders who have great integrity and personal commitment to the Cause and the

Fear of disappointing a respected Boss can be a greater intimidatory dynamic than fearing the wrath of a bully.

people involved, often intimidate their followers with their passion. Fear of disappointing a respected Boss can be a greater intimidatory dynamic than fearing the wrath of a bully. Leaders have to massively compensate for the hierarchy effect, over-indexing on positive behaviours of recognition and reward, and this is exhausting and can feel like a distraction from the 'real' work of leading.

8) Corporapaths absent themselves

Macavity the Mystery Cat defied Scotland Yard, because whenever they were about to catch him in the act, the cry would go up 'Macavity's not *there*' (T S Eliot, 1939). The Corporapath has the supreme ability to disappear when the hard ground work or heavy lifting needs to be done. They rarely put themselves in the front line, where real problems arise, since they would then find it harder to ignore the legitimate pleas of their followers for more resource. How many episodes of *Back to the Floor* or *Undercover Boss* have you watched where it's clear that the leader has never put themselves in the shoes of their employees? Corporapaths love a crisis, but they need to time their entrance so that can be suitably incredulous that the crisis arose, and secretly delighted that the world has yet again proven that bad things happen when they are not around. Truly the Corporapath is indispensable.

9) Corporapaths forget (delete) inconvenient data

Corporapaths 'conveniently' forget things they have said, committed to or previously admitted they know. This is a hugely effective technique of course, since arguing with the Boss that you definitely told them, or scurrying away to look out the email that proves it, feels like the act of a churlish 'jobsworth'. And, of course, proving the Boss wrong is never appreciated. The strange thing about this dynamic is that the Corporapath is conditioned into believing the infallibility of their memory, when they really need to learn that it has holes.

10) Corporapaths create strong teams, but through a fortress mentality

Corporapaths often create what look like admirably strong team cultures, through a form of 'fortress mentality' strategy. Thus everyone in the team (within the fortress) is protected, and all conspire to build a strong ethos and fantastic results, with a powerful PR machine to constantly communicate how wonderful everything is within the fortress. In fact the Corporapath is simply creating a collective version of themselves. The strength of these teams relies not so much on the internal code or mission, but on an enemy to be repelled. As much as those within the Fortress's protection are defended, promoted and rewarded, the real power comes from defeating the enemy without. Every fortress has besiegers at the gates. The more we can demonise the enemy, the stronger we become. The more we can bombard them, the more they will be weakened. This is all fine of course when the enemy is the competition. Analysing how to beat the competition is a legitimate strategic consideration. But what about other external agents – regulators or suppliers? Are we really served by having an adversarial relationship with these third parties? And what if the 'fortress' dynamic spills over against internal agencies – departments within our own organisation that are there to support? Or if customers, or investors become 'the enemy'? I've seen many examples of great damage caused by this style of team performance building.

11) Corporapaths allow their egos to be massaged

It is a quite superhuman act for a leader to keep their ego in check. It suits followers to massage the Boss's ego, since it deflects them from having to talk about problems they are presiding over, and since it fuels the whole hierarchical status system. If followers don't massage the Boss's ego, they risk contributing to a culture whereby, when they themselves assume the lofty pedestal, they won't be able to enjoy the benefits. I am somewhat ashamed now to admit that as a 24-year-old CFO, my ego was rampant. I adored ordering my Ford Granada 2.8GL; there was something intensely pleasing about having a secretary sitting outside my office, making my coffee and fielding my calls and visitors. I savoured the power and I enjoyed the benefits. Even now 36 years later, I noticed on taking up my most recent Chairman's role, that I really enjoyed having the opportunity to once more throw my weight around. Keeping ego under control is a massive ask. There is a natural sense of entitlement built into the Corporate system, that the higher ranks get more of the spoils. So when these are denied, it is a keenly felt loss, and one that is hard for the system to deny. On taking over a failing car dealer group some years ago, when I could have been driving the top of the range luxury car, I deliberately drove the oldest car in stock for two years. I needed to send a strong personal message, and it was 100 per cent the right thing to do, but I had to fight my Ego constantly, for it was my Ego that had to explain to my friends why I was driving an 'old banger' despite being the Group Managing Director. What is the point of climbing to the top of the slippery pole, if you then have to deny yourself the trinkets?

12) Corporapaths can't coach, but think they can and think they are

Most managers think they coach – they will readily admit that they could be better, but they fundamentally believe that they are coaching a lot of the time. They are not. What they are doing is directing people with closed questions rather than statements and showing people what to do and how to do it. The first is called manipulation, and the second is called teaching, or it would be if it were overt. We'll see in a later Chapter just how universal and how powerful this dynamic is. Corporapaths struggle to differentiate the styles of leadership – directing, coaching, educating – both in their conscious self-regulation and appropriate usage of the different styles, and in their contracting with their followers to ensure the appropriate response.

13) Corporapaths won't show vulnerability for fear of losing respect

Corporapaths really struggle with vulnerability. They are so scared of spooking their followers; so afraid that they will lose their followers' respect, that they work incredibly hard to manage their own worries and fears. They seem incapable of saying

'I don't know'; incapable of asking for help. Their explanation is that it is actually their *duty* never to show vulnerability. It's as if it's written into the leader manual. I've seen countless examples of 'the good guy' not getting the promotion because they've not displayed the rock- solid confidence that is so prized at senior levels. In my view this dynamic alone is a major cause of the lack of diversity in boardrooms. But working for an 'invulnerable' leader is exhausting and demoralising. How can any employee get a genuine sense of fulfilment, of adding value or being of value, if their Boss always knows the answer before the employee got there; if their Boss makes it clear that they could do the employee's job (and probably better); if their Boss only asks questions to which he or she has a 'correct' answer in mind; if their Boss's coaching is in fact merely trying to catch someone out?

14) Corporapaths try and hide negative emotions

Corporapaths are afraid of emotions. Fear, sadness, disappointment, anger – these are to be avoided or at least covered up as much as possible. Corporapaths pretend to be confident when they're fearful; they'll avoid conversations where sadness or disappointment will come up; they pretend to be calm when they are angry. While this is understandable on a human level, the insanity is that they believe they can successfully mask what they are feeling, which of course they can't. Numerous times I've had a client admit to me that they were really angry with someone in a meeting, but that 'they wouldn't have known'. Of course they knew! With over 90 per cent of communication happening nonverbally, and with our survival mechanism of fight or flight honed to perfection over 200,000 years, it's impossible for one human being to mask their fear, sadness or anger. We are programmed to pick this up, in case we need to run from a Mammoth that we've not seen yet. Corporapaths do not believe it is right for them to display fear and anger, and so they have no practice at doing so appropriately. And they send the unconscious direction to their followers that they must practice the same behaviours. Always look confident, pacy and in control. Do not let on when you are struggling. I would argue this is the Corporapath's greatest failing, and yet they know not what they do.

15) Corporapaths compartmentalise their lives

This is a common trait among managers, coming to believe that they must have an identity, a persona, a set of behaviours, maybe even morals, at work that must be different from their 'normal' or natural home persona. How many corporate citizens metaphorically change from Superman to Clark Kent on the drive home, treating the car like the telephone box in which to change from the cape and underpants-on-the-outside look, into spouse or parent uniform. The issue of course is that the 'work' persona becomes a manufactured creation. How can that be authentic? One of my favourite coaching questions to an executive is 'what does (insert name of spouse or partner here) think?' I would say in more than 50 per cent of cases, the response is 'I've not really talked to him/her about this'. Some go further and add the overrider 'I try and keep work stresses to myself, I don't want to worry him/her, and besides he/she does not work in the corporate world and therefore doesn't understand what it's like'. Wow.

16) Corporapaths shoot messengers

They don't mean to of course, but they do. One of the scariest things any corporate citizen has to do is deliver bad news to their boss. Legend has it that Sam Goldwyn said that he expected people to give him bad news even if it cost them their job. Was Sam Goldwyn being corporapathic or authentic? I would say the latter, as I believe it is essential that a common commitment to truth is crucial, as is personal accountability. On receiving bad news, it is of course humanly almost impossible not to react with surprise and anger. And even when that reaction is so clearly not aimed at the messenger, it will feel like it is. How do *you* receive bad news? I talked earlier about Major Marsden who taught me to drive, and John Pallin one of my early bosses, and how they reacted to 'bad' news. Reacting poorly to bad news is not only a huge self-indulgence, but it is a massive factor in the culture. And for most 'bad' news, read 'inconvenient' news. It's never *that* bad. So I exhort you to work hard to manage yourself in those moments, focussing on how the messenger is feeling at first, accessing the compassion for someone in pain, then enquiring as to the well-being of the affected parties. You are not important. Of course the bigger question then becomes how you create an environment whereby 'bad' news is rare, since the whole community is always on top of the truth of any situation. Start by managing the first, and the second question will take care of itself.

17) Corporapaths are controllers, if not freaks

I'm not sure I've met another human being who isn't seeking control over their lives. Whether they are all control 'freaks' is only a matter of degree. Corporapaths are so consumed with being in control that they often flirt with freakery, but since these are decent people who are desperate not to be raving autocrats, they develop unconscious controlling habits (more later). The pursuit of control of outcomes is of course Corporatism's greatest illusion. I have no issue with seeking to control inputs. But outcomes are outcomes. The natural world is full of examples of controlled inputs – our biological construction is incredibly ordered and controlled. But outcomes are outcomes. If a golfer tries to hit the ball into the hole from 160 yards, a statistically almost impossible outcome, then their body will likely do things to make that outcome more *unlikely*. All the golfer can really do is hit the best shot they can. Notice how caddies are never overheard exhorting their golfers to 'just hit the thing in the hole'. That would be unhelpful. What they will be heard doing is giving inputs on yardages and wind, and calmly asking the golfer what they are thinking. If they exhort anything at all, just before the fateful shot, it will simply be 'just play the best shot you can'. Corporapaths are scared of this type of 'just do your best' strategising, since it feels impotent. Their fear is that if they stand up in front

> *The pursuit of control of outcomes is of course Corporatism's greatest illusion.*

of their bosses and say 'we did our best' or 'everyone is doing their best' that the retort will be a simple but vapid 'well your best was not/is not good enough'.

18) Corporapaths speak fluent platitude

Corporapaths love euphemisms, acronyms, generalisations and platitudes. Listen carefully to your leaders and when they've stopped speaking just ask yourself what it was that they communicated. It is highly likely that it will have sounded great, maybe even inspiring, but that it will not have been specific. Corporapaths frequently state goals as strategies in the form of 'so what we need to do is make our customers happy' or 'we have to work out what will make our customers happy' or 'we know that making our customers happy is our number one success factor, so let's all go do it!' No one can argue with this, and I get that Henry V was inspiring when he exhorted his followers to go into the breach again, but with Corporapaths it is all they can do, and inspiration needs the addition of perspiration in order to achieve things. We need our leaders to be great storytellers, to bring the mission to life through metaphor and narrative, but we also need a route-map and directions. When you're on the front line, life is simple and real. But Corporapaths speak fluent platitude. If *all* you hear from your leader are beautiful words, then it's just not enough, especially if when it comes to it, your leader's inspiring words are not matched by their actions. And here is where the Corporapath ultimately falls down, for when they speak their words they are absolutely sincere, and everyone believes them. But then they let themselves down by not ruthlessly ensuring that their actions are in 100 per cent alignment with their words.

19) Corporapaths believe the correct sequence is 'Fire, Ready, Aim'

Corporapaths will say that they understand the value of good preparation and that they know that time spent carefully targeting the right results will enhance performance and maximise the chances of success. Corporapaths, ever fluent in platitude, will say they believe in planning – 'To fail to plan is plan to fail' they will hear themselves exhort. But the reality is that Corporapaths value action more than any other commodity, in others but also in themselves. To be 'inactive', to wait and see, feels like simply trusting to luck. Go tell your boss that you've done everything you can, and now you just have to see how things turn out, and see how they react (emotionally). Do they emanate confidence and acceptance, or do they betray doubt? As Corporapaths rise through the ranks, they notice that their opportunities to solve problems and make decisions diminish. As CEO, how many decisions should you be making in a year? As a factory worker, or even as a site manager, you will have to make countless decisions every day. But as CEO you might make only a handful of decisions each year. Corporapaths struggle with this 'inactivity' and will land on the merest hint of an opportunity to pull the trigger. Fire, Ready, Aim becomes an habitual process, and even then the 'Ready' piece can be omitted completely.

20) Corporapaths delegate conflict

As you scale the hierarchy, you get further away from the manifestations of the natural conflicts that arise in any organisation. It's so easy for the Corporapath to say they understand what it's like for their front-line staff to handle difficult customer situations, while at the same time presiding over a woeful lack of resource or support to those staff. I've seen leaders working incredibly hard to build harmonious senior teams, offsite after offsite, but paying no real attention to how they support the next level down to navigate the inevitable conflicts that arise. There are natural points of tension (and therefore potential conflict) in every organisation. Corporations are typically organised to delegate the authority for decisions involving resource allocation to experts and specialists, who will in theory make rational decisions for the good of the Cause. But such situations demand that people understand and accept the outcome, sometimes feeling like they've won and often like they've lost. Our Left Brain says 'winner or loser'. Where in your organisation are those conflicts playing out? And where are your leaders in all of this? It's all too easy for the Corporapath to make the unemotional, the rational, the dispassionate decision, and I'm the first to argue that there are cases where only the leader can make that difficult call. But how does the leader create an environment whereby daily decisions, the need for which arises from the inevitable tensions and conflicts, are best made, and then best executed. A leader who abhors conflict to the point of making everyone else deal with it, is committing their whole organisation to an unnecessarily tough and inefficient working life.

The Effects of Pressure on Managers

While it's convenient to believe that pressure is caused by time, or by our Boss, or by lack of resource, or simply by extraordinary and unpredictable events, that can be a dangerous and distracting fallacy. There will be moments of pressure created by external factors, but most pressure is self-generated. We put pressure on ourselves, and it is caused fundamentally by the weight of expectation we feel.

The greatest insecurity is when people have to guess what their boss wants of them – in the phase when trust is not yet fully established. Pressure comes from feeling like we're being judged by the boss for not meeting expectations – if the expectations are unclear or people feel unsupported in meeting them or in striving for goals, then they get very stressed.

Under pressure and when we get frustrated – we go to one extreme or the other – we either get overly aggressive or overly passive. We either intimidate people with the force of our judgements or our authority, or we withdraw and leave people in a vacuum.

Pressure causes us to act inauthentically. To access my integrity, I need to think calmly and rationally; to be able to weigh up my options and compare them to my internal code.

Pressure means I have to be right and not wrong; conform and not be different; be compliant not disruptive. I know this because my behaviour is rewarded even if it is only the absence or withdrawal of threat if I am compliant and it is sanctioned if I show uncertainty or hesitancy or disloyalty or god forbid that I seem to have retreated from prior forward movements. Pressure creates fear and induces panic. Fear causes fight or flight. In corporate cultures flight is not an option neither is fight so freeze (and therefore denial) is inevitable. Fear causes cortisol levels in the brain to rise. Cortisol levels are a major factor in ADHD and so it goes on.

> *Pressure causes us to act inauthentically. To access my integrity, I need to think calmly and rationally; to be able to weigh up my options and compare them to my internal code.*

Under pressure, and getting frustrated, managers often resort to one of the three default styles of leadership.

1. Bullying (aggression/fight)

2. Manipulation (passive aggression/fight)

3. Hope (hiding/flight)

I've certainly seen a huge rise in passive-aggressive behaviours in the corporate world in recent years.

Unconscious Controlling Habits – We're Addicted to Control

Ninety-nine per cent of managers are striving to do their very best under enormous corporate pressures for results. They genuinely care about their people and they do take their people-management responsibilities seriously. Unfortunately, the pressure often leads managers into situations where it's all too easy for them to judge their people as getting in their way, and then out comes 'the Beast'.

In interactions with others, if I exercise my Left Brain I become separate from you and you become an obstacle to me solving the problem. People have to be more important to us than problems. That's how we hard wire growth into our organisations. The Right Brain is open minded, open to possibilities and new ideas and ways, simply savouring the debate and the relationship. The Left Brain is closed minded, since the answer is clear and 'why are we wasting time?'. The Left Brain uses statements and does not want to consider new data. The Right Brain is curious and asks questions to learn. The Left Brain judges new data as inconvenient, superfluous and distracting – a waste of time and energy. The Right Brain has no judgements and simply wants to commune with the energy around in the present moment. The antidote to control is curiosity.

Our physical default in the face of a problem is to solve it. We need to make our physical default asking questions. The reason so many managers are appalling facilitators is that they are simply out of the habit of building relationships and too into solving problems themselves, so they end up facilitating a group like they would run one of their own team meetings. In a matrix organisation the key component is trust which means that the quality of relationships is key and yet often no explicit investment of focus or time is put into this.

Control Freakery

When asking a roomful of managers 'who would admit to being a Control Freak?' what proportion would you say raise their hands? Well, a lot – and I should know since it's a question I've asked many, many times. And those who do not raise their hands are often dithering for fear of looking silly. So I play a little game with my audience and pose the question in multiple choice form.

A. I am a Control Freak and proud.

B. It's not that I am a Control Freak it's just that I like things to be right.

C. I'm not a Control Freak (but I have a friend who thinks they might be . . .).

D. I got feedback in my last 360 that I can be a Control Freak, but I think I know who said it, and believe me they're the one with the problem.

E. I am definitely not a Control Freak (and I will see anyone who says I am in my office at 9 o'clock tomorrow morning).

Of course, this produces some laughter and a communal acknowledgement that we are all pretty much Control Freaks. In fact I'd go further and say that in my experience most corporate managers are pretty much addicted to being 'in control' (and they thus become highly agitated when their world is suddenly 'out of control').

We seem to work on the basis that everything is within our control – we suffer a poor weekend's retail sales due to the appalling weather, and we feel like it's our fault; our operating costs rise due to a spike in commodity prices, and we feel responsible; we lose market share as a competitor launches a brilliant new product, and we beat ourselves up; we suffer unexpected operating losses as one of our factories has to close following a flood, and we feel the pressure.

And yet all these things are outside our control; in fact it's pretty hard to come up with anything that *is* directly in our control, apart from our own choices and actions. Ah but then there are our employees . . .

Now we get that we can't control the weather, the oil price or the competition, but surely we can control our employees, can't we? After all, they are contracted to us – we give them money every month without fail in return for very specific activities and performance.

So if we can control our employees, why is it so difficult to get them to change? They know the company plan, they know what's expected of them, they even know what's-in-it for them. We pay them well, we keep them informed, we may even have a scheme whereby they bene-fit financially if we hit our targets. So why, oh why can't we get our employees to really buy-in to the changes we need to make – to really own the plan? The answer is simple – because most of our employees are Control Freaks too!

We human beings are simple creatures, and we share one fundamental psychological trait – when change is imposed upon us we go through a five-stage psychological process before we come to fully embrace that change. Not only *will* people go through these five stages, but they *have to* go through them; there is no going straight to ownership and no skipping a stage on the way there.

The five stages are:

1. **uncertainty;**

2. **resistance;**

3. **engagement;**

4. **reflection;**

5. **action.**

We will look in detail at these later in the book.

Ogres may get a bad Press, but They're Still Ogres!

The report into the Smolensk air crash which killed the Polish President and nearly 100 other people in 2010 blamed the Polish pilots, saying they had failed to heed bad weather warnings because they were afraid of displeasing President Lech Kaczynski – the Pilots feared a '*negative reaction*' if they diverted to another airport. The flight recorder caught one of the crew saying '*He'll get mad*'. Poland's Air Force Commander had entered the flight deck and his presence '*put psychological pressure on the crew to decide on continuing their descent in a situation of unjustified risk, dominated by the goal of making a landing at any cost*'. The Polish authorities strongly refuted the findings, saying that the President would have completely endorsed the Pilots' decision had they diverted, and that he did not deserve a reputation for being an 'Ogre'.

So who do you blame? The Pilots, The Air Force Commander or the President? I guess the real question is how would any of us have acted under such pressure? The President might actually have been oblivious of the whole thing. Perhaps his Air Force Commander 'hinted' to the crew that the President would be angry. It would not be the first time that an Ogre's name had been taken in vain.

History is littered with the voices of Ogres incredulous that they have been maliciously misinterpreted – Henry II's frustrated cry of '*Will no one rid me of this turbulent priest*' was interpreted as a Royal Command by four loyal knights who went straight out and murdered the Archbishop of Canterbury, Thomas Becket, in the name of the King. More recently, as we saw earlier, the 2003 headline of 'Shuttle Report Blames NASA Culture' gave strong evidence of how the pressure put on engineers by NASA bosses caused safety to be relegated to a secondary concern – behind costs and deadlines. And in the even more recent financial crisis, how many 'rogue' bankers, having cost their institutions billions, went on to claim that their bosses had known all along what they were up to but put overt pressure on them to keep producing extraordinary returns?

Pressure to cut costs. Pressure to meet deadlines. Pressure to hit high targets? Sound familiar? In my experience the most powerful motivator in corporations is the desire (perhaps the perceived need) to please the boss. Most bosses completely underestimate the power of the hierarchy, believing that they

> *In my experience the most powerful motivator in corporations is the desire (perhaps the perceived need) to please the boss.*

can be seen as 'one of the troops'. The reality is as leaders of people at work, we hold immense power over them. And under pressure, our worst traits appear – we get frustrated with people who should know better and who simply aren't doing things well enough or fast enough or even in the right order!

Mind you, bosses can't win – if they are too aggressive and people fear their reaction to 'mistakes' then everyone plays it very safe. If they are too passive then everyone has to try and guess what they want, so playing safe again becomes the default mode. If they are perfect and become loved, then people fear letting them down or disappointing them, and . . . you guessed it.

The easiest way to stay safe in corporations is to have your excuses ready – the perfect reasons why you did not do what you should have done or what you committed to do. And the easiest excuse of all is to blame the Boss. So things get done in the Boss's name. The Boss is used as a threat by weak and fearful middle managers, and the merest hint of pleasure or displeasure at a situation is taken as direction.

We don't set out to be Ogres, but it can be convenient for others to demonise us, and we may have some Ogre-like tendencies that support the myth. Ogres may get a bad press, with things done in their name that they are completely oblivious to, however a defence of 'I never said that' or 'I never meant that' might be strictly true, but if the plane's gone down already, it's too late.

The most Controlling Thing we do is Doing Nothing

The hardest part of being a leader or manager is to recognise that we don't have to do anything to be feared. We have power. That's enough. Even when we become aware of controlling behaviours, we tend to think of them as always being active – as acts of Commission. And so we stop trying to control, and genuinely start to try to help. But even helping can be experienced as controlling. Boy, we really can't win.

> *Inaction is a powerful, arguably more powerful, controller – acts of omission are the most powerful controlling behaviours of all.*

We don't have to do or say anything for people to be fearful, in fact leaving a vacuum creates more fear than anything. Inaction is a powerful, arguably more powerful, controller – acts of omission are the most powerful controlling behaviours of all. Acts of omission are *never* interpreted positively by followers, but always endowed with a sinister motive. And that's the bummer – it's one thing to acknowledge we need to work on our behaviours, consciously turning a potentially controlling act into one of genuine facilitation or enablement, but now we have to be super sensitive when we are *not* doing anything. This is going to be exhausting.

We think of overt behaviours such as telling people what to do or checking up on them or chastising them when they make mistakes or fail to hit a target. Thus we judge ourselves kindly if we do not engage in these that often. However, the really pernicious controlling behaviours are the unconscious habitual ones we have such as interpreting rather than listening, problem solving rather than coaching or facilitating, and manipulating rather than being clear and up front. Interpretation – seeing the world or another person not as they truly are but as we prejudge them or expect them to be – is the first automatic step to problem solving which is in itself our way of controlling our world. Of course it works because we are constantly proven right, or so we believe, because people also behave in the light of how we are with them, or because our solutions are good. However, we miss any form of potential new outcome, and we completely miss creating positive learning and the potential for extraordinary growth.

How not to Demonise Corporate Customers

It's one thing working for a 'difficult' boss, but frequently it's our customers who are the ones apparently inflicting abusive and intimidating behaviours on us. Individual retail customers can be difficult, but at least if we lose one individual retail customer we will not really notice the fall in revenue. However, where we are supplying a corporate customer, life can be very different, frequently characterised by each customer representing a significant proportion of our sales and organised to procure from us 'professionally'.

Supplying some corporate customers has become a drastically tougher challenge in recent years, with suppliers believing that the financial crisis, followed by just about every industry being 'disrupted', has changed the behaviours of corporate buyers forever. Once reasonably stable partnership-based supply chains have been apparently turned on their head, with not just *price* as important, but an ever-*lower* price, and with no compromise on quality, technical specifications or environmental sustainability.

If you are a salesperson to the supermarkets you have learned through tough experience your core competency in knowing how they operate and knowing how to secure reliable and growing revenues. You have had to lead your customers in the face of sometimes extreme pressure to simply cut prices, and then you have had to come inside your own organisation to lead internal cross functional teams in constantly raising the game on quality, security and logistics.

But no matter how well Key Account Managers (KAMs) perform in their role, they struggle at the best of times to elicit the essential urgency and collaboration from their internal colleagues. How much tougher that has become now that the supermarkets have become 'Men Behaving Badly'. Or have they . . . ?

There are two dynamics at play within any supplier to the supermarkets. First, the degree to which the KAMs feel threatened by their customers with loss of sales is always higher than warranted – I call this the 'Indispensability Gap'. Second, the KAMs are the trusted advocates of the customer when they come back inside the business seeking changes and improvements to the quality, security and price of supply.

Where the Indispensability Gap is 'healthy', ie the degree to which the supplier believes they are indispensable to the customer is *just* below the reality, an appropriate level of humility is brought to bear in strategic account planning, and KAMs remain confident in both their ability and their authority to *lead* the customer (usually manifested in saying 'no' very professionally to some customer request).

This then helps them to be honest internal brokers, in other words where they come inside and genuinely represent the customers' true needs and wishes, the internal departments can respond professionally and creatively. Together, the combined account teams can thrash out the best possible solutions, and the KAMs are then able to go back to the customers and give honest responses, even if they have not been able to secure everything they wanted.

So these two dynamics are crucial to the success of any large supplier to the multiples, irrespective of product characteristics and whether or not the supply is protected in any way by aspects of branding. When healthy and in balance, things work, even if the 'partnership' can feel stressed at times. When out of balance . . . be afraid.

Where the Indispensability Gap has become too wide, KAMs rapidly lose confidence, saying 'yes' to customers when they should not, or even worse, procrastinating over critical tactical questions, thus drastically reducing the customer's confidence. Once strong and trusted supply partnerships end up becoming all about short term 'spot' sales, to mutual detriment.

Again, where this dynamic gets stressed, KAMs feel they have to 'manipulate' the situation and come inside negotiating with their internal teams by mis-stating the customers' position (and communication style) in order to press for more than they feel they would gain by being honest. This can then lead to the internal teams accusing the KAMs of 'crying wolf', and refusing to believe their increasingly desperate advocacy.

The 'demonising' of the supermarkets, though a comfortable and convenient story to put about, is a major factor in unbalancing these two dynamics, and we enter the vicious circle of codependent behaviour – they pick up on our fears, become less trusting of our words and commitments, and so in turn they start adapting their behaviours. We perceive them as bullying us, and so we defend ourselves too aggressively, or perhaps more pathetically, we roll over and take it, while muttering under our breath and painting them as the enemy within our own teams. After all, if we can paint them as the culprits, no one will chastise us when we fail. There is no more successful diversion than uniting against an Ogre.

So we need to get a healthy balance back. And that starts with openly acknowledging the dynamics, and re-calibrating them internally, before going out to our partners, making up and starting over.

So just what are we Supposed to do as Leaders?

Being a leader in an organisation under huge pressure is not easy. It demands qualities of integrity and discipline beyond anything we had imagined when they first gave us the job.

First of all, we have to be more committed to principles and values (the *way* we are going to be) than to the mission and goals (the *what* we are there to do). That does not mean we devalue or belittle the Mission – it remains why we are all here, but the moment we put the end result above principles we are on the slippery slope. And we have to be more committed to the growth of people than any targeted outcome.

Secondly, we have to be super aware of behaviours under pressure, both our own behaviours and the giveaway behaviours of others around us – sycophancy, gossip, over-optimism, blame. In our own case we need to appreciate that although expressing frustration in the face of bad news may be a natural human reaction, it can be very intimidating to those looking to us for a lead. In the case of others behaving 'badly' we need to draw strict and non-negotiable boundaries that let people know that their behaviours are unacceptable.

Finally, we must have an intelligence network of people throughout our domain who will tell us the truth. And the only way to create this is to reward people (be pleased with them) when they tell us exactly what they think and exactly how it is, however painful the news and however inelegant the delivery. Our mantra should not be 'don't shoot the messenger' but 'raise the messenger on high'.

Notes

Deming's 14 Points for Management   Dr W Edwards Deming offered 14 key principles for management to follow to significantly improve the effectiveness of a business or organisation. The principles were first presented in his book *Out of the Crisis*, originally published in 1982 (Boston: MIT Press, 2000).

Robert D Hare   Babiak, P and Hare RD (2006) *Snakes in Suits: When Psychopaths Go to Work*. New York: HarperBusiness.

Robert D Hare 20-Point Test   The Hare Psychopathy Checklist, now revised (PCL-R), is a psychological assessment tool most commonly used to assess the presence of psychopathy in individuals. It is a 20-item inventory of perceived personality traits and recorded behaviours, intended to be completed on the basis of a semi-structured interview along with a review of 'collateral information' such as official records. The PCL was originally developed in the 1970s by Canadian psychologist Robert D Hare for use in psychology experiments, based partly on Hare's work with male offenders and forensic inmates in Vancouver, and partly on an influential clinical profile by American psychiatrist Hervey M Cleckley, first published in 1941.

T S Eliot   *Old Possum's Book of Practical Cats* is a collection of whimsical poems by T S Eliot, collected and published in 1939, with cover illustrations by the author, and quickly re-published in 1940, illustrated in full by Nicolas Bentley.

Back to the Floor   In this six-part documentary series, the CEOs of several major companies, organisations and public institutions were invited to 'spend a week at the bottom of the career ladder'. Specifically, the executives chosen were whisked away from their cushy panelled offices to the workplace itself, where they learned first-hand what it was like to be an ordinary salaried employee. Based on a British original telecast by the BBC in 1998, *Back to the Floor* aired in America over PBS from 14 June to 19 July 2002.

Undercover Boss   A television franchise series created by Stephen Lambert and produced in many countries. It originated in 2009 on the British Channel 4. The show's format features the experiences of senior executives working undercover in their own companies to investigate how their firms really work and to identify how they can be improved, as well as to reward hard-working employees.

Smolensk Air Crash Report   12 January 2011, 'Kaczynski Air Crash: Russia Blames Polish Pilot Error', BBC News website, www.bbc.co.uk/news/world-europe-12170021 (accessed 25 May 2018).

Chapter 6

Introducing the Corporate Hostage – You and I

Corporate Hostages – The Corporate Equivalent of Stockholm Syndrome

'Stockholm Syndrome', also known as 'traumatic bonding', is a condition whereby hostages develop a psychological alliance with their captors as a survival strategy. The feelings that result from such a bond between captor and victim can develop into really strong emotional ties, yet seem wholly irrational in light of the fear and abuse endured by the victims. Hostages come to judge their Captors not by the enormity of their wrongs, but by the tiniest demonstrations of kindness or compassion. The good person is seen within the Beast; the fellow victim seen within the Abductor. The Hostage's compassion is triggered, and their humanity outweighs the Captor's cruelty. Hostages may even come to believe that they alone understand the Captor, and may start to make themselves responsible for their redemption. The ultimate expression of this is when, on release, the Hostage comes to defend the Captor against 'unfair' judgement, often feeling like they are the only ones who have the right to judge.

Ingrid Betancourt (2011) held hostage in the Columbian jungle for six years, summarised that three things happen to hostage takers in extreme situations when Captors have power, no witnesses and a hierarchy above them.

1. **They abuse their power and the control they have over others and they inflict pain and suffering.**

2. **They blame their leaders and abdicate responsibility for their actions.**

3. **They feel they can hide their behaviour as no one is watching or judging from a moral standpoint, so it's as if their behaviour is not real.**

These abuses are ultimately justified by the chillingly prosaic explanation of 'I was only obeying orders', the subtext of which is 'I would have suffered had I not obeyed' or even 'had I refused, someone else would have done it to you, so you would not have been saved anyway'. In the face of seemingly no choice, it is the Captor's subsequent dissociation from their actions that enables them to carry out the abuse.

But how does this relate to the Corporate World? No one is tortured, no one is physically abused, no one is forced to do anything against their will. And surely these days managers are not given 'orders' to obey, are they? Surely corporate citizens are completely free to exercise personal moral judgement. Aren't they?

But a Corporation, by its very construction, does indeed have the three fundamental characteristics for hostage conditions and abuse identified by Ingrid Betancourt.

1. **It gives people power over others.**

2. **It places a controlling hierarchy above the people to whom it has given power.**

3. **It fosters a secrecy that means there are no witnesses to abusive behaviours.**

Let's just look at how each of these plays out in the Corporate World.

People with Power over Others

Corporate entities are organised such that some human beings are deliberately given power over others. That power is enshrined in corporate management hierarchies, backed by the ultimate authority to sack people, and enabled through ever more sophisticated 'People' processes such as recruitment, performance appraisals, training needs analysis, disciplinary and grievance procedures and meritocratic reward systems.

But in the modern business world, rarely are managers sacked, they are instead 'performance managed' or 'managed out'. And so the ultimate expression of management power (managing someone out) is used as a last resort. Now I'm the first to celebrate the dramatic reduction in instances of summary dismissal for the smallest and often most innocuous or even patently unfair of reasons, but the problem now is we've lost the honesty of the fundamental contract of employment whereby if the employee does not do the job for which they are paid, they simply cannot continue to be paid. I believe in giving people chances and support their learning and their confidence, but I am also old-school enough to think that someone who is not up to the job should not be allowed to continue. I will work hard to discover each employee's true potential and even build the organisation structure and products around those amazing skills, genuinely valuing a great attitude, and working with those fundamentally decent people who for some reason have got themselves into a poor attitude. But the bottom line has to be that if after appropriate care and effort, the person is not doing the job, they have to go.

However, what I see often in the more 'enlightened' (frightened?) management cultures, are managers living with poor performance because they are scared to address the problem. And rather than supporting the poor performing employee 100 per cent, they allow their frustration and lack of belief in the employee to show, thus condemning the employee to the corporate equivalent of Death Row. In my view this is one of the most common abuses exercised by people with power – the self-indulgent betraying of feelings of frustration, irritation and impatience; of a closed-minded judgement and condemnation, thus virtually guaranteeing the employee's failure. The very essence of the self-fulfilling prophesy. The very first serial Plc Chairmen I worked under had a wonderfully simple mantra when it came to managing his Chief Executives – he said 'I support my Chief Executives 100 per cent until the moment I cannot support them, and then one of us has to go'. Honest and fair. I believe every employee is owed the same loyalty from their manager.

'Managing someone out' sounds like an active strategy, and in some of the worst cases it is absolutely manipulatively so. It is not wholly unusual for me to hear a manager say that they are trying to make the unfortunate employee's life so uncomfortable that they'll 'get the message'. I call this abuse. What do you call it? 'Managing someone out' is mainly a passive strategy, waiting for the person to come to their own realisation that they need to move on, and I've frequently seen this strategy being allowed to play out for many months and sometimes even years.

The most powerful manifestations of management power exercised actively are the decisions managers can make on promotions, bonuses, pay raises and working conditions. A poor manager will rarely sack anyone, since they cannot bear the discomfort of the final conversation. Poor managers use the carrot of future endorsement, patronage or just plain bribery, and the stick of the threat of removing or withholding these things to exhort desired performance out of people.

Power Affects People

Power does strange things to people. Power causes the brain to work differently, for a start, reducing the ability to read the emotions of others, inducing a form of psychopathy. Jerry Useem (2017) writes about Dacher Keltner and Sukhvinder Obhi. Keltner found in studies over 20 years that people with power acted *as if they'd suffered a traumatic brain injury, becoming more impulsive, less risk-aware and less adept at seeing things from other peoples' point of view*. Neuroscientist Sukhvinder Obhi from McMaster University in Ontario *found in MRI studies that power impairs a specific neural process known as "mirroring" which is often seen as the cornerstone of our empathetic abilities. It's not broken by power, but it is certainly anesthetised*. Useem writes that, since subordinates provide few reliable clues to the powerful, motivated as they are to please and appease, leaders have to work doubly hard to elicit completely faithful reactions and truthful feedback from employees, at the very moment when their natural human ability to empathise goes offline. So leaders have to work quadruply hard. And that is exhausting and for many simply too inefficient a use of their precious time to bother with. And so they fall back on good old 'command and control', albeit exercised in a more manipulative way.

> *Power causes the brain to work differently, for a start, reducing the ability to read the emotions of others, inducing a form of psychopathy.*

Having power over others is in some ways a natural state within the animal kingdom. But human development evolved away from dominance as the prime organising dynamic toward collaboration quite early on, as we spread and grew in numbers. It's only in the last 6000 years that the deliberate acquisition and exercise of power over other humans has come to be so prevalent. So in the absence of war and in the deliberate creation of Corporatism to organise both our daily survival and our creative endeavours, it would have been more 'natural' for Corporatism to be based upon collaboration not power. But that was not even contemplated, since the people setting up Corporatism already had power. They had already acquired land, property, influence and dominion, and they were not about to risk giving it away. So collaboration was never tested as a methodology for efficiency, exploration and innovation. Worse, slavery was arguably the most logical use of power: just look at what the powerful achieved with cheap and compliant labour. And how many of the enslavers were 'good' men, who firmly believed that they had taken men and women from un-Godly and desperate lives in Africa, to the relative safety, security and piety of their lives in the sugar and cotton fields? How many of those paternalistic attitudes remain in the powerful today, justifying both the retention of power, and the absolute mistrust of collaboration?

Once acquired, the holding of power lessens the need for a high level of skill in influencing others. It also lessens the need to have and develop the skill of forming a really nuanced reading of people. Now I have power, I don't need to cajole you to do what I want. I can order you, or better still I can rely on the fear you have of my power to know that you will control yourself. And since I am now less able to detect a single individual's unique traits, I find myself stereotyping and generalising, and thus leaping to incorrect conclusions about how individual people are feeling and what they are thinking. I group people together into as large a homogenous cohort as possible, since then it is easier for me to make environmental changes that work for everyone. But this is the start of the dehumanising process, and before long I am guilty of treating you as less than human, and of compensating for my lack of human connection by valuing causes and material outcomes over people. The cycle is completed by my feeling alone and massively unappreciated. Don't they know what I do for them? Don't they know if it weren't for me and the sacrifices I make for them, they would be suffering? Cannot *someone* just once say thank you to me? And the Corporapath is fully fledged.

Stephen Karpman's Drama Triangle, the endless ping pong and table-end changing of the roles of Persecutor, Victim and Rescuer, does not come about because one person serially persecutes a victim – it comes into play because both parties are complicit. Karpman (1968).

> *Power creates the conditions for what Lord David Owen calls 'Hubris Syndrome', when an individual with power becomes deluded as to their skills and/or lack of weaknesses, and deluded in the breadth and unilateral expansion of their remit.*

Finally, power creates the conditions for what Lord David Owen (2008) calls 'Hubris Syndrome', when individuals with power becomes deluded as to their skills and/or lack of weaknesses, and deluded in the breadth and unilateral expansion of their remit. They come to believe they are superior to all others (or at the very least that their responsibility is to have greater wisdom), and that therefore they have licence, in fact a duty, to go way beyond what they were hired or elected to do. And they create a cadre of eager supporters and protectors around them, who obsequiously feed the ever-bloating ego of their master. If we ever needed an example of this in action, proving the deluded nature of hubris, surely it was when US President Donald Trump asked each of his Cabinet, in a televised meeting, to publicly praise him for his extraordinary talents. How is it possible that a human being can be so deluded as to think that was normal, appropriate, inspiring behaviour?

Returning to the more mundane matter of our day to day lives as corporate managers, let's turn to the question of how many people one manager can effectively exercise power over? Conventional corporate wisdom these days seems to say it's somewhere between 8 and 12. The phrase 'Span of control' itself hints at the reason for limiting the number of direct reports, with the implication that effective control can only be exercised with a level of detailed knowledge of what the employee is up to day by day. I do not subscribe to such notions and I hate the term itself. In my Dale Carnegie days, the head of the organisation was a wonderful guy called Olly Crom. He'd married Dale Carnegie's daughter Dorothy and had taken the reins of what was by then a worldwide training organisation when Dale Carnegie died. Olly Crom had 180 direct reports, for that is how many Sponsors there were across the world. Of course, they were all franchise holders, business people in their own right, and he therefore did not feel the need for a complex multi layered hierarchy of control. Of his 180 Sponsors he would say *'there's no problem we can't solve between us in 15 minutes over a cup of coffee'*.

Small numbers of direct reports also mean that managers rely heavily on 1:1 sessions, which by definition are private – secret even – whereas a large number of direct reports means that a manager has to do far more in groups. I believe this group or team focus to be a far more effective management methodology. First of all, a group of individuals can 'manage' each other, giving succour and support to an individual who may be struggling, and holding a poor performer to account for letting the group down. Secondly, the greater openness and transparency means that problems surface and are dealt with far more quickly, efficiently, creatively and perhaps more critically, and opportunities for abuse are minimised. Finally, the manager saves an enormous amount of time by only having to communicate once on an issue, plus the group can then agree on and embody the right meaning and a unified strategy. 1:1s are important for personal well-being, but group work is critical for maximum effectiveness.

A Controlling Hierarchy Above the People with Delegated Power

Even a CEO has to answer to someone. If that someone is a supportive, nurturing, pro-fessionally respectful and challenging Chairman, then the CEO has the best opportuni-ty to be authentic and to exercise power and control in a humane and ethical manner. But many CEOs have to answer to a range of stakeholders who either have or seem to have power over them, such as other Non-Executive Directors, investors and analysts. The judgemental, even gladiatorial, dynamics of the results-presentations and trading-update conference calls, can create a fear within even the most self-assured CEO, such that they feel that they must take actions that are in fact out of their integrity. At the very least they may feel that they have to communicate in a language that is not authentic. There seems to be a 'licence to invoke fear' that goes along with formal scrutiny; that governance pro-cesses are heavily reliant on interrogation techniques; that managers are 'fair game' for torture since they are so generously remunerated.

If even corporate CEOs, who on paper might not look as though they have a hierarchy above them, have their strategies and behaviours influenced, contaminated, neutered or even downright changed by the fear they feel from above, what hope does a middle manager have, buried deep within the organisation, away from any public light?

I've known many decent men and women in senior leadership roles who've acted in ways that clearly sit outside their personal values and human integrity. Their excuse? If I hadn't done it, I would have been replaced. As an Executive Coach, I will ask clients wrestling with this dilemma, 'what strategy or action, motivated by your most profound personal integrity, could you execute that would fall just short of getting you fired?' In other words I challenge clients to test the boundaries of their fears, rather than gradually and inexorably becoming slaves to fears that are not justified. Whenever I hear the words 'I would do that, but my boss would not let me/not like it/fire me if I did' I challenge back for evidence to support such strong beliefs. Rarely am I given concrete evidence; in fact on most occasions the client ends up admitting that not only have they not tested it out, but that in fact their boss might well be supportive. When I dig further, the client often reveals evidence to themselves of how their boss is actually positively supportive. What is most illuminating to me when this happens, is how often the client still hesitates to trust. Fear is powerful.

I recall an occasion coaching a CFO who was struggling in his relationship with his CEO. The CFO had convinced himself that his boss wanted him out. His fear was beginning to turn into a paranoia where everything the CEO did was interpreted negatively, where every action the CEO took was endowed with a deliberately negative motivation. At one point, under challenge from me, the CFO handed me a copy of an email the CEO had written to him the day before – he handed it to me as a falsely condemned man would present the ultimate damning evidence of his persecutor's abuse to an impartial judge, with the hope and expectation that I would immediately see the injustice and irrevocably join his cause. What I read was a wholly supportive message. It was 100 per cent clear to me that the CEO had taken great care to balance legitimate challenge with human support. The email addressed the issue at hand (the CFO was not denying the issue, he was simply blaming other factors) and it conveyed total support. But the CFO had read the email in a semi-paranoid state, and so he'd heard what he expected to hear in the tone and interpretation of the words. While I might have been critical of the CEO for trying to address the issue over email, I could find no fault with what he had communicated.

Secrecy Meaning no Witnesses to Their Abusive Behaviours

As we saw in earlier chapters, the power of fear is immense. It breeds exponentially like a virus. It chokes a culture within a very short time frame. Fear breeds fear. Insecurity breeds insecurity. And it is fear that drives unethical behaviours. To an extent this would be resolvable, certainly not terminal, if these behaviours were observed, since then they would be sanctioned, and cultural order would be restored. But they are not observed.

Adrian Furnham, in a lovely *Sunday Times* article entitled 'I Didn't get Where I am Without Being Toxic' (2016) wrote: '*So how is it that sociopaths go unchallenged and succeed?*

At the heart of the problem lie organisational processes and structural complexity. In essence, this means all bad behaviour can be hidden.'

Corporatism is very definite in what it does, and it engages the whole weight of culture and an army of advocates and promoters to justify these things. But Corporatism is also very definite in what it does not do. Having chosen not to do something, it cannot risk that thing arriving in the culture through the back door; it cannot afford, therefore, to leave anyone in any doubt as to why the thing is not done, and not to be done. Corporatism does not want observation and witnessing of management behaviour, and so it actively discourages it. Corporatism is also obsessed with competition, and this has fuelled the 'need' for confidentiality. Senior execs are so scared that employees will run to the competition with trade secrets that they utterly justify their opaqueness or even just downright lies. Corporatism creates a legitimacy around confidentiality and uses highly coercive tactics to dissuade openness and transparency. You may well not be fired for serial abusive behaviour towards employees, particularly if you continue to preside over 'great' results. But you will surely be fired for a breach of confidentiality. If you are 'managed out' because you are a poor performer or because your abuses of the employees are simply too great, you will leave with the dignity of spending more time with your family or to explore new opportunities. If you are fired for breaching confidentiality your head will be paraded on a stick through the office corridors and factory lines as a traitor. You can abuse people, but do not betray the company.

> *Corporatism creates a legitimacy around confidentiality and uses highly coercive tactics to dissuade openness and transparency.*

A Plc Director client, having decided to merge two operations together with the unfortunate but inevitable closure of a plant employing 4000 people, was clearly told by his IR Director, his in-house Legal Counsel and his HR Director, that he was not to tell any of the 4000 employees until the decision had been announced publicly. When he pushed back, saying he could not accept a situation where 4000 people would hear the news first on the Radio 4 Today programme, his peers were adamant that he had no choice – that the decision constituted an announceable event for the City, and that he would be in breach of Company Law were he to tell the employees first. I was able to help him have the courage to stand up to his colleagues and, lo and behold, they found a way for him to do it without anyone breaking any law. He personally delivered the news to the employees on site, and while it was a horrendous event in their lives, at least they were given the dignity and respect of their leader telling them in person and being with them as they vented their anger and grief. To this day, he recounts that story as a defining moment in his leadership confidence.

I often advise executives not to accept the ridiculous tyranny of so called professional advisers and to find creative ways of doing the right and ethical thing. I recently helped a very senior client complete a change of role within a global organisation, despite an absolute diktats from HR that it was not possible. His new boss, a VP based in a Germany, had originally said the role needed to be based there. My client was clear he would only take the role if he could stay resident in London. Between the two of them they worked out a modus operandi and shook hands on a deal. They had not bargained for HR however! The (relatively junior) HR person tasked with facilitating the change of role retorted that it was not policy to support such changes to role location and that the VP would have to find another candidate. The VP was made to feel that he had done wrong, and my client was made to feel guilty for being trying to organise the company around his personal circumstances. Such is the power of HR in this company that both the VP and my client were on the verge of accepting the position. I encouraged my client to present a joint front with the VP and firstly to ask a specific question of the HR guy on the policy that would be breached. They got an irritated but interestingly vague response: three paragraphs that basically said 'because I say so!' It was clear that no such policy existed. They then communicated a form of 'the decision is made, now please advise how we can best complete this from an internal process and policy angle'. The HR guy gave up, sending back three paragraphs that basically said 'do what you like!'

Secrecy is the key enabler for how corporate cultures can become and be sustained as places where fear rules. I understand how fear can create the initial abuses. But it is the secrecy that allows abuses to perpetuate, to grow and to become systemic.

It is often said that our real integrity is how we act when we know we have no witnesses; when we know we can get away with things because no one is looking. So it would make sense, if corporatism were really intent on having integrity, to systemically build observation and witnessing into the processes. But the critical interactions between manager and employee (between the powerful and the subordinated) are not observed. The 'time and motion' studies of mid-twentieth-century corporatism were an attempt to systemise observation, but were wholly productivity-focussed, with an agenda for reducing waste and cost. Corporatism has never embraced observation and witnessing either as a legitimate tool for improving management performance, or as protector of employees against the abuses of power.

So what are the critical interactions? Literally anytime a manager with power and authority over an employee interacts with that employee. There are, of course, the formal interactions of 1:1s and meetings, where the manager and employee have some chance of preparing and behaving calmly and rationally in relation to each other. And then there are the multitude of daily on-the-job or ad hoc interactions, which are mostly unplanned (even if they are somewhat routine) and are most open to unguarded behaviours driven not by ethical or values-guided considerations, but by pressure and unconscious controlling habits. Since most managers are under pressure most of the time and are therefore managing near-constant states of impatience, frustration, irritation and low-level anxiety, it is no wonder the predominant managerial behaviours in that multitude of daily on-the-job and ad hoc interactions are unconsciously threatening. There is no overt threat of the 'do this or I'll fire you' kind, but a constant, pernicious, low level, background soundtrack of judgement. Now if you and I listened to some of these interactions, the chances are we'd conclude that actually nothing at all threatening is occurring. We might think the manager was a bit clumsy, but we would not necessarily be able to point to any direct threats or even jarring judgements. But we would not be listening in a state of anxiety, hearing what is said, and what is not said, through the filter of a heightened state of agitation – threat. We would not be hearing the words and automatically giving them a Machiavellian twist, as might the actual recipient. We would not be hearing the tone of voice through the recipient's filter of anxiety which turned those words into way harsher and more pointed a meaning. Of course if we genuinely observe the interaction, we'll see the truth of the dynamics, and the recipient's anxiety will be palpably obvious. There is a skill in observation that is simply unpractised in organisations. Even where observation takes place, most observers make the mistake of putting their calm rational selves into the recipient's place and working out how they would respond. They in fact do not observe what is actually before their eyes, rather they see a false version of the interaction as if they were tasked with sorting out a problem. They are not observing in order to give feedback; they are observing in order to correct people.

But even where these critical interactions are witnessed, it is all too easy for the witnesses to pretend or be persuaded that what they have seen is in fact acceptable. It's just the way things are done around here. It's why so many companies have 'honesty' (or any wordsmithed variations on that theme) in their Corporate values – to give an appearance of openness, or at least the desire for it, and to facilitate the stakeholders in accepting any absence of openness since clearly the leadership's aspiration is noble. But those same companies with openness, honestly, transparency in their values, and the same companies who are so desperately wanting to be seen to enshrine whistle-blowing protection into their cultures, are still persistently presiding over a massive systemic secrecy.

And so we have the ultimate killer condition of ethical behaviour – conditions where employees feel fundamentally insecure being manipulated by well-meaning managers who don't actually want to fire them, and may in fact think the world of them.

What Happens when People feel Trapped

Investors and Corporate leaders talk openly about 'locking people in', devising reward and incentive schemes that have the express aim of making it near impossible for managers to leave. Managers become trapped not just of course by the high salaries, but because they have commensurately high fixed 'living' costs. So these Hostages are created almost openly. The Hostages are most frequently people earning way in excess of the average, but with lifestyles to match, and financial commitments that cannot be discharged without continuing the Faustian Pact entered into with the Corporate Master. I've known so many executives on £100K, £200K, £500K, even £1 million plus, yet absolutely trapped, and certainly feeling like they could not even contemplate swapping their current imprisonment for a job that pays less. Earn less money? Unthinkable.

Big house?

- big mortgage.

Spouse sacrificing their own career to look after the children?

- requirement for material lifestyle – cars, holidays etc;
- second properties;
- promise of financial security with time left to enjoy proper togetherness.

Children?

- school fees;
- clubs, activities, equipment;
- electronic devices;
- private tutors, nannies.

Parents needing care?

- care fees;
- sibling conflict;
- guilt.

Friends needing attention?

- expensive hobbies, weekends, trips.

Me?

- poor health;
- toys, distractions;
- resentments, guilt, shame.

Oh and those resentments . . . the all-comforting and all-knowing and all-caring Corporate Mother seduces the poor unfortunate manager, whom no one appreciates, and showers them with what they crave – power through which they can exhort love and respect from their followers, money through which they can acquire their toys and distractions, and freedom (secrecy) through which they gain protection from the consequences of indulging their resentful behaviours.

And we're back at Stephen Karpman's Drama Triangle. In the workplace, the Persecutor, having created the Victim, then becomes the Victim's Rescuer, and the Victim then becomes a Persecutor of others. And in the home, the Rescuer returns to those who (should) wait in eager anticipation of their hero's stories of derring-do and the size and contents of the swag bag. But how quickly the Rescuer becomes the Victim of the unappreciative.

As a Corporate Hostage, when I get home, even if welcomed by the supremely apprecia-tive, I simply cannot talk about my day – I've lived it once and I cannot and will not go through it all again. It would be too exhausting and distressing. My work is to be endured until I can escape, and that's just life!

But it's not just the underlings that are held captive by their masters. Frequently leaders find themselves held captive by one of their own team. An SVP client talked to me one day about a member of her team whose behaviours were becoming unacceptable, admitting that the person's own team were afraid of him. My client was fully aware of the morality of the situation, and that she was ducking responsibility – she was, after all, a very senior, very experienced executive. So why was she incapable of resolving this 'unacceptable' situation? Because she had come to believe that the consequences of action were un-thinkable. In her own words 'if he were to leave, the company would be screwed'.

Wow! That's not only an extreme belief to hold but a belief that shuts down any possible entertainment of alternative actions. It's the power of denial. It took some tough coaching, some 15 minutes of asking, digging, challenging on what 'screwed' actually meant, of pre-cisely would happen if the executive were to leave, for my client to admit to herself that the company would not in fact be 'screwed'; that in fact the team reporting into the executive would be released with all the unleashing of potential, energy and creativity that would follow; that in fact, things would be so much *better* without him. And as with every other example I've ever seen of this, most of the evidence of the executive's indispensability had come from him – had been carefully manufactured and stage managed by his own hand.

LTIPs – Ethical Rewards or Corporate 'gin trap'?

Everything that supports the executive career has a high cost. Forgetting the emotional cost for the moment, everything else can be compensated for with money. Now if only there were a way for owners to provide enough money to compensate for the emotional damage; oh and a way of hedging that cost. Now *that* would be worth having.

And so the LTIP (Long Term Incentive Plan) was born. LTIPs have become popular in re-cent years as Corporate Governance efforts have sought to better align Executive rewards with the interests of shareholders. These schemes have noble motives – to reward Exec-utives for long-term sustainable growth – and have been put in place (pretty much univer-sally in the quoted company and private equity sectors) to negate the ability of Executives to earn excessive amounts from the procurement of short-term (and thus potentially tran-sitory or even damaging) results. The corporate world got sick of the army of itinerant mercenaries, banking huge amounts of cash for 'turnarounds' that fundamentally could not be sustained after their departure to their next feeding ground.

Unfortunately the LTIP very quickly became a self-serving vehicle – one that almost immediately pro-duced the opposite effects to those originally desired. The reason? Once again, an invention born of the no-blest motives of corporate governance was quickly hi-jacked by the professional support services sector, to

> *Once again, an invention born of the noblest motives of corporate governance was quickly hijacked by the professional support services sector.*

whom the notion of lower short-term costs is always attractive, and for whom the granting of a promise of a seemingly generous share of something yet to be created has no cost whatsoever. No wonder the LTIP became popular. As an owner I can now attract Executives by offering them life-changing wealth in just five years, and I only have to pay it to them if they in turn have made me fabulously wealthy. What's not to like? In the old days, as an owner I had to match the cost of employing managers to run my investments with the returns I was getting in dividends and reasonable capital growth. That meant I had to care about and manage their emotional state, making sure they were pretty happy along the way. Now with LTIPs I can leave it to purely financial motivation. And if my chosen servants screw up, there'll be plenty of others who would kill for the opportunity to flog their guts out for me.

I remember floating a small company on the AIM market some years back. We floated at an Enterprise Value of £4.5 million and, lo and behold, the shares achieved the projected 10 per cent uplift on Day 1 on the market. But that float cost the company £900,000. It cost us 20 per cent of the value of the company just to place the shares on the stock market. The estimate for fees when we started the process was just under £0.5 million, and I thought *that* was excessive. As the floatation process progressed, continuing further and further to a point of no return, the list of professional advisers to whom we 'had to' pay fees grew. I learned that there were specialisms in the field of corporate finance that I'd never known about, and of course these specialisms involved employing monumentally expensive specialists who needed to be engaged to solve the impenetrable problems that came up as the float progressed. In addition, the fees we'd agreed to the original cohort of advisers also grew as they discovered elements they'd not quoted for. In all of this, the single energetic impulse was the value we would create/unlock by floating. Yes £900,000 was a lot of money, but we would all look back and see it as money well spent when we were rich. And I was as guilty as anyone of being seduced by those arguments. The fact is that once we'd entered the dark arts world that is corporate finance, we were lambs.

Looking back on that transaction, I noticed that a significant proportion of the fees had been incurred to advise on, design and enact the share options scheme – the LTIP. Oh and I noticed that the starting point for any adviser's fee quote, sort of the equivalent of a restaurant's cover charge, was £20,000. That figure today might well be £50,000. These types of fees are only justifiable in terms of the riches to come. And so the seduction is powerful.

Now I acknowledge that there are many good examples of where share options schemes have worked and are working well for all parties. But of all the Executives I've coached, I've only known a small handful of schemes that worked. I've encountered far more schemes that have back-fired, creating hugely negative executive behaviours.

Dealing with one global tech company client in the years straddling the millennium, I learned quickly that I had to allocate the first part of any global meeting of their managers to them circling each other on the question of the value of their stock options. Their culture was such that managers somehow needed to calibrate their relationships based upon their paper net worth. Those managers who'd been around for a long time, and who'd achieved a certain management grade, simply *had* to communicate their net worth, which was always north of $1 million, and in some cases north of $10 million. I noticed that if I did not give them time to converse and trade this information, they would not settle. In the run up to the millennium, the personal fortunes ballooned. When the tech crash of 2000 happened, and the share options of those managers dropped through the floor the mood in the meetings turned to abject despair, as the managers mourned the loss of their fortunes; in many cases the loss of every cent. Of course this was money they never had. They were grieving for the loss of something they'd never ever possessed. But this is the power of the share option scheme. It's not perceived or valued as a potential future bonus (where 'bonus' is understood in its truest definition). It's valued as a current asset, albeit one that cannot be turned into cash just yet. Many eye watering interest only mortgages have been secured and justified by the absolute certainty of the future cash fund to pay off 100 per cent of the capital.

The flaw is the promise of life changing wealth. Here we go again with Corporatism's promise of its 'something for nothing' alchemy, imploring the seduced Executive to 'give me your life for five years and you'll never have to work again'. This is the classic Faustian Pact that sits at the heart of all those spoken and unspoken agreements between corporate executives and their spouses and families – we'll all be in hell for five years (emotionally anyway, but the material comforts will mask that), but then we'll be free.

> *The flaw is the promise of life changing wealth. Here we go again with Corporatism's promise of its 'something for nothing' alchemy, imploring the seduced Executive to 'give me your life for five years and you'll never have to work again'.*

How can I be a 'good Leaver'?

The ultimate expression of the madness of LTIPs is when executives ask themselves (and me as their Coach on occasions!) 'how badly can I behave for them to want to get rid of me, but as a "Good Leaver?"' Of course they never ask it that honestly, but that's what they mean.

In the Corporate world, a 'Good Leaver' is basically someone who has done nothing wrong, certainly nothing that could remotely be punished with summary dismissal, but where they have arrived in a place where the company does not want them in the role any more. Even if there is an element of under-performance, their prior loyalty or the company's sense of culpability in co-creating the conditions for them to underperform, mean the company classes them as a 'Good Leaver'. This is important within their contract of employment, since this status avails them of their full contractual entitlements. Their full notice period is honoured, normally in a single compensatory payment, and crucially they will receive an element of the value of the potential future LTIP payout, since the company is denying them the opportunity to be around when the scheme vests. Good Leavers get assistance with outplacement, the promise of glowing references, and even sometimes the effective extension of a contractual notice period as they assist the company to find and bed in their successor. The value of being a 'Good Leaver' can typically be anything between six months and five years of salary.

A 'Bad Leaver' on the other hand leaves with nothing. Not only do they leave with no money, they leave immediately with no cashflow so they have to dig into savings to fund their high fixed costs. And they leave under a cloud at best, and at worst with a public humiliation. And they can forget the reference. You do not want to be a 'Bad Leaver'. You *really* don't want to be a Bad Leaver.

So for an executive who is so demotivated in their role that they want to leave, the question of 'how can I behave badly enough for them to want to fire me, but as a Good Leaver, not a Bad Leaver?' begins to sound reasonable. What else is the executive with integrity supposed to do, for it would be grossly unfair to have to walk away with nothing? But this is to betray the dishonesty of the original 'agreement'. When the executive signed up to the remuneration package, either they wilfully misunderstood the notion of 'bonus' or they lacked the courage to fight for the fixed salary they really felt would value the role properly. They gambled and they lost. Get over it and move on. The 'justification' for poor behaviour in the Executive who feels unfairly treated by their LTIP is the exact same 'justification' that the under-paid and under-valued employee on minimum wage feels. It is the doorway to the delusional self-righteousness that allows decent law-abiding persons to fiddle their expenses, steal company stationery, lie about taking time off, falsify records and see harm done to others in pursuit of personal gain. Corporatism, in the way it rewards human effort, commitment and talent, conditions people into an unhealthy selfishness, one that leads to behaviours that would be abhorrent to people in their 'normal' lives outside work. For me it has always been a clear and simple ethical question of leaving a senior role. As an authentic leader I have never felt comfortable with the self-protective notion of 'find a job before you leave a job'. For me that would have put me unacceptably in a disloyalty and dishonesty with the people around me, and how could I put my heart and soul into a cause I secretly wanted to leave? And how could I be loyal to my cause and my followers if I was out there hawking my services around to a 'better' cause? In my corporate career as a salaried executive I have twice left a very senior role without any role to go to; on the first occasion I was 'between jobs' for three months, on the second occasion it was eight months. I have been called naive for holding such a principle, and I was criticised on both occasions. Interestingly it is a strategy that has not let me down. On both occasions I went on to bigger roles.

As a Consultant, one of Collaborative Equity's Operating Principles is 'We will risk future work to tell you what we see and what we really think'. I have walked away from projects where I felt either it would not achieve what the client wanted, or indeed where I felt that I was not the best agent for them. And I have on many occasions persuaded a client to change their approach, by laying down very firm boundaries on what I would support or do on their behalf.

As a Chairman, I have stepped down from each of my three biggest Chairman's roles and been asked to stay on each time. And it was not a question of my being bored or running away from a problem I couldn't handle. The first time I stepped down from a Chairman's role was after nine years and two successful rounds of investment, involving Private Equity and a Stock Market float; the second occasion, after six years, was a large Public body where I had already agreed to stay on for 12 months after my initial five-year term as the Regulator had failed to act in time to recruit my successor; the third was after nine months, when I had been explicit at the outset that I would be Interim Chairman while the business was in crisis turnaround mode, again staying beyond my initial commitment of six months. In each case it would have been very easy for me to carry on, take the money, pitch up and do my job. I had no other Chairmanships to immediately step into so in each case my income reduced. Had I stayed on in each one I would have done an effective job, but I was simply no longer the best person for the role. I simply had to do what best served the company and the company needed a different leadership. On each occasion I personally aided the process of ensuring the incoming Chair was the best possible candidate.

What has been the result of my integrity? After a 40-year career, there is of course a chance that had I chosen a different approach, I could be sitting here contemplating retirement with a very much larger pile of cash. I accept that my integrity might have 'cost' me money. But I would not trade my life for any amount of money. By any standards I am a wealthy man financially. But more than that I am rich in my relationships, my health, my freedom and my reputation. Pompous and smug I may be, but I sleep gloriously.

Who'd be a Whistle Blower?

I admire whistle blowers. I admire them for the same reason I admire workers that go on strike. Now I am not so naive that I don't realise that some are maliciously motivated, but I believe these to be in the minority. In my experience the majority of whistle blowers and the majority of strikers are justifiably at the end of their tether. As my wife Rachel says, *'Have you ever tried to get people to go on strike? It's a tough sell; no one takes strike action lightly.'*

I admire whistle blowers because they have a courage that I do not possess. I'm not sure I've ever seen a whistle blower treated well, in fact most are treated appallingly, having to endure the harshest and most unfair of judgements, and often enduring great intimidation and hardship for their pains. Who'd be a whistle blower? Not me. At best they're pilloried for disloyalty. Their bosses argue that, even if they're right (and of course every whistle blower is accused of being selfishly motivated or having a destructive agenda), their actions are so disloyal to the company that they will make matters worse and not better. See how it serves human beings to depersonalise things when it suits them. Bosses will defend the company even if admitting the issue exposed. They'll even say that it's not personal, it's not about them as leaders, that they can take the personal criticism, but how dare you damage the company. And the Whistle Blower's peers and colleagues, who all know what's been happening and who may well have been negatively affected by the issue exposed, may well be hugely critical, fearing as they do that they will suffer for their colleague's folly, and experiencing a silent shame that they have been complicit all along. Or the whistle blower will be bought off and made to sign an NDA, designed to serve as a terrible threat to ensure the issue exposed is buried forever. How come paying someone to stay quiet about a crime is legal in the corporate world? Immunity once again.

And when should we blow the whistle? On the first signs of misbehaviour or wrongdoing? Surely that would be overreaction. On the second or subsequent occasions? But how many instances need to be endured before I start feeling that actually I've now left it too late? If only I'd had the courage to highlight the issue at the earlier opportunity. But since everything is secret, either no one else is noticing it, or if they do they don't seem to be that bothered. Maybe I'm wrong. Maybe it's me.

'Maybe it's me' – the most undermining and soul-destroying place to live for a corporate employee. Every fibre of your being knows that it is not right, not ethical. And yet the psychological mass hypnosis around you makes you question yourself.

'Maybe it's me' – the most undermining and soul-destroying place to live for a corporate employee. Every fibre of your being knows that it is not right, not ethical. And yet the psychological mass hypnosis around you makes you question yourself. A tiny minority have the courage to stand and challenge. The rest of us? We endure or we leave.

Modern Slavery

Slavery is defined as 'a civil relationship in which one person has absolute power over the life, fortune and liberty of another'. It was abolished 150 years ago, yet it is clear that some corporate employment practices and many corporate supply chains enable 'slave' conditions to exist, so much so that the Modern Slavery Act had to be passed in the UK in 2015.

Slavery is rightly associated with disadvantaged, vulnerable and very low paid workers. It is completely understandable how people fall victim to such exploitation, even in the twenty-first century. But surely the term slavery cannot be used to describe the working dynamics of relatively highly paid professional staff, can it? Well it probably can't, since no one in that cohort could possibly identify with that term – even if they feel themselves to be trapped, possibly even enslaved, pride alone would stop them accepting the epithet Slave.

Yet take away the typical staging of low pay and poor or even squalid conditions, and the characteristics, or at least the individual's reactions to perceived constraints, are remarkably similar. With senior executives, due to the pummelling they receive in their roles, they can suffer a gradual and progressive diminution of self-confidence; their self-esteem is eroded with the ebb and flow of every pressured interaction; so they come to believe that they would never get another job anywhere else at anything like their current salary.

The 'employee' version of this of course is not so prevalent. Yeah right. Employees are after all two for a penny – if some leave, then no problem because there's an endless supply of pathetically grateful job hunters to fill their places. Remember we can take this approach to employees since our isolation and the sheer effects of power on our psyches have caused us to think of employees as a single homogenous cohort. And if there isn't an endless supply of employees to fill vacancies, well that's just a sign that we need to automate or outsource or offshore. What other alternatives are there?

And now we have zero-hour contracts and the 'gig economy' – after 200 years of progressive employment protection legislation, we've arrived at a place where arguably employees suddenly have less legal protection now. It is estimated that there are over 900,000 workers in the UK on zero-hour contracts (2.8 per cent of the employed workforce) which is four times higher than in 2013 (ONS 2017).

There is no doubt that zero-hour contracts have been hugely beneficial for many thousands of people, who really appreciate the flexibility. The question is whether people have a genuine choice as to their nature of their employment contract, and the number of people feeling that they have no choice but to take work under a zero-hour contract, when they really need a secure level of income. Frequently workers under zero-hour contracts are denied holiday pay (which is illegal) and in some cases sick pay. UK employment legislation makes a distinction between a mere 'worker' and an 'employee', an employee having more legal rights than a worker. Whether a person working under a zero-hour contract is an employee or a worker can be uncertain. I wonder how many employers, when it comes to practical matters of employee protection or anything that would involve 'unnecessary' or 'discretionary' cost, drop down on the side of people being 'workers'.

And where do you stand on the 'gig economy'? This is the very modern dynamic whereby web platforms and mobile apps have been set up to broker dealings between private citizens. Uber and Airbnb are the largest and most high-profile examples, and who could not be massively impressed by their achievements. From nothing to global brand awareness, hundreds of thousands of transactions, and billions in enterprise value. Uber is currently valued at around $50bn, and Airbnb around $30bn – making them amongst the most valuable companies in the world. Justin King, former CEO of Sainsbury's, called the gig economy *the greatest increase in piece-work since the nineteenth century*' (2018).

As with zero-hour contracts, where people have genuinely and freely chosen to get into 'employment' in that manner, contracting with an Uber-style business is brilliant. There is an honesty to the whole arrangement, with the 'contractors' free to work when they want to, and reasonably rewarded for the use of their asset (their car) and reasonably compensated for their time.

These disruptive technologies are the modern-day equivalent of the Spinning Jenny, or the Steam Engine, revolutionising industries and working practices and conditions. Assuming the Ned Ludd role (the man who gave his name to the 'Luddites' who destroyed machinery in a vain attempt to keep human being employed) in trying to defy them doesn't ennoble anyone. But corporatism never fails to take a brilliant innovation and try and exploit its more insidious aspects.

The more sinister examples of the gig economy are where companies deliberately 'swap' jobs that previously had 'employed' status, with employees' welfare protected by legislation, for engaging self-employed 'contractors'. In my view the worst offenders in this regard are in the online purchase/fulfilment/delivery sector that has seen explosive growth in recent years. I have no issue if someone decides, through a genuine free choice, to invest in a van, set themselves up as a self-employed delivery contractor, and start offering their services to potential customers. But what happens is that the many delivery companies *only* offer contracts – they do not offer to employ delivery drivers full time on their payroll. And yet their 'contractors' are not free to ply their trade to other customers, surely the true test of whether someone is employed. While stories of warehouse order pickers peeing in bottles in order to earn 'bonuses' may be exaggerated, the pressure people are working under to facilitate our right to cheap deliveries surely cannot be worth the dehumanising existence it means for some.

Do me a favour – next time a delivery driver comes to your door, ask them what their working life is like. That's if you are prepared to engage with how your fellow human is living in order to service your rights. Modern slavery indeed.

It's not 'just Obeying Orders'

Much has been researched and written about the 'only obeying orders' syndrome. From the most hideous excesses of genocidal regimes, to the excuses offered up by weak corporate managers, the upward delegation of any personal responsibility is a convenient but ugly self-protection. That is not to say I don't understand or have some sympathy. Who is to say how I would have behaved in similar extreme circumstances? I'd love to tell you that I would have stood firm, but I know that is not true.

We saw in Chapter 4 how one of the most famous experiments into how people behave when given orders was conducted by Stanley Milgram in the early 1960s. Milgram concluded that we humans are incredibly susceptible to obeying authority figures. His research and his conclusions have been widely accepted ever since as evidence of our capacity for blind obedience – that our inhumanity springs not from pathology, but from a more mundane programming to defer to authority rather than thinking for ourselves.

But recent research and recent re-interpretation of Milgram's work and other work in the field of human coercion and authority have revealed that there is something else going on, and that 'only obeying orders' is just way too simplistic a conclusion. Alexander Haslam and Stephen Reicher argue that a re-analysis of the film footage of Milgram's experiment shows a different potential interpretation: that the study participants were motivated more by sense of duty that they owed to the cause they were serving (that cause being the study of punishment on learning) than by the individual instructions from the authority figure or any fear they felt of consequences of refusing such.

The study participants identified more with the cause of science than they did with the plight of the ordinary citizen . . . those who shock do so not because they are unaware of the consequences of their actions, but because they know what they are doing and believe it to be worthy. Rather than being blindly obedient, they are actually engaged followers, contributing to vitally important work.

Alexander Haslam and Stephen Reicher, 2014

When you believe in the cause (and Milgram worked hard on this aspect with his study participants) then you will be far more open to actions that would be inconceivable to you in a vacuum.

Haslam and Reicher also draw on another famous experiment from 1971 conducted in Stanford Prison by Philip Zimbardo.

This involved randomly assigning roles of prisoner and guard to study participants in a mock prison. Within a few days, the 'guards' were subjecting the 'prisoners' to a host of degrading and abusive treatments. Zimbardo concluded that people descend into tyranny because they conform naturally and unthinkingly to the toxic roles and scripts that accompany particular contexts.

But as with the Milgram experiment, Zimbardo had given the 'guards' clear guidance beforehand, and Haslam and Reicher argue that '*the behaviour of the "guards" was not the result of blind conformity but the result of engaged followership*'.

I absolutely subscribe to Haslam and Reicher's 'Engaged Fellowship' theory. One set of values overrides another, and while the worst behaviours are unethical, abusive and ultimately damaging, the motivation behind them is arguably quite principled, driven by a set of values that place the company above people.

There is also more evidence supporting this theory coming from our growing knowledge of neuroscience. Laura Spinney reinforces the theory that '*people perform brutal acts because the "higher" more evolved brain over-reaches*'. The set of brain changes involved has been dubbed 'Syndrome E' – with E standing for Evil – by neurosurgeon Itzhak Fried originally in a 1997 paper. Spinney reports that Fried suggested that this '*is the result of "cognitive fracture" which occurs when a higher brain region, the pre-frontal cortex, involved in rational thought and decision making, stops paying attention to signals from more primitive brain regions and goes into over-drive*'.

Spinney continues

Fried's theory starts with the assumption that people normally have a natural aversion to harming others. If he is correct, the higher brain over-rides this instinct. It is normal, not pathological, for the higher brain to over-ride signals coming from the primitive brain. Fried believes this process goes into overdrive in people with Syndrome E.

Laura Spinney, 2015

I contend that Corporatism creates the conditions in which people are far more suscepti- ble to 'Syndrome E' kicking in or being exacerbated. While not overtly coerced, corporate citizens become so conditioned by anxiety that they come to have a different neurological experience of authority, one in which they are able to unconsciously distance themselves from the unpleasant event they are living through, and the damaging impact of the behav- iours they may be exhibiting.

In addition, our evolution as ultra-social animals means we feel less empathy towards people outside our groups, and we can literally dehumanise them. With Corporatism based on and driven by competition, it's easy to see how demonising our competitors, or indeed anyone painted by our masters as a threat to our existence – governments, regulators, community action groups, trades unions, even suppliers – creates a strong cause that unifies us.

Corporations are clever at getting people to relinquish their own identity and adopt the ideology of their master. Corporations are fantastically skilled at creating cultures of dedi- cation to causes. The twenty-first-century workplace is extremely unlikely to be character- ised by managers issuing orders. In fact we've bred a generation of managers who seem scared of exercising their authority; scared to be directive for fear of being thought of as arrogant, micro-managing, autocratic, intimidating, a bully. It is both overly simplistic and unhelpful to our analysis and our creation of solutions to say that the worst excesses of unethical behaviours are down to blind conformity. Corporatism has developed phenom- enally powerful dynamics around Missions, Purposes, Values, Visions, Big Hairy Goals – building cultures of engaged followership, and that is great news for us. People desire to be engaged followers; they want to follow a cause. All we need to do is to ensure that the Cause itself is ethical (not merely about money) and that the fine words in the Values are actually focussed on, rewarded and genuinely lived out.

Notes

Betancourt, I (2011)   *Even Silence has an End: My Six Years of Captivity in the Colom- bian Jungle.* London: Virago.

Jerry Useem   'Power Causes Brain Damage: How Leaders Lose Their Mental Capacities – Most Notably for Reading Other People – That were Essential to Their Rise' *The Atlantic*, Business Section (July/August 2017 issue), www.theatlantic.com/magazine/archive /2017/07/power-causes-brain-damage/528711/ (accessed 25 May 2018).

Dacher Keltner   Psychology Professor at UC Berkeley.

Sukhvinder Obhi   Neuroscientist at McMaster University Ontario.

Stephen Karpman   The Drama Triangle is a social model that was conceived by Stephen Karpman, a student studying under Eric Berne, the father of Transactional Analysis. Berne encouraged Karpman to publish what Berne referred to as *'Karpman's triangle'*. Karpman's article was published in 1968. Karpman received the Eric Berne Memorial Scientific Award in 1972 for this work.

Berne, E (2016) *Games People Play: The Psychology of Human Relationships*. London: Penguin Life. (First published 1964)

Lord David Owen   Neuroscientist and former UK Foreign Secretary. 'In Sickness and in Power: Hubris Syndrome and the Business World' was a speech he gave at The Association of British Neurologists Joint Annual Meeting, Liverpool, 25 June 2009, and was in itself an extract from his book *In Sickness and in Power: Illness in Heads of Government During the last 100 Years* (London: Methuen, 2008).

Donald Trump   45th President of the United States and, depending upon your point of view, either the most authentic or the most narcissistic occupier of the White House in history. Maybe he's both. On 12 June 2017 he invited each member of his cabinet to praise him in front of the TV cameras. It's hard to watch, but excruciatingly compelling.

Olly Crom   J Oliver Crom joined Dale Carnegie in 1957 (the year I was born) and was President of the Dale Carnegie Organisation during the time I held my Dale Carnegie licence from 1989 to 2001. I met him twice at Dale Carnegie conventions in London and in Charleston.

Adrian Furnham   'I Didn't Get to Where I am Without Being Toxic', *Sunday Times*, 'On Your Head' article (27 November 2016).

Faustian Pact   Faust is the protagonist of a classic German legend, an erudite who is highly successful yet dissatisfied with his life, which leads him to make a pact with the Devil, exchanging his soul for unlimited knowledge and worldly pleasures. The Faust legend has been the basis for many literary, artistic, cinematic, and musical works that have reinterpreted it through the ages. 'Faust' and the adjective 'Faustian' imply a situation in which an ambitious person surrenders moral integrity in order to achieve power and success for a delimited term.

Rachel Young   My wife, Founder and Director of the Banbury Therapy Group.

ONS   Office for National Statistics, www.ons.gov.uk/employmentandlabourmarket/peopleinwork/earningsandworkinghours/articles/contractsthatdonotguaranteeaminimumnumberofhours/mar2017 (accessed 25 May 2018).

Justin King   Chief Executive of Sainsburys Plc from 2004 to 2014. He was known to quote 'consecutive quarters of growth' as a mantra like achievement at every results announcement, culminating in the 35th consecutive quarter, achieved just a few months before he stepped down. I heard him talking about the Gig Economy on the Radio 4 Today programme in March or April 2018, and I was struck by his likening of its employment practices to the piece rate methods rampant in the nineteenth century.

Ned Ludd   Ned Ludd, possibly born Edward Ludlam, is the person from whom, it is popularly claimed, the Luddites took their name. In 1779, Ludd is supposed to have broken two stocking frames in a fit of rage. After this incident, attacks on the frames were jokingly blamed on Ludd. When the 'Luddites' emerged in the 1810s, his identity was appropriated to become the folkloric character of General Ludd, the Luddites' alleged leader and founder.

Alexander Haslam and Stephen Reicher 'Just Obeying Orders', *New Scientist*, 13 September 2014.

Stanford Prison Zimbardo The Stanford prison experiment was an attempt to investigate the psychological effects of perceived power, focusing on the struggle between prisoners and prison officers. It was conducted at Stanford University 14–20 August 1971, by a research group led by psychology professor Philip Zimbardo using college students.

Laura Spinney 'Roots of Brutality', *New Scientist*, 14 November 2015.

Itzhak Fried Professor of Neurosurgery and Psychiatry and Biobehavioral Sciences and Director of the Epilepsy Surgery Program. Dr Fried's research and clinical work is dedicated to the treatment of intractable seizure disorders and epilepsy and to the study of human memory from single neuron level to clinical intervention.

Chapter 7
Corporate Pathology

The two Prime Causes of Stress at work

Stress is the number one cause of absenteeism from work. While we human beings need some stress in our lives, there is a big difference between positive and negative stress and the effects on our bodies. Positive stress comes in two forms – the very necessary and extremely valuable stress that accompanies real physical danger and which galvanises forces in our bodies (attention, focus, strength and speed) to survive, and the stress that comes from pursuing a chosen goal and which gives us excitement and motivation to keep going as we solve the puzzles and overcome the obstacles in our path. Neither of these types of stress (in 'normal' doses) is harmful to us – the first since it keeps us alive, and the second as it provides us with purpose, mastery and pleasure.

And then there is negative stress, which has a harmful effect on our physical and mental well-being; the stress we feel from perceived threats to our reputation, our material lifestyle and our self-esteem. Since arguably the worst excesses of fear-based management have been exorcised within Corporations over the last 30 years, our corporate workplaces should be places of relatively low levels of negative stress from threats to our lifestyles and our self-respect, and yet the opposite seems to be true. The corporate world seems to be a place of greater stress than ever before.

> *Our corporate workplaces should be places of relatively low levels of negative stress from threats to our lifestyles and our self-respect, and yet the opposite seems to be true.*

Why is this? The greater prevalence of stress in the corporate world is, in my view, down to two significant factors.

1. An almost continual and unbroken state of uncertainty

2. The experience of a perceived ever-present state of judgement

Uncertainty creates the very same physiological dynamics as physical threat; and remember, our brains cannot distinguish between the two. You would think that our brains would work out the difference, since uncertainty does not of itself tweak our amygdala into sensing 'incoming' on our threat radar. But herein lies the real problem of today's corporate world and the stress it creates and nurtures – the stress that leads to trauma – we are living in a near constant state of altered brain chemistry. Whereas the occasional adrenaline rush or cortisol burst can be both life-saving and indeed life-affirming, the constancy of high levels of these chemicals is creating responses and conditioned learning that are ultimately destructive. It's as if we are being perpetually traumatised.

And then there is the awful fear of judgement, which in the good old days was a rather beautifully simple fear of being sacked for not performing, and which has now morphed into the near constant fear of condemnation. It is this extension of fear, from judgement to condemnation, that is a major factor in the extreme stress levels within companies today.

Judgement is scary, of course, but it is delivered and then it's over. If I am called in by my boss and legitimately 'told off' for something I've done wrong, it's not a nice experience, but it's over quickly, I learn a positive lesson and my boss still loves me. I live to fight another day, now better equipped and knowing I have positive support to succeed. The feedback had the desired effect – I learn and feel motivated to improve.

But condemnation is terrorising, petrifying even. It is final – there is no way back. I am the walking dead, I am on Death Row. My fate is assured, it is only a matter of time. It is delivered by a look, a single damning comment, or even a passive aggressive, faux positive sop to keep me unsuspecting (and still performing) while those around me plan for my replacement. But while condemnation is often real, it is all too frequently a fantasy of a growing paranoia. And of course it ends up becoming the classic self-fulfilling prophesy. If the mark of death is on me; if I give off the all too familiar whiff of desperation, then others will soon learn to avoid me 'like the plague'. And since we live in competitive environments where everyone is scurrying to find the merest morsel of something with which to please those in power, avoidance turns to active predation. I become prey; I become the sacrificial offering to the Gods.

It is delivered by a look, a single damning comment, or even a passive aggressive, faux positive sop to keep me unsuspecting (and still performing).

The Medical and Neurological Effects of Stress

The major medical manifestations of stress are headaches, stomach upsets and back pain. These conditions can of course be caused by some form of physical trauma or ingested foreign body – stress is by no means the only culprit. But in the absence of a physical agent, mental stress is likely to be at the root. The body reacts (experiences pain) to having stored up the stresses and unexpressed emotions for a period of time, until it has to demand attention (rest or treatment) through rendering its owner incapable of work.

We become jumpy, easily spooked, 'on the edge' – in this heightened state the merest hint of threat can set us off. This is why people get into states of near paranoia. A CEO client recounted how, despite truly Herculean signals and evidence from her Chairman that she was fully supported, valued and thought to be doing all the right things, she lived in fear of being sacked. Irrational, yet undeniable and unconquerable. It culminated in being asked to meet her Chairman late one afternoon, and her enduring the discussion simply waiting for the axe to fall. When it didn't, since the meeting was wholly positive and supportive, my client came away still believing that her fate had been decided but that the Chairman had bottled it! Insanity!

A VP client recounted the story of feeling so unwell at a company offsite (one that he had organised for his own leadership team!) that he travelled all the way back from London to his home in another country on auto-pilot – literally unable to recall any of the journey, save for one hazy recollection of finding himself sitting on the floor in the middle of the departure hall in Terminal 5 of Heathrow, being surrounded by concerned airport staff, and being helped through security. He collapsed the moment he walked through his front door and spent a week in bed. This client is very successful, hugely respected by his team and his boss alike. So where did the extreme stress come from?

One can only conclude that so much of the stress in today's managers is utterly self-generated, but that would be to deny the power of the system, and to place too simplistic a responsibility on individuals to 'grow up and snap themselves out of it'. Corporatism is creating a form of mass hypnosis, and although its defenders will argue that the system cannot be blamed, that is the start of the witch-hunt to find the scapegoats. If the defenders of Corporatism accept that this extreme self-generated stress is endemic, then they must seek to analyse why and how it happens.

So how does it happen? There is a lot of research now centring on inflammation being the critical factor in neurologically based conditions. When parts of the brain become inflamed, they cease to function normally, as with any other part of the body that experiences damage. But with the brain, we are unable to use the inflammation as a signal for us to act to repair the damage, and so the inflammation, unnoticed and unattended, goes on to cause greater and greater damage.

On external parts of our anatomy, inflammation is visible to us due to abrasion or redness, plus we experience pain or discomfort that is clearly physically located. Even when the inflammation is internal, we still feel pain from the area concerned. So we seek medical assistance or we bathe and dress the wound ourselves, and we also make adjustments to our daily routines to give the inflamed area time to heal. This strategy has served us beautifully throughout our evolutionary history. But as Caroline Williams says:

Modern life is stacked against this delicate balance. Obesity, stress, pollution, bad diet and aging can all tip us into a low-level state of inflammation that, rather than being confined to a specific tissue, keeps the entire body in a perpetual state of readiness for a threat that never comes.

Caroline Williams, June 2017

The problem with the brain however is not just that we cannot see the inflammation, it's that we simply don't know that we are suffering, since there are no pain receptors in the brain. We may experience headaches when the inflammation has been left long enough to run riot, but headaches are pains felt not in the brain, but in the muscles of the head, in the dura (the membranes between the skull and the brain) and in the nerves in the scalp.

The problem with the brain however is not just that we cannot see the inflammation, it's that we simply don't know that we are suffering, since there are no pain receptors in the brain.

Andy Coghlan writes frequently on the effects of stress on our bodies and our brains. In a November 2017 article 'How Bullying Can Lead to Depression' he writes:

Experiences like bullying make the blood brain barrier leaky, leading to brain inflammation and leaving you vulnerable to depression. Anything that threatens your sense of worth is a type of social stress . . . for example a hostile work environment. First the stress kicks off inflammation in the bloodstream. This weakens the blood–brain barrier which normally protects the brain, making it more likely to let substances in. This enables large molecules like inflammatory substance interleukin-6 and aggressive white blood cells called monocytes to pass into the brain. Here they seem to disrupt signalling in the nucleus accumbens, which helps evaluate threats and rewards.

Andy Coghlan, November 2017

Aggressive, warlike language, so beloved of the Corporate leadership rhetoric lexicon, actually serves to supress the immune system.

So our brains are secretly suffering, throwing our normal cognitive functioning out of kilter. As Caroline Williams concludes,

The hormone noradrenaline, which is released in anticipation of an impending life or death situation, sets off the same chain of events as an infection or injury. Yet although stresses passed quickly in our evolutionary past, these days many of us are walking around with a ticking time bomb of stress-induced inflammation that never quite goes away.

Caroline Williams, June 2017

Anxiety Disorders

Anxiety disorders, including generalised anxiety, panic attacks, social anxiety and phobias, have one central ever-present dynamic – a constant feeling of dread or foreboding, either that something bad is literally just about to befall us, or that we've forgotten some important responsibility or commitment. It's the powerlessness to predict the threat or to remember the promise we've made that seeps into every pore, building an ever-increasing irrationality to our state of anxiety.

Anxiety disorders cost Western health care systems billions each year. Anxiety disorders are the most common mental illness in the US, affecting 40 million adults or 18.1 per cent of the population every year. On average one in six of us in the West will contend with an anxiety disorder at some stage of our lives – that figure in 1980 when first measured was 1 in 25 (ADAA 2018). What's going on?

And surprise, surprise, we're back again to our basic neuroscience. In normal working, our amygdala senses threat, and acts like a circuit breaker between the ancient parts of our brain that look after our basic survival, and the neocortex that runs our rational systems of learning, decision making and communication. In threat situations the amygdala shuts off the circuit to the neocortex, since all available blood must go to our arms and legs and the neocortex is a very blood hungry organ. Anyway, it is simply not required in emergencies and would in fact be dangerous and way too time consuming to consult. In life or death situations it's usually the thinking part of our brain that gets us killed! Then the moment the threat has passed, probably after just a few seconds, the amygdala switches the circuit to the neocortex back on. In healthy people, the switch to the neocortex is in the open position probably 99.9 per cent of the time, allowing the neocortex near free rein to do its job of managing the process of learning and conscious action – of taking in data, comparing it to everything we've ever learned in the past and either reinforcing learnings, or overwriting with new memories to adapt or even change our beliefs.

But in people with anxiety disorders, this circuit gets stuck in the off position, which explains why it is almost impossible to think calmly and rationally when we're anxious. Telling someone to calm down, get a grip and pull themselves together is futile, and if this exhortation comes with an added invective of frustration (threat) will only serve to make matters worse.

Doctors use the GAD-7 test to help assess whether someone has an anxiety disorder. For each question here, answer as follows and note the score.

'Not at all'	score 0
'Several days'	score 1
'More than 50% of the days'	score 2
'Nearly every day'	score 3

Over the last two weeks, how often have you been bothered by any of the following problems?

1. Feeling nervous, anxious or on edge?

2. Not being able to stop worrying or control worrying?

3. Worrying too much about different things?

4. Trouble relaxing?

5. Being so restless it's hard to sit still?

6. Becoming easily annoyed or irritable?

7. Feeling afraid as if something awful might happen?

Scores of 5–9, 10–14 and 15–21 indicate mild, moderate and severe anxiety respectively. Doctors recommend further evaluation if your score is greater than 10.

Dare you take the test? And if you do take it and your score is greater than 10, will you seek medical advice?

Dare you take the test? And if you do take it and your score is greater than 10, will you seek medical advice?

Why Sleep is Critical

We are hearing more and more now about the benefits of sleep. How insane, that we have to be persuaded of the value of sleep by scientists! Surely our relationship with sleep is one of the greatest examples of how we have come to believe that our minds can have absolute dominion over our bodies. We dismiss millions of years of evolution, with the utterly insane belief that we can now do without so much sleep.

Sleep basically anaesthetises us from the constant and inescapable stimuli flooding in through our five senses from the outside world when we are awake. In our waking state, our brains are having to manage so much – from the ceaseless watchfulness for threat, to the focussed attention on whatever chosen task is at hand, be it searching for food, courting a mate, caring for a child or managing our own daily maintenance. Our brains are learning all the time, firing new neural pathways and laying down new memories, to the extent that our brains could be overloaded very quickly by the explosion of new data to process.

Sleep is therefore essential, for it is when we sleep that our brains have the respite to do some fundamental maintenance work. First of all we need to 'delete' learnings and memories that we no longer need, through a process called 'synaptic pruning', performed by microglial cells. Our brains brutally cull things we no longer need, with a callousness that members of Clutterers Anonymous (there is such a fellowship) would find abhorrent.

How do our brains decide what's no longer needed? Simple – if it hasn't been used recently, it goes. No storing things 'just in case they'll come in handy later on'.

How do our brains decide what's no longer needed? Simple – if it hasn't been used recently, it goes. No storing things 'just in case they'll come in handy later on'. Our brains do not believe in putting things in the loft. Synaptic connections that have not been used or that get used infrequently are marked with a protein called C1Q. When the microglial cells detect the protein, they bind to the protein and destroy (prune) the synapse. In the process, our brains are able to develop more streamlined, efficient pathways, enabling the new learnings that are really serving us to literally flow more freely. When we sleep, our brain cells shrink by up to 60 per cent to create the space for our 'glial gardeners' (or to give them perhaps a more prosaic metaphorical title 'glial night soil workers') to come in and take away the waste.

Sleep is absolutely essential for us – not simply for our physical health, but fundamentally for the efficient operating of our brains – enabling the most efficient process of learning and then being able to recall and act on that learning. Sleep is essential for the creation of the physical space we require for us to learn more.

According to Alice Klein,

Our brains can't generalise when we're tired . . . well rested brains use associative memory to link concepts together . . . the brain cares less about individual data and more about the gist of what it means. Sleep deprivation inhibits this – not only are we less able to learn individual items, we are less able to extract their meaning.

Alice Klein, January 2017

Sleep restores and reboots our cognitive functions, necessary for the processing and correct filing of memories.

Research clearly shows that around eight hours of sleep is what we are designed to function best with. Actually we are genetically hard wired to sleep in two shifts, which is why some cultures still to this day enjoy a 'siesta' as part of their normal daily routine. A 10- or 20-minute nap gives our 'glial gardeners' the chance to come in, clear away some unused connections, and leave space for new ones to grow.

But, critically, sleep also heals any low-level inflammations that may have started to develop during the day. If these inflammations are allowed to fester and develop, they soon start to cause us major problems, and the real risk is that they are cultivated to the point

Sleep also heals any low-level inflammations that may have started to develop during the day.

where permanent damage is done to our systems. There is increasing research showing links between sleep deprivation and just about every neurological condition going, including Alzheimer's. A single night of poor sleep is enough to see damaging effects in the brain. We go without sleep at our peril.

With the cult of busyness holding sway, going without enough sleep is not just a painfully 'normal' way to work and live, it can be part of the working cultures whereby any form of rest is seen as weakness, and where competitiveness rewards the sheer number of hours worked. In Japan they even have a word for it – 'inemuri', falling asleep in meetings. As a young executive working for Fujitsu I was introduced to this first hand. I would pick my boss up at the airport in the middle of a working day, with him having flown 14 hours from Tokyo, and I would have to bring him straight to the office and into a meeting. Inoue-san would then take up his unique physical position for such meetings – he would draw his chair a little way from the meeting table, sit bolt upright with knees apart, clamp his hands on his knees with his elbows sticking out at 90 degrees so that he could take the weight of his upper body on this carefully constructed frame, and he would then duly go to sleep, without any of that ridiculous head lolling that we westerners go in for, and certainly no snoring and no dribbling. It was amazing to witness. The meeting would carry on (in English, so Inoue-san would not have understood a single word anyway) and, eventually, usually after about 30 minutes, he would wake up, give a short head bow to the assembled group, and get up and leave. Having satisfied this rather ridiculous ceremony, he could then go to his hotel with honour intact.

That was over 30 years ago, but I wonder if anything has changed? Maybe not. In 2016 in Japan, there were 1456 cases of 'karoshi' – death by overwork. This covers death by cardiovascular illness or stroke as well as suicide. Surviving family members can claim compensation but only if the deceased had clocked up a minimum of 160 hours of overtime in one month, or an average of 100 hours of overtime for three successive months.

In the UK, employees working for global businesses have the triple whammy of being physically located at the perfect epicentre of global trading time zones. The Americas are 5–8 hours behind us and MENA and APAC are 5–10 hours ahead of us. While we in the UK should be resting or sleeping, our global colleagues are working. And so we wake up to a world that's already been changed by our Middle Eastern and Asian colleagues since we had the temerity to go to sleep last night. And we get home from our long working day to find that our American cousins want (and expect!) to 'hangout' with us. Video calls (VCs) have now become the far more invasive version of the conference call. Conference calls were relatively invasive, but at least we couldn't be seen, so we could go onto mute and do other/family things while still being on the call. Now with VCs there is nowhere to hide.

So our working day is not only hugely extended, it has seeped into our 'family' time in a manner that literally allows no respite. And while we still go through the self-calming ritual, every night at around 11pm, of assessing that we have everything under control and that we know what we're doing and what we must achieve tomorrow, we awake to a world that has gone out of control as we slept. The following morning at 6am I reach for my mobile device and, although my intellect implores me to go and make a cup of tea, counselling me that the emails can wait, my addiction gets the better of me and I check the mails that came in overnight. I don't even have to read some of the emails to find my amygdala being tweaked. I only have to see the name of the sender, or the ridiculous subject title. It's 6am and I am already running adrenaline and cortisol. I truly live in a mad world, but it's not real. It's a world that is a construct and that I have voluntarily joined.

How many hours a week do you work? Let's look at a not untypical working week for a corporate citizen. Rising every day from Monday through Friday at 6:30am. Since reading and answering emails likely starts pretty much straight away, the working day has begun. Travelling in by car means making lots of phone calls to get the day underway. Travelling in by train means reading and preparing reports. Meetings, calls, emails all day. Probably leaving the office around 6pm, since anything earlier just looks like indolence. Calls or reports on the way home. We've now been going for 12 hours, but of course we're not finished. Put the kids to bed, have dinner and catch up with family life, then just a few quick things before bed so that we can start the new day in control. If we work for a US company then we'll have the ubiquitous conference call as well. So into bed and we've clocked up probably 14 hours. Five days is 70 hours. We are already way over the number of hours proven to increase the risks to our health. Ah, but we still have the weekend. Probably a couple of hours on Saturday, since we're now a bit pissed off with it all, plus our spouse has sneakily arranged things to distract us. We maintain this distraction through most of Sunday, but then that Sunday evening feeling starts to grow (around late afternoon) and we know we need to get the new week prepared. So we do a few hours on Sunday evening – of course we're watching TV and our body is physically present with the family, but actually we're at work. How frequently our spouses complain that we're 'not present'. We get defensive because we know they're right. Total number of hours for the week – likely to be around 80.

Working 55 hours or more per week is linked to a 33 per cent greater risk of stroke and a 13 per cent increased risk of developing coronary heart disease.

Increasingly we are seeing the links between long working hours and physical and mental illness proven. Working 55 hours or more per week is linked to a 33 per cent greater risk of stroke and a 13 per cent increased risk of developing coronary heart disease compared with working a standard 35- to 40-hour week (Science Daily, 2015). And we're doing 80! God help us when we try and keep up with machines.

So even if we sleep well, and many of us do through sheer exhaustion, we are ramping up the likelihood that we will succumb to physical and mental issues at some point – and maybe dangerously so. Headaches, stomach upsets, back pain – early warning signs of anything from stroke to heart attack, gastric problems to diabetes to cancer, depression to psychosis.

But overwork and sleep deprivation often go together, in some crazy dance of dependency. Sleeplessness can set in, further exacerbating the physical strain on our bodies. You may recall Antonio Horta-Orsorio, the CEO of Lloyds, being signed off work for two months in 2011 with what was publicly communicated as a chronic case of insomnia. Some of us self-medicate (the ubiquitous couple of glasses of wine in the evening to wind down).

In suffering a cataclysmic result of extreme stress, and the poisonous cocktail of over-work and sleep deprivation, you may not go the straightforward route of having a stroke or heart attack. You may end up going the far more complicated route of some form of mental breakdown. 'Burnout' is a pretty common corporate phenomenon these days, with many senior leaders reporting being burned out to some degree. But what exactly is 'burn-out?' In 'normal' life we'd probably simply diagnose the individual as being depressed – emotional exhaustion, low self-esteem and possibly even self-loathing, helplessness, hopelessness, isolation, loneliness, futility, impotence etc.

One of the most extreme manifestations of 'burnout' is the condition known as Chronic Fatigue Syndrome, an extreme example of how initially neurological issues come to be manifested in completely physical conditions. Cara Tomas is a PhD student at Newcastle University, now studying Chronic Fatigue Syndrome. She had herself been rendered bed-bound with CFS 13 years earlier.

White blood cells in people with CFS are as listless as the people themselves often feel. She found that mitochondria in CFS cells can't produce energy properly, pointing to a phys-iological, not a psychological disorder. Control cells consumed twice as much oxygen as the CFS cells, with the disparity widening dramatically when the cells were stressed. Cells from people with CFS can't raise their output to meet the energy demands of routine tasks.

Andy Coghlan, November 2017

Stress is the number one cause of absenteeism, and as we've seen the most seemingly all-pervading stress on corporate citizens today is not caused by the reality of any fear they should have over being sacked, it is almost entirely self-generated and self-inflicted. I am not saying that corporate leaders can absolve themselves of any responsibility in this, since they are ultimately responsible for the working cultures that foster such self-inflicted torture.

Under pressure and in a heightened threat state, people will surely misinterpret the mo-tives of their colleagues, to the absolute detriment of trust going forward. These dynamics become the classic self-fulfilling prophesy – if I perceive you as untrustworthy, I will become so myself and we will both be proven right.

It's also the source of us being quicker to go to Child or Victim mode in reaction to an undesired event – we throw a strop, we sulk, we bemoan our fate, we jump instantly to condemn and blame others, endowing them with a pre-meditated malice that really does betray the start of madness.

Our responses to human distress malfunction – we seem to be suffering from a form of empathy burnout, where either we are just plain immune to the plight of others, or at the opposite extreme we are almost overwhelmed as we feel the pain of others who are unknown to us (even though we are not necessarily motivated to take action to salve it for them). In this state we really shouldn't watch that documentary on the famine in South Sudan, or walk past the homeless beggar in the street, and if we do then we can at least have some legitimacy in adopting a 'but what can I do?' impotence. The more pragmatic question is whether we can walk past the immoral or unethical or even illegal thing that is happening under our very nose at work.

Family, Social and Psychotherapeutic Dynamics

Transference and Projection are theories in psychology in which humans defend themselves against their own unconscious impulses or qualities by denying their existence in themselves while attributing them to others (projection) and by unconsciously redirecting feelings about a second person to a third person (transference).

The most abusive form of projection in the corporate world is the bully. We know that bullies are actually insecure, and that their aggressive and intimidatory behaviour is them over-compensating for this. They play this out by projecting their insecurity onto others (by assuming weakness) and then by pretending to be strong. In fact, in the particular instance of bullying, psychology terms this 'projective identification' – literally 'what I cannot and will not feel in myself, I will make you feel'. If I am insecure, since I cannot allow myself to feel fear, I will develop strategies that make others feel fear in my presence. In all the thousands of managers and leaders I've encountered, I have come across many who are fundamentally insecure – not all of them turn into bullies, since many of them have a high level of self-awareness and can develop counter-strategies to compensate for their insecurity. But it seems as though the corporate world loves the insecure over-achiever in positions of leadership, since they drive others as they feel they themselves deserve to be driven. This is of course the basic flaw in the noble sounding tenet of 'lead people as you would wish to be led'. That's fine in the hands of the secure; but you wouldn't use that principle with a sado-masochist, now would you?

This is of course the basic flaw in the noble sounding tenet of 'lead people as you would wish to be led'. That's fine in the hands of the secure; but you wouldn't use that principle with a sado-masochist, now would you?

Insecurity and projection are also at the root of all blame ascribing and blame shifting. Why would I try and move the blame for my mistake or inaction onto someone else? First of all I will feel guilt and shame from that act, even if I deny them in myself, and secondly I won't learn the available positive lesson of how not to repeat my mistake, since I cannot get honest feedback. The most toxic corporate cultures of course take blame allocation one step further by systemising the advance allocation of blame should something go wrong in the future. It's called arse-covering. In dealing with representatives of organisations with such cultures, notice that their sole motivation for any act that they take is so that they cannot be blamed if something goes wrong. Dropping a colleague in it is a form of advance defence. It doesn't matter what the outcome is as long as I won't be blamed. The most pathetic extension of this is how we feel when someone else in the team is getting it in the neck. Do we jump in to defend them? Do we give them genuine support to recover? Or are we (even ever-so-slightly) guilty of glorying in the fact that since someone else is getting it today, I am safe.

Corporate hierarchies recreate the parental structure where Mum and Dad are to be obeyed – Mum and Dad had knowledge and power and dominion, and in return they gave protection and security and nurturing and learning. So people automatically bring stuff from their family and the way they were parented into the workplace. They project and transfer emotions onto others around them in this new family.

How many managers have you known, ones you may have come to respect and maybe even love, who's predominant strategy was actually to build a family? To provide strength and protection for their charges from the big bad world; to assume massive responsibility for others. This can be a quite intoxicating style to work under, since it is so evocative of the profound nurturing emotions and conditions we felt as a child (or that we *wish* we had experienced . . .). How many of us are unconsciously playing out unresolved issues with our parents in the way we interact with our boss? Even a perfect boss can't really influence the way I react if I'm unconsciously reacting to my father!

Even a perfect boss can't really influence the way I react if I'm unconsciously reacting to my father!

One major issue of course with a paternalistic style of management is that it cannot help but infantilise those we lead; leaders who act like parents inevitably create 'families' of dependent and increasingly rebellious children as followers. This is such a common dynamic in corporate cultures, and a major source of the systemising of bright, decent, hugely resourceful and potentially creative souls simply waiting to be told what to do.

Leaders who act like parents inevitably create 'families' of dependent and increasingly rebellious children as followers.

Our corporate environments are crucibles for us playing out the many and varied relational dynamics we bring from our family and social lives. We project and transfer our emotions onto others, the start not only of a profound misunderstanding and mistrust between people at work, but of vast swathes of unnecessary conflicts and the ensuing waste of creativity needed to handle them.

Another significant psychodynamic factor playing out in the relationships we build at work is codependency. Codependency is a form of dysfunctional 'helping' relationship where one person supports or enables another person's refusal or inability to take personal responsibility. A chronic codependent is someone who cannot function from their innate self and whose thinking and behaviour is instead organised completely around another person. Over time this produces the paradox whereby the helper colludes with the other to keep them firmly in their addiction, disability or personality disorder. The last thing they would want is for the other to be 'cured', since their raison d'etre would cease.

There are of course some positive sides to codependency – surely there is no deeply loving relationship in the world that is not codependent to a small degree? Loving someone involves an element of codependency, otherwise losing a loved one would not cause such deep pain; would not evoke an almost physical sense of not being able to live without the person we've lost. Loving someone *does* involve us in taking some responsibility for them, but here's where the line gets crossed: we should take responsibility for how we are in relation to them rather than assuming near total responsibility for their happiness and well-being. *'Please fit your own mask before attempting to help others around you'* would seem to me to be a good general guide.

The true codependent can only experience happiness when the other is happy (and even then it may well be fleeting since we project that the other's happiness is a temporary illusion). When the other feels 'negative' emotions of sadness, discomfort, anger etc, the codependent feels these more painfully than if they were happening to them!

The corporate world is full of codependent relationships.

The corporate world is full of codependent relationships. First of all, thousands of people bring their codependent tendencies in to work from their home life. When you've lived a certain way, to the point where you are completely unaware of the madness, it would take some pretty dramatic induction into work, to break a replication of that way of life. Why would your new 'family' be any different from your old one? Secondly serial codependents are attracted like magnets to the helping/rescuing professions. Nursing, counselling and social work are the obvious examples, but what about helping professions in the corporate world? HR is the most significant one, but as we saw in an earlier chapter, there has been a massive growth of professional 'support' functions in recent decades, where their whole (unconscious) motivation is to keep those they support dependent upon them.

The bottom line for the majority of corporate citizens is that their life is fine, maybe even joyous, when their boss is happy with them, and truly awful when their boss is not.

And then we add in the dynamic of the relationship with our boss – a relationship that is ripe for codependency. The bottom line for the majority of corporate citizens is that their life is fine, maybe even joyous, when their boss is happy with them, and truly awful when their boss is not. There is of course some naturally occurring and valuable output from this (assuming our boss is pretty decent) in that our boss's happiness with us is direct feedback on our job performance. But corporatism has overlain two further dynamics that completely screw with any notion of positive feedback. First, the pursuit of exceptional and urgent objectives has created environments where moments of tension and overreaction are rampant. If these moments are rare, as they are in 'real' life, then our brains and bodies have time to lay down routines and rituals of trust. When a moment of drama arises, it is far easier for all parties to handle it rationally and absorb and process any feelings of hurt or being judged or treated unfairly. But when these moments come at us like machine gun fire, our limbic systems are agitated to the point of disturbance and even trauma. It's why so many clients express a near perpetual state of feeling 'unsettled' to me, even when things are going really well (which interestingly they are the majority of the time; it just doesn't *feel* like it).

Secondly, it has become almost impossible to distinguish just who our boss is unhappy *with*, in fact in pretty much 100 per cent of interactions where our boss expresses displeasure (verbally or nonverbally) it will feel as though they are pissed off at us; that we are the cause of their unhappiness. Since bosses are suffering from an endemic lack of self-awareness of their controlling habits, they fool themselves into believing that they are hiding this (at least well enough) leaving them unable to even acknowledge there is a problem for them to solve. The most ridiculous thing about the drama of the moment when bosses expresses displeasure is that more often than not they are actually angry with themselves. But that is not how it will feel to any poor subordinate witnessing the reaction of the moment, even the mentally healthiest without a codependent cell in their body. It's why I always work hard, in moments of anger (which are inevitable even if we use the more PC label of 'frustration') to own it myself and to communicate as calmly as possible to those around me that I am absolutely not cross with them.

These dynamics are so prevalent, so institutionalised and so damaging, one would think that all management training would have a module covering transference, projection and codependency. But I have never once come across any such thing. Why is that? Frankly, it is because corporatism does not recognise 'real' human emotions, dynamics and frailties. It cannot bring itself to do so, for then it would not be able to treat humans as mechanical resources. It would have to embrace the gloriously costly and inefficient acceptance of having to pander to human weakness. And furthermore, since the development of management skills has been sucked into the domain of codependent HR professionals, the accent in training is on ever-more-shiny intellectual models and frameworks.

So there are many differing family dynamics and neuroses. But where did they come from? Intuitive knowledge is passed down the generations genetically. When violent conflicts between collectives of people really started around 4000 BC – when the strong started to systematically exercise dominion over the weak – a growing amount of fear, guilt and shame started to pass down that inevitable genetic channel.

Fear, guilt and shame. The fear of difference – someone different to us needed to be instantly categorised into superior or inferior, as threat or no-threat, to be avoided or to be exploited. We learned quickly that one effective self-preservation strategy was to ensure that someone else was being persecuted. We learned to create scapegoats – people whom we could use to deflect attention from a potential predator away from us. This intuitive knowledge passed genetically plays out in the school yard, with any kid unfortunate enough to be different singled out. This damaging comparing of ourselves to others (inferior and superior) has fed our competitiveness. And now here we are with Corporatism banging the drum of competition as a virtue. Competition breeds fear. Competition ultimately breeds violent acts. By all means extol the virtues of competition but please don't deny the potential pitfalls.

> *This damaging comparing of ourselves to others (inferior and superior) has fed our competitiveness. And now here we are with Corporatism banging the drum of competition as a virtue. Competition breeds fear. Competition ultimately breeds violent acts.*

And guilt? Ignited when we feel that something has happened to others and not to us, or vice versa, even when it is clearly not our fault. When someone suffers a misfortune we often feel guilty that it did not happen to us. When something joyous happens to another person, how many of us can say that we haven't felt the merest pang of envy or even resentment? And since we are good people at heart, we'll feel guilty of these emotions. I can't be certain of course that no one ever felt guilt before 4000 BC. But we can be certain that guilt has become an enormous factor in our psyches as we relate to others in our families, our friendships, our communities, our institutions and our workplaces, fuelled by our comparing of ourselves to others. We do not do this from a place of malice – we do it from a place of survival instinct, so deeply ingrained are the genetic messages passed through 250 generations.

And when guilt ignites, even the merest pilot light at first, shame will not be far behind. We feel shame from our culpability in the plight of others. We feel shame in breaking promises. We feel shame in disappointing people. We feel shame in acting in ways that may well ensure our personal survival but which we know are not in service of our fellow men and women.

And notice that managers who adopt an overly parental style from noble motivation, often slip into using guilt and shame to manipulate their followers. This is largely unconscious of course, and can even be almost wholly nonverbal, for instance cues and signals around working hours and methods (tell me honestly you feel no guilt when 'working from home' or walking out of the office at 4:45pm), but frequently it morphs into an ever-present 'style' of overtly using guilt and shame as motivators. It's why the fear of 'letting someone down' is so profoundly omnipresent. How many of us, despite our protestations of 'family first', prioritise things for the benefit of our work colleagues far above things for our family. Our fine words are simply not matched by our actions, our prioritisation and our behaviours.

Finally, think about the conditions and the normal dynamics of the cycle of life, that exist in family and social groups, such as anxiety, isolation and loneliness, alcoholism and addiction, domestic violence and abuse, depression and grief. These play out and become integrated within corporate cultures.

Addiction to substances is replicated by addiction to work, control, power and status, and now increasingly to internet material, smartphones even, and the 24/7 access they give to stimulus. We've already seen the mirror of domestic abuse in the Corporapath and the Corporate hostage. Depression and anxiety are constant bedfellows from the pressure of expectations. Isolation and loneliness come from the systemising of individual targets and performance management, and the fostering of blame driving mistrust between colleagues.

Grief

Whereas the other dynamics have found equivalent and comparable outlets, the one that stands out as different and hugely exacerbated is grief. Our corporate world is ever changing; but with those changes so frequently out of our control, we live in a near constant state of handling enforced change. All change involves loss, and so as a corporate citizen I experience grief on a very regular basis. Now in 'real' life, I don't experience grief that much. Someone close to me might die every few years, and while the grief I feel is deep and can be even be extreme in its pain, it is after all 'natural': people die. Of course if the person who has died was young, or died in tragic circumstances, the trauma of the grief can take many years to be healed, if ever. But, again, we are experiencing these naturally occurring emotions singly and serially, for a short burst each time, and with plenty of time to process and heal between occurrences. And grief teaches me appreciation of others, gratitude, patience and humility.

But the grief I experience every time my working environment changes (I don't recognise it as grief of course) becomes that self-same low level constant bedfellow as anxiety from pressure.

Elisabeth Kübler-Ross (1969) described the 'Cycle of Grief' in five stages:

Anger, Denial, Bargaining, Depression and finally Acceptance.

I believe the corporate equivalent, which I call the 'Cycle of Ownership' goes like this:

Uncertainty, Denial, Engagement, Reflection, Ownership

The point here is that since change in the corporate world is so rapid and unrelenting, we get no real chance to go through the whole grieving process. While change in 'real' life is also constant, it does at least have some rhythm of the seasons, so we have a chance of anchoring the constant flux to a pattern in our lives. But in the corporate world, despite the annual budgeting cycle, we are never anchored in the same way. In real life, when someone close to me dies, I usually get the time, even if I don't get the counselling, to go through the Cycle of Grief and to receive sufficient healing to return myself to strong mental health, recovering from the temporary and transitory trauma. But at work, I just begin to come out of uncertainty and bang! I'm hit with the next change.

From my experience, I believe it takes around two years for people to successfully navigate all five stages of the Cycle of Ownership following a significant change such as a restructuring, a new owner or boss, a relocation or a redundancy. And as with grieving for a loved one, normally mentally healthy people can and will successfully navigate this cycle on their own. The problem in the corporate world of course is that change does not come along serially once every two years. In fact, in the twenty-first century, with the digital revolution, we might not even get two months.

It's why my definition of leadership differs from any definition I've ever read. My definition is: 'A great leader takes people through the Cycle of Ownership faster than they could get there on their own, and just in time to successfully manage the next change.'

> *A great leader takes people through the Cycle of Ownership faster than they could get there on their own, and just in time to successfully manage the next change.*

I have a second definition which is: 'A great leader takes an entire community outside its collective comfort zone and makes that journey exciting and not frightening.' But more on that later.

The Corporation goes one stage further in causing people to grieve over the loss of something they never had in the first place! Corporatism is a master of offering future rewards as present-day motivators. All it needs to do is convince you of the absolute certainty of their 'promise', and you'll be hooked. Then of course when the reward is not forthcoming . . . . Well, we saw in the earlier section on LTIPs how this plays out for senior executives, but it is also present every single time a corporate citizen allows themselves to be seduced by the promise of something for nothing, somewhere not too far down the line.

The alchemy of 'something for nothing' once again becomes an engine, an accelerator even, for human effort. When this is channelled honestly and openly into an enterprise with an ethical purpose and where the relative values of 'something' and 'nothing' have a grounding in reality and fairness, then it works spectacularly.

Psychological and Personality Disorders and the DSM-5

Working in a corporate environment duplicates, amplifies and even creates the many and varied personality disorders and mental conditions that human beings can suffer from in 'normal' life: conditions such as paranoia, obsessive-compulsive disorder, conditioned anxiety disorder, narcissism, autism, ADHD and, in extreme examples, psychopathy and psychosis. Corporate cultures create conditions where people who have even the merest psychological pre-disposition towards a mental condition, but suffer no impacts or issues from this in their everyday life, can experience a rapid develop of the condition as they work. The issues this causes at work soon then leak back into their everyday life.

The *Diagnostic and Statistical Manual of Mental Disorders*, Fifth Edition (DSM-5) serves in the US as a universal authority for psychiatric diagnoses and treatment recommendations. Payments by health care providers are routinely determined by DSM classifications.

When referencing the manifestations or even outcomes of psychological disorders, DSM-5 lists the 'Three Ds'.

1. Distress

2. Dysfunction

3. Deviance

It categorises disorders into Three Classes.

Class A – Odd or Eccentric Disorders (paranoid, schizoid and schizotypal disorders)

Class B – Dramatic, Emotional or Erratic Disorders (antisocial, psychopathic, borderline, histrionic and narcissistic disorders)

Class C – Anxious or Fearful Disorders (Avoidant, Dependent and Obsessive disorders)

I want to draw attention here specifically to disorders in Class B, since in my view these play out so frequently in the corporate world. I challenge you to read the following brief descriptors without smiling in recognition of the characters in your working life.

Antisocial/Psychopath Personality Disorder

These individuals are manipulative, irresponsible, and have a history of legal difficulties. They show little respect for the rights of others and feel no remorse for their actions. They leave a trail of unfulfilled promises and broken hearts. They seldom suffer from depression or anxiety, but often use drugs, alcohol, gambling or sex to relieve boredom and irritability, and as 'rush seekers' they are at high risk for addiction.

Borderline Personality Disorder

Borderline personalities are impulsive and have extreme views of people as either 'all good' or 'all bad'. They are unstable in relationships and have a strong fear of abandonment, demonstrating attention-seeking and destructive behaviours.

Histrionic Personality Disorder

People with this condition engage in persistent attention-seeking behaviours often including inappropriate sexual behaviour and exaggerated emotions. They have an excessive need to be the centre of attention and constantly seek reassurance or approval from others. They blame others for their failures.

Narcissistic Personality Disorder

Narcissistic personalities have an over-inflated perception of themselves, with a false sense of entitlement, and an excessive desire for admiration. They have no respect for other people's feelings, yet are hugely oversensitive to criticism. Prone to outbursts of anger and irritability, the narcissistic personality is manipulative in relationships. But deep beneath the surface lies a vulnerable self-esteem, susceptible to depression and feelings of inferiority. 'Narcissism has to be channelled into achievement or violence' (Terry Bogg, October 2016).

People with personality disorders feel and then act immediately – the 'normal' mechanism of a split second of self-control is fundamentally lacking. Since they are unable to control their impulses, they have to invest an enormous amount of time and massive amounts of creativity in 'recovering' from the fallout of their impulsive actions. They not only become hugely skilled at managing this fallout, they also develop phenomenal powers of predicting and thus pre-empting their inevitable future lapses. So they put themselves in environments where they are unlikely to be found out, or where others will more than compensate around them. Since their impulsiveness and outward bravado is frequently mistaken for confidence and therefore competence, and since they are experts at creating narratives where they are the hero, it is not at all uncommon to find these 'time bombs' in positions of power and influence. Handing power to someone with a personality disorder is like handing a loaded AK47 to a toddler.

Handing power to someone with a personality disorder is like handing a loaded AK47 to a toddler.

Corporatism loves these people – their confidence in risk taking and their ability to manipulate people make them natural corporate leaders.

We saw earlier how many people are suffering anxiety, and so corporatism has a ready-made supply of people in early incubation of personality disorders, particularly as the corporate world offers so many of the environmental attributes valued by such people – power, money, status, control, something for nothing, rewards for confidence (over achievement) and a 'blind eye' tolerance of unethical and inappropriate behaviours. In fact, corporatism so loves these people that it breeds them from the merest hint of early signs and symptoms. Corporatism can take a decent, ethical, mentally healthy, utterly psychological disorder-free human being, and turn them into a sociopath in a very short space of time.

Corporatism can take a decent, ethical, mentally healthy, utterly psychological disorder-free human being, and turn them into a sociopath in a very short space of time.

It does this this by simulating the conditions of early and adolescent brain development.

Think about the process of joining a company. First there are the immediate attachments, just as in the first two years after birth – to a first boss or peer designated to train us, without whom we would fail since we know nothing. We are wholly reliant upon them in the early days of our new position, and while we may overtake them quite quickly in status or competence or recognition, we will always 'owe' them. Then we start to make our own way in this new world, mirroring the early years of childhood as we make friends, learn the unwritten rules of conformity and acceptance, and now attaching to people of our own choice. In this phase peer influence is paramount, and the fear of social exclusion is extreme. Next comes adolescence as we contemplate and plot rebellion and start to do things our own way – anything, actually, rather than conform to company processes, since we are different and special and unique. In this phase we also start to notice and enjoy the opportunity for dominion over the newbies and so we set about creating our Acolytes.

But do we ever get to maturity? Real life gives us real feedback – rewards for good and desired behaviour and consequences for bad and undesired behaviour. And real life is ruthless; it simply doesn't care about fairness and so we frequently have to endure the consequences of quite random and chaotic outcomes, not always purely of our own making. So we learn to live by rules and we learn to trust and to rely on people around us – doctors, cab drivers, waiters, police officers, tax collectors – without ever feeling the need to 're-educate' them to our particular unique needs. They don't care anyway. Who the hell are we? But corporate life is different. The rules of rewards, feedback and consequences are entirely different and utterly open to manipulation. We can be rewarded despite breaking the rules or acting in blatant contradiction to the written values. We can avoid the consequences of poor behaviour, either because frankly there are none, or through ensuring that blame is cast elsewhere. And since tangible results and outcomes are so spurious or nebulous, we can only really be judged on how we appear – and we've got that cracked.

Corporate cultures are veritable breeding grounds for Corporapaths. No wonder attempts to persuade or even regulate corporations to be more ethical have failed miserably.

ADHD

We saw in an earlier Chapter how high levels of Cortisol cause long-term damage, and Cortisol levels are characteristically high in people with depressive disorders. But one disorder where Cortisol is now known to be a specific culprit is in ADHD – Attention Deficit/Hyper Activity Disorder. ADHD sufferers are living with a consistently and unnaturally high level of cortisol in their system, causing them to be on a permanent high state of alert.

ADHD symptoms and manifestations include forgetfulness, poor concentration, insomnia, running late for appointments, interrupting people, untidiness, impulsive and inappropriate behaviour and risk taking, boredom, frequent changes of jobs and partners, and restlessness or hyperactivity, often including constant tapping with feet or fingers. ADHD sufferers just cannot sit still. I often look out at a team as they work and see the number of foot tappers, finger tappers and pen swivellers, and at just how many are constantly checking their phones.

ADHD sufferers just cannot sit still. I often look out at a team as they work and see the number of foot tappers, finger tappers and pen swivellers, and at just how many are constantly checking their phones.

Thom Hartmann's 'Hunter and Farmer' hypothesis about ADHD is that genetically we retain many characteristics of the Hunters that we were for many hundreds of thousands of years, and that we are still only slowly developing the characteristics of farmers, from a mere 10,000 years of our most recent evolutionary history. Where this is interesting for the corporate world is the degree to which 'Hunting and Farming' has entered the world of professional sales, with Hunters winning new business and Farmers retaining those new customers over the long term.

Antony Jay echoed this in his amazing book *Corporation Man*:

At the basis of modern business is a pattern of behaviour some 15 million years old. It is not logic and reason but the ancient survival imperatives of aggression, status displays, territorial defence, hunting comradeship, tribal gatherings and appeasement rituals that dominate the modern corporation. We've had 10,000 years as farmers, but we had 15 million years of hunting. Hunting is in our genes. Male genetics are to band together in aggression . . .

Antony Jay, 1972

Hartmann matched the 'disorder' characteristics of ADHD to the characteristics that make Hunters good at new business. Impatience means that Hunters are capable of huge bursts of energy and focus in pursuit of a sale. Impulsiveness means that Hunters can spot and tackle an opportunity with no fear of rejection. Easily bored and distracted, Hunters have no emotional attachment to the last sale, and can move quickly onto the next prospect. With their distorted appreciation of time, Hunters are flexible to change strategy in the moment. The Hunters short attention span leads them to constantly scan their world for new opportunities. And since ADHD sufferers struggle to convert concepts into words, and frequently also have some form of reading disability, don't expect your Hunter to keep the CRM system up to date! I am often perplexed by how frequently I see senior leaders trying to get their salespeople to be both Hunters and Farmers; to be good at making appointments as well as good at converting them into sales; to be excellent administrators as well as excellent trust builders. It's not just that the skillsets are different, since anyone can learn new skills. It's that the fundamental motivations and characteristics for success are different. People who love engaging face to face often hate using the telephone and people who live to build relationships would die rather than fill out forms. Thom Hartmann's hypothesis gives a clear psychological reasoning for the allowance of specialisation, and the trick then becomes how best to support the 'annoying' characteristics of the Hunter.

Observers and practitioners are increasingly pointing at environmental factors exacerbating ADHD suffering, with behavioural therapies and lifestyle changes as the solution. Many children's diagnosed ADHD is down to purely genetic factors, but how many children are living in chaotic and even unsafe family environments, leading inevitably to persistently high levels of cortisol?

And in the corporate world, it's no wonder that people start to demonstrate and then embody the symptoms and characteristics of ADHD, given the unnaturally high levels of cortisol running through the collective corporate brain. We are becoming overloaded, with many corporate citizens feeling overwhelmed most of the time. Our brains evolved to be good at concentrating on one thing at a time, and our capacity to retain information, to learn cogently and consistently, while efficient, is pretty limited. Every day the neurons in our brain have a limited amount of energy to do what we ask of them, and small decisions can be just as mentally costly as major ones. Adrenaline and Cortisol disrupt memory and therefore learning. Our bodies can retain the conditioned learning of fear and response, but our higher emotional and intellectual learning is shut off, since recallable memories to learn from are simply not created. So we don't learn the right lessons. We don't even remember accurately.

All of this conspires powerfully against the formation of anything that is sustainable; of anything that requires careful and patient nurturing, like growing a business organically or building human relationships. It's just too much like hard work; too boring.

> *All of this conspires powerfully against the formation of anything that is sustainable; of anything that requires careful and patient nurturing, like growing a business organically or building human relationships.*

Fear in the System

In the Corporate World, pressure and fear rule. Unreasonable and unnatural expectations create cultures of fear, dishonesty, manipulation, unethical and even illegal behaviour. The quality of human experience is subordinated to the achievement of purely financial objectives. What's worse is that frequently a serious diminution of the human experience is legitimately called into the service of the achievement of those objectives. I've seen countless examples where the weight of expectation is harmful and abusive – where share prices or aspirational company valuations are shored up by systemised unachievable forecasts.

How many times have I exhorted my clients not to rely on hope as a strategy? Yet no one can accept realistic forecasts from their people, since that would be to accept failure. But who will be the one who has the courage to hold their hand up and say 'Enough'?

Of course, that person might get shot. A worse fate would be that they may be allowed to stay but be labelled weak, ineffective, naive and destined for demotion. At best they might just trigger the guy next to them to follow their lead in a kind of 'I am Spartacus' moment, but this will feel a hopelessly remote possibility.

The result of all of this is that decent people (whether managers or employees), who have huge potential to be successful, creative, hard-working and dedicated corporate servants, feel like failures and endure the most fearful working conditions. Over time they become culturally hypnotised into behaving the same way. If they are managers they come to act cruelly in the name of maximising performance, but actually in punishment for not achieving what was impossible to start with.

Even in 'enlightened' and highly engaged, open and trusting working cultures, the fear of disappointing people – the fear of being not just judged, but also condemned and ultimately rejected – creates a frustrating and stifling paralysis. So many Corporate cultures are driven by a form of 'dynamic inertia' whereby a vast amount of energy and creativity is used to maintain the status quo.

In all my years as a manager I used a disciplinary process on probably only three or four occasions. I rarely needed the shock factor of such a process to clearly communicate the seriousness of a person's situation. I remember a boss of mine criticising me for putting one of my managers in a position whereby they were clear that if their performance did not improve within three months, I would remove them from their role. But it worked, and more importantly the recipient completely respected the process. I merely treated them like an adult, clearly outlining the inevitable consequences of their continued poor performance, outlining very specifically what they had to do to improve, and offering my wholehearted support for them to do so. I wanted them to win and they knew that and felt it. So it was up to them, and they respected that.

The finest example of a disciplinary process I ever saw was when the CEO of a Divisional MD client of mine suspended my client for a week. My client was hugely respected, in total command of his job, achieving great results and having built a hugely engaged culture. He was, however, still quite young and a little immature, and would occasionally drink too much at customer hospitality events. His CEO had spoken to him about this and told him clearly that he needed to address this behaviour. He was absolutely clear that drinking too much at customer events was no longer acceptable. Witnessing my client's drinking at one such occasion was the final straw for the CEO, who took him outside, told him he was suspended from work for a week, and put him in a taxi. My client duly served his week's suspension and his behaviour was corrected. He recalls this act as the greatest gift his CEO ever gave him.

The dynamic of fear around targets and forecasts is most prevalent in operational and commercial functions within companies where KPIs are clear, transparent, and most easily symbolised in financial terms. So this is another reason why people at the centre, acting in support of those with financial KPIs, create arbitrary and intangible objectives for themselves, so no one can ever put them in a position where their 'underperformance' is so starkly obvious. Management careers and the 'professionalisation' of manual work and the provision of care have become first a parallel and now frequently a paramount purpose to the original one of serving people and improving the quality of human experience.

How does this all break, since break it must? Often this is through a new leader coming in. Why do incoming CEOs reset expectations as their very first priority? Why do they 'kitchen sink' their first set of results? Because they can. Because they can legitimately argue, in the Corporate version of whistling and exclaiming 'Cowboys!', that the previous regime was simply not telling the truth about reality.

I cannot understand why so many Non-Executive Directors survive such dramatic re-sets. What were they doing beforehand? How could they not have known the reality of the company's situation? There is no defence.

As an incoming CEO or even Chairman, I have frequently found myself faced with cultures of fear around targets and forecasts. Many, many times I have had to repeat the phrase 'I don't care what the number is', as I've gone about removing fear from the system. This might sound naive, and you'll be asking yourself but what if the number they come up with really is unacceptable? Then we deal with reality. Since I believe in being transparent with people as they go about creating their budgets, or forecasting their future results, they have the information they need to put their assessments in context. In creating a budget, if the 'best' they can come up with would make a loss or would not give a sufficient return on capital employed, then they will know

Many, many times I have had to repeat the phrase 'I don't care what the number is', as I've gone about removing fear from the system.

this and be party to discussions and debates on the bigger issues thrown up by their budgeting. In forecasting a result that falls short of the plan, or short of what everyone has been expecting, then they will know this and will accompany their forecast with an action plan.

Fear will cause a manager to believe that forcing a person or team to continue with an unrealistic forecast will cause that person or team to work harder and/or to think more creatively and thus make up the shortfall. Fear will also cause a manager to believe that the moment they accept a degraded forecast, the person or team will breathe a collective sigh of relief, and all go back and metaphorically put their feet up having been rewarded for poor performance. Fear will then cause that manager to resent the situation they've been put in (yet again) by lazy, feckless, uncaring, disloyal, incompetent employees – that while the employees go happily back to their workplace exonerated of all blame and free of any stress, the poor manager is the one who now has to give bad news to the Ogre above. It's not fair.

Notes

Caroline Williams   'The Fire Inside: Stress Fuels Inflammation, the Hidden Cause of Many Modern Ailments. It is Time to Put Out the Blaze', *New Scientist*, 17 June 2017.

ADAA   The Anxiety and Depression Association of America 'Facts and Statistics' https://adaa.org/about-adaa/press-room/facts-statistics# (accessed 25 May 2018).

GAD 7 Test   Generalized Anxiety Disorder 7 is a self-reported questionnaire for screening and severity measuring of generalized anxiety disorder.

Alice Klein   'Our Brains can't Generalise When We're Tired', *New Scientist*, 7 January 2017. Klein quotes the work of Alex Chatburn of the University of South Australia.

Science Daily   The largest study in this field so far involving over 600,000 individuals, published in *The Lancet*. www.sciencedaily.com/releases/2015/08/150819211119.htm (accessed 25 May 2018).

Andy Coghlan   'How Bullying can Lead to Depression', *New Scientist,* 18 November 2017, p 11.

Kübler-Ross, E   (2008) *On Death and Dying* (1969). London: Routledge. (First published 1969)

DSM-5   DSM-5 is the taxonomic and diagnostic tool published by the American Psychiatric Association (APA), first published in 1952 and most recently revised in 2013. It now contains over 150 'recognised' psychological disorders.

Terry Bogg   Psychologist, General Manager and Expert in the field of Addictions Treatment and Policy, and a personal friend who died in April 2018. This was in my notes from a workshop Terry ran for Banbury Therapeutic Training in October 2016.

Thom Hartmann   Thomas Hartmann is an American author, psychotherapist, businessman, and progressive political commentator. Hartmann has hosted a nationally syndicated radio show, The Thom Hartmann Program, since 2003 and a nightly television show, The Big Picture, between 2010 and September 2017. In an article on his website he wrote about his beliefs and findings on ADHD. www.thomhartmann.com/articles/2007/11/thom-hartmanns-hunter-and-farmer-approach-addadhd (November 2007) (accessed 25 May 2018).

Jay, A   (1972) Introduction to *Corporation Man.* London: Jonathan Cape.

Chapter 8

CTSD – Corporate Traumatic Stress Disorder

Trauma and PTSD

The defining characteristic of a traumatic event is one that has the capacity to provoke fear, helplessness or horror in response to the threat of injury or death.

Under high stress, it is difficult to remember what to do, or even if we do remember, to actually do it. Many companies, public institutions and government agencies where employees are likely to be exposed to potentially traumatic situations put their employees through specific training to equip and protect them as best as possible. Training for emergencies works, since the way people respond in high-stress situations depends upon what they know. Prior knowledge is crucial, because when our threat responses are triggered, the brain is in no state for any rational deliberation, since the instantaneous functioning of the amygdala and hippocampus shut down the areas of the brain that govern working memory and that process new information. If the threat situation is one we've never experienced before, there's almost zero chance of us figuring out an escape. But if we've sort of been there before, if we've been through enough drills, our bodies will draw on the conditioned learning that sits in our reptilian brain and our limbic system – literally our muscle memory, and we stand a good chance of surviving.

In PTSD, sufferers become pre-occupied with thoughts, re-living the event, often with an 'if only' soundtrack, yielding further emotions of anger (why me?) or shame (why didn't I?). PTSD first came to public attention after the first Gulf War of the early 1990s. There was even something termed 'Gulf War Syndrome', and people speculated that as well as the stresses of combat, the soldiers were dealing with the effects of breathing a polluted cocktail of air on the battlefield.

PTSD was added to the DSM in the 1980s, and in DSM-5 it has the following diagnosis.

1. **Exposure to a traumatic event (directly witnessed or experienced indirectly)**

2. **Persistent re-experiencing**

3. **Persistent avoidance and emotional numbing**

4. **Hyperarousal (aggressive and self-destructive behaviour)**

5. **Duration of one month**

6. **Significant impairment**

As we learn more about trauma we've come to accept two other categories – vicarious and complex. Vicarious traumas arise from a cocktail of psychological dynamics and environmental factors, but are characterised by feelings of overwhelming responsibility, feelings of anger at injustice, and feelings of hopelessness. We literally live the trauma of others, including in its deepest madness, those whom we've never met and with whom we have absolutely no connection. We bear the weight of the world and it's truly traumatising.

Complex traumas arise from a series of what would be relatively minor traumas if experienced as single events, but which are connected by sheer repetition of traumatic features. These small 't' traumas, as they are also known, are an accumulation of small but nevertheless unsettling and distressing events that culminate in our capacity to cope being exceeded, resulting in a disruption of emotional functioning. While these traumas have no accompanying threat of physical harm, crucially they are ego threatening, due to the individual feeling a notable helplessness, with the layering of guilt and shame that ensues.

> *In the corporate environment, people are frequently contending with a cocktail of such ego threatening events.*

In the corporate environment, people are frequently contending with a cocktail of such ego threatening events – a challenging relationship with their boss, dysfunctional relationships with colleagues, the prospect of failing, conflicts at home due to work pressures and anxiety over finances. And since small 't' traumas tend to be dismissed by the individual sufferer, who will rationalise the experience or situation as being both common and completely normal, a cognitive shame reaction is triggered for allowing themselves to be affected. This avoidance only serves to make matter worse, adding to the accumulated effect of multiple compounded small 't' traumas. With PTSD it is the re-living of the experience that re-traumatises the sufferer; with small 't' traumas it is the integration of the shame.

Exposure to traumatic situations does not lead to PTSD in all cases, of course. In a classic 'fight or flight' situation, the surge of energy created is vented through the extreme physical exertion of the fight or the running away. Even in lower-level threat situations where a physical response would be inappropriate, if we find some physical outlet within a reasonable elapsed time – running, punching a bag, screaming while playing or watching a football match – these responses allow the temporarily trapped energy to be dissipated.

But if we are unable to get rid of the energy, if the body holds the trauma as trapped energy because the person 'freezes', then the trapped energy becomes stored in the cells which then inflame. Of course even then, over time the body can gradually release this trapped emotional energy. If the person is returned to normal life relatively quickly and with relative ongoing stability (love, companionship, respect from finding meaning and purpose) then this will be so in the vast majority of cases. If the person receives professional therapy, then the chances are greatly increased, but even the 'therapy' of loving relationships can do the trick.

If the trauma is extreme then just returning to a 'normal' life of loving relationships and respect won't be sufficient, since the level of shame may be too great, or the brain simply won't allow the person to forget. So they continually re-live the trauma, effectively re-traumatising themselves continuously and progressively, until something breaks. But even minor traumas are hard to recover from if the person goes straight back into a stressful ongoing situation – a controlling relationship, precarious financial circumstances, insecure employment, bereavement etc.

In situations of extreme threat and danger, our most primal hard-wiring is triggered – our brains are flooded with stress hormones; our hippocampus shuts down, we get a surge of cortisol for focus, and of adrenaline for strength and our most basic 'flight or fight' response ensures we survive. Trauma affects the operating of the dentate nucleus in the brain. This is a cluster of neurons, or nerve cells, in the central nervous system, and is responsible for the planning, initiation and control of voluntary movements. It is another part of the 'break' between the limbic system and the neocortex. When we experience 'normal' trauma and trauma responses (fight or flight) the amygdala flicks the circuit breaker to the neocortex, instantly shutting down the hippocampus and dentate nucleus, which are then fired up again seconds later when the amygdala throws the switch again after the immediate threat has passed.

But when the trauma is low-level and constant, the amygdala can't quite decide what to do, and it sort of short circuits, fluctuating wildly between on and off, effectively blowing a fuse in the dentate nucleus, causing cells to die. When the cells re-generate, they emerge into an unstable environment and malfunction.

War veterans with PTSD have abnormally low levels of activity in their pre-frontal cortex, and unusually high levels of activity in their amygdala. They are in effect being constantly re-traumatised by fairly innocuous daily events, and they will re-experience their past traumas very much in the present moment. This is because the normal processing of events as memories in the past has not taken place. If the hippocampus shuts off, then memories can never move to being in the past. When we're triggered we re-experience the fear of the trauma as being right here in the present. We are continually re-traumatised. PTSD is a memory-filing error.

If the hippocampus shuts off, then memories can never move to being in the past. When we're triggered we re-experience the fear of the trauma as being right here in the present.

Research into PTSD has shown that when we suffer trauma and take positive action, then we minimise our risk of suffering afterwards. Our risk comes from when we do *not* act; we do *not* fight; we do *not* run away – we in fact freeze, and when we freeze we hold the trauma in our cells – we go into victimisation and will actually feel responsible for what has happened to us. Crazy of course, but inevitable.

With freeze comes shame. And with freeze comes a constant re-living of the trauma. When I re-live my personal experience of being carjacked, I am rather proud of myself, and I am able to laugh at how ridiculous I must have looked flailing my arms around, waiting for the Rocky style 'thunk' sound as my fist landed on my assailant's chin, which of course it never did. Had I frozen, and simply let them do what they did to me with no defence or resistance, I suspect I'd still be traumatised; the shame would be so great; the 'if only' would still be driving me mad. The trauma would be unfinished and constantly re-lived.

CTSD – Corporate Traumatic Stress Disorder

Perhaps the central tenet of this whole book is my 'discovery' of the existence of CTSD – Corporate Traumatic Stress Disorder – as a separate and distinct condition.

> *CTSD is an anxiety disorder caused through constant and persistent exposure to the low-level psychological trauma of working in corporate environments.*

CTSD is an anxiety disorder caused through constant and persistent exposure to the low-level psychological trauma of working in corporate environments. I believe that the continued, relentless, harmful and poundingly repetitive exposure to states of anxiety and stress within the corporate environment have led to this new form of PTSD.

I am now openly asking interested parties to engage with this belief and to take up research and do further analysis, with the aim of gaining appropriate recognition of CTSD, culminating in its inclusion in the DSM – maybe in DSM-6?

The Corporation is the perfect crucible for creating trauma – the perfect petri dish for growing cultures of fear, anxiety, competition, isolation, threat – trauma. Although we associate PTSD with extremes of experiences and genuine traumas – war, violence and terror (conditions that are clearly not present in the corporate world) and although we also associate PTSD with dramatic but actually short-lived or even momentary trauma, I believe CTSD has arisen as a recognisable psychological condition, through the lengthy layering and the sheer intensity of repetition of lower-level anxiety and threat conditions and thus responses.

In 'real' life, humans go into either fight or flight mode in the face of threat, and rarely 'freeze', but in the corporate world the pre-dominant response to threat is freeze, because neither fight nor flight are acceptable, viable or possible. Freeze, and in the truest sense of the word 'petrification', is a key cause of PTSD, and since this is the more usual response in the corporate world, my contention is that most human beings in working in corporate environments are suffering from at least a mild form of CTSD, and some are suffering in the extreme. Since this condition is unrecognised, it is undiagnosed. My sincere hope is that this book will start to change that.

Trauma is indeed a strong word to use when we think of how people suffer anxiety and stress at work. However our workplaces are our twenty-first-century savannahs – we may not have to encounter predatory animals or cannibalistic tribes, and we do not live with the threat of death or injury as a daily companion. But we do have to live with near constant uncertainty, the daily fear of making mistakes, of not being capable of what is asked of us, of being condemned. And our brain chemistry is being altered, to a pathological extent. We are living with such extreme neurological changes that we are in effect being permanently traumatised – an absolute parallel with what happens in cases of PTSD.

Our pre-historic forbears dealt with their occasional traumas with a medley of flight and fight. But in our modern workplaces these survival tools are not available to us. The hierarchy has ensured that we are scared of fighting (challenging or 'pushing back') since we risk criticism, alienation, demotion or being managed out. And we cannot take flight (leave) since we are true corporate hostages, trapped by our financial commitments and perceived status.

So we freeze – we have in fact mastered the art of looking like we are working hard and looking like we are in complete agreement with the corporate master plan, when in fact we are giving as little of ourselves as possible. We are doing the minimum expected of us, but we are using all our creative energy in a debilitating and soul-destroying dance of dynamic inertia. We are in survival mode for sure, playing small and staying safe. And in a corporation the easiest ways to remain safe are a) to say yes to the boss and b) take no risks whatsoever. And we do this for years, and our cellular make up changes. We suffer a silent and unconscious CTSD.

The by-product of 'freeze' is that the body is left holding the massive undischarged energy surge and has no other place to store it than in healthy cells that then become inflamed. Trauma gets stuck in the body. Trauma is a strong word to use for people suffering anxiety and stress at work. And when it comes to PTSD, we associate that with extreme human suffering – war, kidnap, murder, rape, car crashes . . . but remember the brain cannot distinguish between a genuine life-threatening event and one that involves no mortal threat whatsoever.

Interestingly, in March 2018 the BBC Newsnight TV programme, in a piece covering claims of bullying against the Speaker of the House of Commons, John Bercow, reported that Kate Emms had been diagnosed with PTSD after working for Mr Bercow for a year.

Uncertainty in corporate life is at higher levels and is more frequent a state for people than ever before. So people are less able to pay attention and are easily distracted. Emotions can suddenly take them by surprise, the onset surprising them and threatening to overcome them, with the most extreme example being the panic attack. Many managers frequently experience a near-panic-attack moment. Since emotions are not to be expressed at work, people have once again to supress the emotions, reinforcing the dynamics where their body has to trap and then store the emotional pain. At work we become practised at *not* feeling, which is why when you ask someone how they are feeling, I guarantee they will start their response with the words 'I think . . .' or at best with the words 'I don't feel . . .' Denial!

Denial is an amazingly powerful force in The Corporation. It allows us to know, but not to know. I know that what I am doing is pointless and even damaging, but I cannot know it, since I would then have to change and I cannot afford to do that, so better that I pretend I do not know, and since I am an honest person of real integrity, and I cannot therefore lie or live openly with falsehood, I need to not know. It is truly staggering to the emotionally separate outsider, what they find in organisations, and they ask themselves 'how is it possible that people did not know this was happening?'. The answer is that they *did* know it was happening, but they were in a state of corporate hypnosis, and so they were genuinely unaware. They were in denial, on auto pilot, in a collective blind spot, sleepwalking through the day. They had been suffering from CTSD.

> *They ask themselves 'how is it possible that people did not know this was happening?'. The answer is that they did know it was happening, but they were in a state of corporate hypnosis.*

CTSD has become a pathology within the corporate world – CTSD is a 'Corporapathology'. The strict definition of the term 'pathology' is the science of the causes and effects of physical or mental diseases. But the term has extended into a more informal use in regard to abnormal behaviours which are actually symptoms of a diagnosable psychological condition. Compulsive, obsessive, depressive, dysfunctional and deviant behaviours which have gone beyond the 'normal' in the corporate world, and are so clearly controlling the individual, have become 'pathological'. The behaviours have become so conditioned, so routine, so automated, so unconscious, that the 'disease' has permeated the cells and infected all. CTSD is the new pandemic.

In the Corporate World it very often seems as though a collective psychosis (total loss of reality) has taken hold, where thought and emotions are so impaired that contact is lost with 'real' life. So CTSD is highly contagious, but no one knows they've been infected! CTSD hijacks the normal, mentally healthy methodology for how humans decide to behave. John Wymore describes this 'normal' process, in that every individual has a relatively objective model of reality in their unconscious, created through myriad learnings and interpretational instincts interacting with past experiences, and future (Darwinian) aspirations. The unconscious mind also contains the self-deception mechanism that is guided by a relatively objective cost-benefit analysis of a multitude of real and imagined contexts. All sensory input comes first into the unconscious which then decides what version of reality to download into the conscious, with the content of the download determined by the self-deception mechanism. This selected and potentially altered version of reality then appears in the conscious mind as felt emotions and knowledge – as the truth. It is this version of reality which then directs an individual's behaviour.

Notice how even in normal functioning we have enormous scope for self-delusion, truly believing that our version of events is the truth, and given that our values are fine and noble and right, our ensuing behaviour was not only justifiable, but the only possible choice of integrity. But Corporatism adds a sinister dynamic to this, since it is the collective 'truth' that holds sway. With so many suffering CTSD, it's no wonder why corporate memories are completely unreliable, and why corporate behaviours are so unnatural and inhuman.

Corporate citizens are well practised at dissociating – the conscious mind is cut off from the body and the feeling; cut off from the morality and the emotions. We saw how a key Corporapathic characteristic is the ability to compartmentalise the various parts of our lives, acting and behaving in different ways as we assume almost different identities in each of those compartments. If we are different at home than we are at work, which is the authentic us? Dissociation is the emotional, often almost physical, detachment from immediate surroundings and events – from reality. It's how a nurse can walk past a distressed patient. With psychosis being a *complete* loss of reality, dissociation is an inexorable step down that path.

> Dissociation is the emotional, often almost physical, detachment from immediate surroundings and events – from reality. It's how a nurse can walk past a distressed patient.

With PTSD being a memory filing error, notice in CTSD how corporate managers have developed a wonderfully convenient amnesia. There is no memory since we didn't really take the information in in the first place, being such appalling listeners. And being skilled at compartmentalising and dissociating, information is literally deleted as if it never existed.

Corporations push normal people towards the extremes of their psychological preferences due to the excessive working under pressure. Corporations are often guilty of favouring a particular psychometric profile, valuing urgency, confidence and talking, for example, anathema to, even alienating or intimidating to Blue preference types. Look at the dominance of the Red or ENTJ (Extraversion, Intuition, Thinking, Judgement) preference profile in positions of leadership, understandable in some ways due to the inherent desire of those types to take responsibility, but potentially reinforcing many undesired and skewed behaviours. The extreme psychological manifestation of the Red or ENTJ psychometric preference is narcissism and paranoia, another reason that so many sociopaths end up in positions of leadership. By the way, for completeness, and very crudely, the psychological extremes of Blue preference types is OCD, of Yellow preference types is Bi-Polar and ADHD, and of Green preference types is Depression and Codependency.

I wonder what the cortisol levels are like in corporations compared with normal control groups. If we could scan the brain circuitry of corporate managers what would we find? Have we bred a generation of anxious fearful change agents? Malcolm Gladwell's '10,000 Hour Rule' could apply to being in cultures. Just why are managers so incredibly skilled at manipulating? The simple answer is they get enormous amounts of practice. 10,000 hours is just five years of an executive's life. We become conditioned to feeling predated, so our behaviours are conditioned to be survival based. We play safe. We conform. We lose our personal integrity. And since there are so many distractions in the form of mass stimuli coming at us, we don't realise. We've lost our self-awareness.

CTSD will lead to psychosis in extreme cases. Denial is so strong and dissociation so practised that psychosis awaits us at the bottom of the slippery slope. Corporapaths may be relatively benign, but once CTSD gets hold, how quickly they become sociopaths.

We need a massive, and shocking dose of self-awareness.

Test for CTSD

To repeat: CTSD is an anxiety disorder caused through constant and persistent exposure to the low-level psychological traumas of working in corporate environments.

How would we know if someone was suffering from CTSD? There are many and varied tests that people can take as a guide to whether they may be suffering from any of the multitude of psychological disorders recognised in the DSM-5. Of course, a clinical diagnosis requires more than a simple test, however many of the tests are excellent guides, particularly as to whether someone should seek medical or psychological help.

If we take PTSD for example, a simple online search brings up a whole host of tests, but if we stick with the DSM-5 for the moment, and look at the initial, simple test for PTSD that it recommends (PCL-5) it has 20 yes/no questions divided into seven sections. I won't repeat the full test here, but the sections are:

1. **Have you experienced or witnessed a life-threatening event that caused intense fear, helplessness, or horror?**

2. **Do you re-experience the event in at least one of the following ways? (three listed)**

3. **Do reminders of the event affect you in at least three of the following ways? (seven listed)**

4. **Are you troubled by at least two of the following? (five listed)**

5. **Have you experienced changes in sleeping or eating habits?**

6. **More days than not, do you feel . . . (three listed)**

7. **During the last year, has the use of alcohol or drugs . . . (four listed)**

You'll notice that the initial question is a single gateway – if you have not witnessed a life-threatening event that caused intense fear, helplessness or horror, then you *cannot* be suffering from PTSD. You may well be depressed or have an anxiety disorder, but you don't have PTSD. And that is important because the treatments and remedies for treating different disorders must themselves be different, guided by the nature of the disorder. The clearer the diagnosis, the easier it is to prescribe the treatment, and the more effective those treatments will be.

If you're through the initial gateway, the implication is that you could very well be suffering from the disorder, even before the 'tester' has gained any knowledge of your symptoms of anxiety. The 'tester' is completely open to you being a sufferer. This is not a test to prove that you are a faker or shirker or attention-seeker. This is a test that presumes suffering.

All the research into PTSD as a separate and distinct anxiety disorder has shown that it is characterised by re-experiencing the traumatic event, and being frequently and disturbingly reminded of it. Hence the next two sections of questions are looking for evidence of this, through a number (10 are listed) of typical scenarios or psychological reactions or projections – ones that will therefore be very familiar to genuine sufferers.

Since PTSD is an anxiety disorder, it has many behavioural or impulsive manifestations common to all anxiety disorders, and so the fourth section asks about more general emotional or impulsive reactions or behaviours.

Section 5 asks a single yes/no question about changes in sleeping or eating habits – again this is a common manifestation of behaviour change in many anxiety disorders. Section 6 returns to common emotions experienced by sufferers of anxiety disorders in general and then Section 7 concludes with four questions specifically about your use of drugs and alcohol. Since PTSD was recognised as a separate anxiety disorder, it has become clearer that many sufferers turn to substances to self-medicate, and hence it has become another reliable indicative factor (given the evidence of the other questions) in diagnosing PTSD.

In arriving at a test for CTSD, I have therefore followed a simple template.

1. **A single initial gateway question to establish whether you work in a corporate environment.** If you don't, you might have an anxiety disorder, but it's not CTSD. But if you've only worked in a corporate environment for a very short time, you will also not suffer from CTSD – it is the repetition, frequency and persistency of the low grade 'traumas' that build up into the disorder, so the question needs a time bound gateway. I've chosen 12 months.

   Someone could easily argue that they have anxiety after working for a new boss for just three weeks, but I would say that's not CTSD. A change of boss would see the anxiety lifted instantly with no lasting effects. CTSD is a condition that sits below a level of self-awareness, built up over time, with sufferers not 'knowing' that they are suffering, and thus believing that while all is normal around them, that they are the problem.

2. **There will then be some questions that are 100 per cent specific to the corporate environment and our understanding of the dynamics arising from the abuse of power and control, and from the psychological effects of fear and stress.** As CTSD is not caused or triggered by a single 'traumatic' event, it is not appropriate to use the term 'trauma' in the test. Part of the issue with CTSD is that sufferers will be in massive denial that they have any type of disorder, or indeed that there is anything unusual about their life at all. If we've seen a fellow soldier blown up in front of our eyes, we have something dramatic to point to that completely legitimises our temporary 'weakness'. If, on the other hand, 'all' we can point to is having to keep up with 400 emails a day, our fear is that we will be completely ridiculed if we 'complain', especially if we are well paid. So the questions have to tease out the symptoms in a way that allows the person taking the test to acknowledge the reality of their situation and of their suffering. Therefore, as with the PTSD test, there will be an implicit acceptance of suffering within the test, and the questions must use an 'inside knowledge' of the negative dynamics of corporatism as their root. As such, let's understand in advance that critics will jump on the questions as leading perfectly healthy people to come to believe they are sick!

3. **There will then be some questions that are generic to all anxiety disorders.**

4. **Next comes the question around eating and sleeping habits, which should be included as it qualifies under the 'generic' category, but with the addition of a question around the attempted control of sickness, since that is so characteristic of corporate citizens.** And rather than have a separate question about drugs and alcohol, my test will roll this into the section on health and self-management. I believe that drugs and alcohol are a big issue in the corporate world, but I further believe that other addictions are important to include, such as gambling (since so many corporate roles involve risk taking, playing the odds, and winning or losing dynamics) and sex (how many extra-marital affairs are you aware of within the workplace?). Addiction is also important in workaholism, and in the seemingly addictive usage of smartphones, tablets and laptops.

Test for CTSD

So here is my 'First Draft' CTSD Test:

Yes   **No**   Have you worked in a corporate environment for more than 12 months continuously?

Do you have any of the following experiences at work?

Yes   **No**   A feeling of being overwhelmed by the volume of incoming information and requests eg emails, meeting invites etc

Yes   **No**   Feeling pressure to take on projects, tasks or commitments beyond your capacity to do them all to a high standard

Yes   **No**   Feeling guilty when having to ask things of your direct reports especially when you see that they are already very busy

Yes   **No**   Nervousness in communicating anything 'negative' to a superior

Yes   **No**   Feelings of anxiety when looking ahead at your diary

Yes   **No**   Feelings of dread in the lead up to certain meetings

Yes   **No**   Procrastinating over tasks even though you know this will lead to problems for you

Yes   **No**   Feeling a sudden palpable anxiety from an unexpected request to speak to your immediate line manager

Yes   **No**   An awareness of a constant low-level feeling of being agitated, unsettled or on edge

Yes   **No**   Frequent feelings of irritation, frustration and impatience with people that you are reliant upon in order to do your work well

Yes   **No**   Agreeing to take on work commitments knowing that it will cause problems at home

During the last year/six months have your work commitments

Yes   **No**   resulted in your failure to fulfil responsibilities or promises to family or friends

Yes   **No**   placed you in a situation where you've had no alternative but to take an action that you are ashamed of

Yes   **No**   caused you to lie or act dishonestly

Yes   **No**   caused you to bend, push the very limits, or even break the law

When you are at home or with friends or family, do you experience any of the following?

Yes   **No**   Avoiding discussion of negative aspects of your work for fear that people will naively expect you to do something about it

Yes	No	Finding yourself regularly moaning about things at work to the point where you are almost boring yourself now
Yes	No	Losing interest in previously significant activities in your life
Yes	No	Feeling increasingly detached from friends
Yes	No	Feeling that your work is causing a disconnection from your life partner
Yes	No	Sensing that your future has shrunk (for example, you don't expect to have a successful career, to have a happy marriage, to be a good parent, to have the material success you desire)

Are you troubled by any of the following?

Yes	No	Problems sleeping
Yes	No	Irritability, impatience or outbursts of frustration with people who don't deserve it
Yes	No	Falling ill whenever you take any form of extended break from work
Yes	No	Feeling unsettled or on edge
Yes	No	Detrimental changes in eating habits?

During the last six months, has the use of alcohol or drugs, or gambling, or sexual activity or online activity, or any other compulsive/addictive behaviours

Yes	No	resulted in failure to fulfil responsibilities or promises at work or with family?
Yes	No	put you in a dangerous situation?
Yes	No	put you in a situation where you came close to being caught out for something you are ashamed of?
Yes	No	continued despite causing problems for you or your loved ones?

This is my first draft – there are 30 yes/no questions after the initial gateway question. Half of them are specific to work, and half are more generic to emotions and experiences outside work.

My instinct is that the scoring and 'ratings' could look something like this (it was interesting that as I wrote these, I had to acknowledge the dynamic whereby someone could score very low, not because they were emotionally well balanced, or had high self-esteem or supreme self-awareness, but because they simply don't care about their work!) This of course brings up the question as to what a 'healthy' score is – I've landed rather arbitrarily on a score of between 5 and 10.

0–5 yes's   You may work in a corporation but you seem utterly immune to the potential pressures, although your level of detachment might indicate a lack of interest or commitment to your work and your organisation. Action – consider whether you're in the right role.

5–10 yes's	You seem to have a good grip on things at work and a pretty healthy balance between the commitment you give to your work and the importance of your life outside. Action – stay in this emotional space for as long as possible and be a proud role model for others.
10–15 yes's	Your working life is just starting to have an impact on your emotional well-being and your sense of being a good person outside work. Action – recognise that this dynamic is OK in the short term but ensure that you have a medium-term end in sight.
15–20 yes's	The pressures and strains of your work are taking are starting to damage your relationships both inside and outside work in such a way as the damage may not be recoverable. Action – change something now. This does not necessarily mean leaving your current role, but will involve an honest acknowledgement of your responsibilities outside work and how you will discharge them differently going forward.
20–25 yes's	You are approaching a dangerous situation where the stress you are experiencing and the behaviours it is causing in you could result in some form of breakdown or burnout or a dramatic event or situation. Action – make a dramatic change, either leaving your current role or insisting upon a reset of expectations. Seek assistance from people around you and most likely also from a professional.
25+ yes's	You are either having a breakdown, or may even be approaching a semi-psychotic state. Action – seek professional help now.

So I offer this test, not as a proven methodology but as a starting proposition. I invite others now to join me in developing this further.

Dare you take the test, even as it stands?

Something struck me after I'd completed designing the test above – I've long been a huge fan of the work of the Gallup organisation, often recommending their employee engagement system 'Q12' to clients, since it is a both simple (based on just 12 questions) and in my view beautifully observational of the factors that actually matter to people in the satisfaction they feel in their work. One of the 12 questions is: 'Do I have a best friend at work?' – on the surface this would appear to have nothing to do with whether the employer is good or bad, in fact a high score on this question could indicate a very poor employer, but with a strong internal survival conspiracy in place. Was the Artful Dodger not a 'best friend' to Oliver Twist? But Gallup's research is both sound and comprehensive. They worked out a long time ago that cultures of friendship at work produce high levels of employee engagement, and since Faginesque leaders have largely been seen off, we can trust that this is indeed a reliable indicator. Having a 'best friend' at work is a hugely important part of overall psychological safety, since that friend will not only look out for us, but critically will keep us sane. The biggest risk to our contracting CTSD is not the trauma of working for an Ogre, but the self-delusionary paralysis that creeps over us from our self-inflicted anxieties. A friend can truly keep us grounded.

Notes

DSM-5   American Psychiatric Association (APA) (2013) *Diagnostic and Statistical Manual of Mental Disorders*. 5th ed. Washington, DC: American Psychiatric Association.

BBC TV 'Newsnight'   'House of Commons Speaker John Bercow Named in Bullying Claims', reported by Chris Cook and Lucinda Day, 9 March 2018. www.bbc.co.uk/news/uk-politics-43339116 (accessed 2 June 2018).

Wymore, J   (2006) *Gestalt Therapy and Human Nature.* Bloomington: AuthorHouse.

Blue and Red personality types   Insights Discovery is a globally recognised and very widely used psychometric tool. www.insights.com/products/insights-discovery (accessed 2 June 2018).

MBTI   Myers Briggs Type Indicator is another globally recognised and widely used psychometric tool. www.myersbriggs.org/home.htm?bhcp=1 (accessed 2 June 2018).

Gladwell, M (2009)   The 10,000 Hour Rule, *Outliers: The Story of Success.* London: Penguin.

PTSD Test   Designed by the Anxiety and Depression Association of America (ADAA), the PCL-5 is a 20-item self-report measure that assesses the 20 *DSM*-5 symptoms of PTSD.

Gallup and Gallup Q12   Referenced in Chapters 1 and 2.

Oliver Twist   is the eponymous hero of Charles Dickens' 1837 novel. Born in a workhouse and sold into apprenticeship with an undertaker, Oliver escapes and travels to London, where he meets 'The Artful Dodger', a member of a gang of juvenile pickpockets led by the elderly criminal, Fagin.

Additional Acknowledgements

While I've not quoted directly from the following articles, workshops and publications, the contents were useful in helping me shape my thinking on the links between PTSD and CTSD.

Fiona Dunkley   Banbury Therapeutic Training workshop 'The Physiology of Trauma' (11 March 2016).

Linda Geddes   'Worry, worry, worry, worry . . .', *New Scientist*, 8 October 2016.

Sathnam Sanghera   'Burnout may be just Another Name for Depression, and a Spa won't Help', *The Times*, 2 December 2016 (accessed 23 June 2018).

Jessica Hamzelou   'The Aftermath', *New Scientist*, 17 September 2016.

Section 3
Corporate Emotional Intelligence (CEQ)

'Men's courses will foreshadow certain ends, to which, if persevered in, they must lead,' said Scrooge. 'But if the courses be departed from, the ends will change. Say it is thus with what you show me.' 'Good Spirit,' he pursued, as down upon the ground he fell before it: 'Your nature intercedes for me, and pities me. Assure me that I yet may change these shadows you have shown me, by an altered life.'

Chapter 9

Introducing the Four Pillars of CEQ – Corporate Emotional Intelligence

Waking up in a Corporapathic World

Why 'waking up'? Because first of all we need to physically shake ourselves awake from our convenient and self-serving collective unconsciousness. And then when we do wake up, we'll realise we're waking up in a truly Corporapathic World – a world that has become controlled not by humanity but by corporate systems, strategies and cultures.

The change I am evangelising involves known strategies, but ones that are simply not being implemented. Corporate leaders either *think* they are implementing them, in which case they would see this book as simply yet another tome on a worthy subject, or they believe the strategies don't work, in which case they'll dismiss this book without ever reading it. The vast majority of managers I've met really do want to believe that these strategies can work, but their fear is so great that they cannot be persuaded to implement them confidently, wholeheartedly and irrevocably. Their fear may even stop them from admitting their beliefs openly. My experience is that the managers who have tried these strategies and failed (thus learning never to do that again) have implemented them hesitatingly, half-heartedly and conditionally. Many think they've implemented them, but in fact they haven't. That's an incredibly tough barrier to get past. The forces lined up against the strategies I advocate are so entrenched and so powerful that the merest flicker of equivocation will herald doom.

> *The vast majority of managers I've met really do want to believe that these strategies can work, but their fear is so great that they cannot be persuaded to implement them confidently, wholeheartedly and irrevocably.*

CEQ involves a new, profound and unshakable self-awareness, one that is incapable of being overridden with denial; one that is only arrived at through a profound physiological journey of self-discovery of who and what we have become, and of the behaviours we have become guilty of in the defence of our corporate master. It is not the knowing of our intellect, but the knowing of our very soul. And once we know, we cannot unknow; and once we know, we cannot in all conscience pretend that we don't.

This profound self-awareness will change us, even if we don't consciously act differently. When I check in with managers about one month after they've been through coaching training with me, and I ask them what they've done differently, the vast majority can't wait to tell me of the conscious change they made and the amazing results they've had. But a small number struggle to recall anything they've done differently, so I dig a bit, and in most cases just a few moments later they are realising that they *have* acted differently and seen a benefit. They honestly believed that they had yet to put anything into conscious practice, but they'd had *such* a profound shift in awareness that they had discounted the ensuing change. So this new awareness will of itself deliver change in the corporate world around us even if we don't take radical action, and even if we feel we've not done anything differently. There is power in true self-knowledge, and while we can deny any conscious change, it's amazing what our subconscious does with heightened self-awareness.

But this is not to say that we don't need conscious, radical change nor actively strive for it. I'm not letting anyone off the hook here. So CEQ also gives a clarion call for us to be courageous. It takes courage for us to confront our fears, and to first challenge and then defy the forces conspiring against the necessary changes. My experience is that the initial challenge is usually all that's needed to dissolve potential obstacles and barriers in front of our very eyes. But make no mistake, the depth of ingrained abuse of power within corporatism is so great, that radical action will be required to effect cultural change.

CEQ is therefore the essential bridge between the old world and the new, between denial and change, between fear and joy – and at the risk of sounding overly melodramatic, between doom and salvation.

Changing corporatism does *not* require a revolution, and even if it did, the weaponry against the forces of change would surely prevail. But changing corporatism does require us to be shocked out of our denial and into a collective determination and collaboration of change for good. With this new and profoundly different self-awareness, we have a new and previously undiscovered opportunity to behave differently and to herald a new age of corporatism that is genuinely moral, healthy, sustaining, nurturing and collaborative.

EQ and CEQ

Before I outline the four pillars of CEQ, I must give a hugely respectful nod here to Daniel Goleman's work on EQ – Emotional Intelligence, which has the following five aspects:

1. Self-Awareness

2. Self-Regulation

3. Empathy and Social Awareness

4. Social Skills and Relationship Management

5. Motivation

While Goleman was not the first to use the term 'emotional intelligence', it was his 1995 book that brought EQ to a global audience in a way that allowed people to understand the concept and to improve their relationships.

Having good EQ means we have an ability to regulate our behaviour in relationships with other people; good EQ gives us the awareness and the openness to look at ourselves and our part in any dynamic of conflict; and good EQ gives us the willingness, if not always the skills, to exercise some control over our emotional responses. I believe that an appreciation of EQ combined with an honest conscious effort at developing it in ourselves can only be good for us and the people with whom we commune.

But I am wholly concerned here with the unique and unnatural environment created by corporatism, and therefore with the specialised emotional intelligence we need – to first understand what working in a corporate environment is doing to us, and then to be far better equipped to handle the changes that are required of us.

Both EQ and CEQ are fundamentally about self-awareness, since without it no change is possible, but corporatism is such a powerful contaminator, such a despotic controller, that our self-awareness cannot merely be intellectual. As we've seen, it is often the case that corporate citizens are in denial, on auto pilot, almost hypnotised into believing that they are behaving in ways that are normal, justifiable, moral even, when the opposite is true. And so the self-awareness that has to come with CEQ has to be awakened physio-logically in our bodies; our bodies have to know before our minds get involved and hijack the situation. We can of course learn how to be more self-aware, but even that conscious decision, that choice to do some learning, will only come from a physiological imperative. With CEQ our self-awareness has to be felt physically, or else our powerful intellect will seduce us into denial.

The Four Pillars of CEQ

The Four Pillars of CEQ are:

1. Awareness of Our Unconscious Controlling Habits – OUCH!;

2. Promoting Positive Learning;

3. Transparency and Vulnerability;

4. A Grip on Reality.

The next four chapters go into detail on each of these Pillars, but here's a quick summary of each.

Awareness of Our Unconscious Controlling Habits – OUCH!

The biggest single obstacle to our changing anything about how we behave at work is our complete lack of awareness of our controlling habits. Why would we change if we are un-aware of how we are really behaving, particularly if we already think we're doing the right things? Even when we flirt with more 'enlightened' strategies we first of all believe that we need a huge amount of time to change and then we fool ourselves into thinking that we will get that time when the world settles down a bit. The problem is that we simply do not know how to change our behaviour when we are feeling pressured and frustrated and still get the job done. So we tell ourselves that all we can do is work harder and longer, trying to control more things, and this therefore becomes completely cultural. The vicious downward spiral continues – we get more frustrated and so do our people. At the very instant we require people to step forward in all of their brilliance and fabulousness, our unconscious controlling habits make them play safe and small.

Promoting Positive Learning

We are either learning 'negatively' through our increasingly conditioned responses to threat, or we are learning 'positively' through conscious consideration, deliberate action and immediate feedback in the form of consequences. It's not that 'positive' learnings are by their very nature more elusive, it's more that the 'negative' learnings are so dominant. Remember our brains are five times more sensitive to negative feedback than positive, so we have to work five times harder on nurturing the positive learning. It can be exhausting of course. The worst aspect of the unbridled impact of Our Unconscious Controlling Habits is the learning it creates and embeds. Instead of creating positive learning, where our team member learns that they are the solution, our crass and lazy habits teach them that they are in fact the problem. So, positive learning is not a 'nice to have' – it is a complete essential. If we do not create the environment and the cultural conditions for positive learning, it's not just that we'll suffer the frustrations of unrealised potential, it's that we'll actively do harm. There is no neutrality here, since we are learning all the time, with every nanosecond seeing neurons in our brain firing and creating new neural pathways.

Transparency and Vulnerability

As we've seen, secrecy is the facilitator of fear and control, and the disease attacking organisational health. Add to that our seemingly total unwillingness to show normal human emotions at work, and we have a recipe for the worst excesses of corporatism to thrive. Even when the corporate values espouse openness and honesty (or some wordsmithed variation), the manifestation of these words is that we are only trusted with information our corporate masters deign to believe we'll understand, and only with information that won't cause problems should it get into the public domain. Truly we are both thick and untrustworthy. Human beings are naturally messy, emotional, clumsy, imperfect. Corporatism desperately tries to condition these unhelpful and inconvenient dynamics out of its employees. But human beings are also fabulously talented, creative, extraordinary and resourceful, and Corporatism loses most of this amazing potential in the process. This for me is the true meaning of diversity. So leaders have to create and then nurture a working environment that allows people to be human, developing skills in observation, coaching and facilitation. And rather than introducing vulnerability as a quasi-manufactured device, designed to show authentic leadership and trustworthiness, the vulnerability that comes with transparency is real and palpable.

A grip on Reality

How often have I concluded a tough coaching session with a senior client, having worked to help them navigate the often-extreme stresses and pressures of their role, with the words '*And remember it's just a job; it's a game; it's important, but it's not real life*'? And I say these words not to belittle the massive investment of personal time, energy and skill that the client has made, nor to downplay the difference the client's company is making to people's lives. I say it because the client is in danger of taking their role so seriously, as to potentially damage themselves and their families. Without a strong touchstone to reality, we simply won't have the humility we need to be trusted and to lead with real authenticity, and therein lies the road to hubris. If we believe we are indispensable, then we will surely be proven wrong sooner or later, but after a huge self-inflicted cost and cultural infantilising of others. So it doesn't work. However, while I am of course concerned for the well-being of *all* clients, the open acceptance of the Faustian Pact means that at least the most senior ones are getting very well rewarded. My main concern therefore is the damage caused to those who have the misfortune to be led by the seemingly omnipotent ones. Our belief in our indispensability will cause those we lead to learn that they are lesser mortals, incapable of doing what we do, thinking like we think, moving as fast as we can move, caring as deeply as we care. And they will learn that they *are* dispensable, with all the fear that this creates for them. If indispensability is the gateway to hubris, then dispensability is the crevasse to living in fear.

Bio/Psycho/Socio/Spirito

I came across the Biopsychosocial Model during my research into psychotherapy and addiction. But it seemed to me that there was a missing element – the magical and always surprising results and outcomes that seemed to flow for so many people as they sought to recover from disease or addiction by consciously using the first three steps.

In order to save corporatism from itself, we are all going to have to embark on a profound change. But attempting to change our behaviour won't do it, and the more we focus on *thinking* our way through this, the more we collude with corporatism to stay exactly as we all are, and the less likely we are to save ourselves from the destruction that corporatism quite likely has in store for us.

We don't just need to change our behaviour, we need to be cured of CTSD. We need to go into 'recovery' – in exactly the way addicts do to save their lives. We have to have the gut wrenching, solar plexus hitting moment of awareness that we simply cannot go on as we are. We need to be sick and tired of being sick and tired. This is the Bio Step – the biological knowing in our bodies. Of course our intellect has known for some time, but knowing is simply not enough; we have to feel it. As a participant on one of my training courses, a Sales Director

> *We don't just need to change our behaviour, we need to be cured of CTSD. We need to go into 'recovery' – in exactly the way addicts do to save their lives.*

in a global corporation, said to me after a self-awareness exercise, '*I've had feedback for 25 years that I can intimidate people, and I've sort of worn it as a badge of honour. But I've just felt what I do to people, and I never want to do that to a human being ever again*'. Gut wrenching. How could it be that an intelligent person can have 25 years of consistent feedback and not act on it? Easy – her behaviours were (more than) acceptable to her, she got good results, and no one ever complained. Why would she ever have decided to change?

Next is the Psycho Step – we need to engage our psychological selves, first of all to catch ourselves when we are about to slip back into old behaviours, then to give us immediate handy tools to use, and then to rationalise and learn why the 'enlightened' collaborative strategies work. So first we need a knowledge of our own psychological triggers so we can catch ourselves before we are guilty of acting from sheer habit. Second we need some memory triggers or easily actionable frameworks that we can pick up and use in that split second of choice – some handy tools that just get us through the immediate critical 'sliding door' moment. And finally, as the adrenaline subsides and the cortisol starts to dissipate, we engage our rational minds on the logic and sheer common sense of the efficacy of the 'enlightened' strategies. We become more confident in our advocacy, and we enter that wonderfully human domain of proving ourselves right, finding all the data and every available anecdote that conveniently supports our argument, and ignoring and deleting anything that might prove the opposite. I understand when a prospective client asks me to prove in advance that my training programmes work, and I believe more than most I am able to make the direct link between training and improved business KPIs, but I also know that anyone who needs proof in advance that training works will probably turn out to be a 'high maintenance' client. Experience tells me if they start with too high a degree of scepticism, no amount of data will win them over. Clients who 'get it' on the other hand, and who fundamentally trust the whole process, don't need proof, and only ask for data if they have some annoyingly suspicious stakeholder looking over their shoulder.

> We need a knowledge of our own psychological triggers so we can catch ourselves before we are guilty of acting from sheer habit.

Then comes the Socio Step – we need to come together in honest, self-supportive and self-determining groups, to go about our common enterprise – to help each other stay in recovery, and to genuinely collaborate (not compete!) to ensure the enterprise flourishes. We are essentially social animals and although certain of our leaders in the recent past have tried to tell us that there is no such thing as society, the truth is we die if we are alone. The story of Homo Sapiens is a rip-roaring, rollercoaster of a saga, involving war, power, conflict, love, beauty, exploration and death. But it is fundamentally one of social collaboration. We survive in groups. We thrive in groups. We are not built to live solitary, isolated lives. And actually we are not programmed to compete, other than through childhood, as we compete naturally with our siblings to learn survival and relationship skills. We *can* compete, of course, and will most certainly do that when we are threatened. But we've already seen that violent conflict on an organised scale is a very recent factor in the history of our species. There is no doubt that the seven billion of our species currently occupying the planet have some major conflicts going on. But the bottom line is that despite the macro threats we may face, when you zoom in on individual towns and villages, on individual companies and families, you'll find social groups collaborating brilliantly.

We are dependent upon our parents or prime carers for far longer than other animals, realistically until we are at least teenagers (I understand if you've just rolled your eyes at that because you still have a 28-year-old living at home with no real evidence of an ability to look after themselves) and then at whatever age we fly the nest, we go and find other social groups to join. Our need to attach in our formative years is fundamental to our healthy development, both physically and psychologically, and then our need to belong becomes equally important for our sense of self-worth and the development of our emotional intelligence.

The final step – Spirito – cannot be manufactured; we cannot do anything specifically in order to feel spiritual joy, in the same way that it's impossible to plan to be spontaneous. It comes as a result of doing right and it is both a surprising bonus rewarding us for our faith, and an inspiring motivator to continue. We 'decided' to change in order to survive, purely and simply because we just couldn't go on as we were. And we survived. But the thing we never expected is that we would come to thrive; to experience joy. What a surprise; what a delightful bonus! That joy might not be in the form of a promotion, a bonus or an accolade, although it might very well be those things. The joy will come in the form of continual sublime moments of human connection, freedom from the fear of being threatened and controlled by those with power, sincere and heartfelt validation from people we respect, and the sheer pleasure of a profound mastery of our chosen craft.

The Johari Window

I received the wonderful gift of going through two amazing leadership development programmes in my late 20s. The first was the Dale Carnegie 'Management Seminar', which so profoundly affected my attitude and my development, that I was inspired to train to run the course in my spare time. The licence I held for ten years to lead Dale Carnegie training programmes across the world, while all the time running companies, remains one of my proudest achievements. The second programme was a Diploma in Management at Bradford University. It was there that I was taught the Johari Window, a framework I have used in almost every aspect of my work in the 30 years since.

The more I've used it over the years the more I've adapted it for maximum effectiveness in practice, so what I'm describing here is my own accenting of what I feel to be the critical aspects and priorities when using it as a framework and as a guide.

The Johari Window is in my view fundamentally a model of the progression of healthy (and non-codependent) human relationships.

The Johari Window is in my view fundamentally a model of the progression of healthy (and non-codependent) human relationships. As with many things in microcosm, what is true for individuals is also true for organisations, and so my real breakthrough in utilising the model was in understanding how to use it in cultural development. I've heard thousands of managers talk passionately about uncovering and unleashing the potential in people, but then observed them fail in their efforts to do just that, and I've learned that fundamentally this is because they fail to follow what the Johari Window really teaches us about human psychology and human behaviour.

Here's the way I draw the Window (and I've drawn this hundreds of times on flipcharts and whiteboards).

Known to All **OPEN** **(STAGNATION)**	**Observation** **and** **Feedback**	**Unknown to You** **Known to Others** **BLIND** **(SELF-AWARENESS)**
Clarity and **Vulnerability**	**Coaching and** **Experimenting**	
Unknown to Others **Known to You** **HIDDEN** **(TRUST)**	**Unknown to All** **UNKNOWN** **(GROWTH)**	

'Open', 'Hidden', 'Blind' and 'Unknown' are the traditional titles of each section of the Window, and the 'Known/Unknown' headings describe the fundamental state of each.

'Clarity and Vulnerability' is how we move from Open to Hidden; 'Observation and Feedback' is how we move from Hidden to Blind; 'Coaching and Experimentation' is how we move from Blind to Unknown.

Finally, 'Stagnation', 'Trust', 'Self-Awareness' and 'Growth' are the outcomes in each section.

Let's take each section of the Window in turn, since the progression to our desired destination of growth must follow a sequence in order to be effective, sustainable and psychologically safe for all.

Open

The OPEN section is first impressions and early disclosure between us. How we dress, how we hold ourselves, the things we choose to disclose to each other. As our relationship starts, we are already making judgements based on what we see and what we perceive, and many relationships don't progress beyond this most basic stage. This is OK if our relationship ends right here, but it's a problem if we have to work together. If I am guilty of judging you on first impressions or on our earliest encounters and exchanges, I could put you in an unfair 'pigeonhole', one from which it might be very difficult for you to persuade

me to re-classify you in the future. Our highly transactional corporate world means we often deny people
any possible chance to change our minds about
them, and such is the power of expectation in falsely
colouring what we believe to be a truthful version of
events, we frequently get just what we expect from

*Our highly transactional
corporate world means we often
deny people any possible chance
to change our minds about them.*

people, since we unconsciously set it up in that way. I frequently coach clients that in order to 'jump pigeonhole' with their masters, they need to do something dramatic to grab
attention.

Our opportunity in this section, before we appropriately venture out into the others, is to
lay down an honest contract, to give people the best possible chance of making realistic
first impression judgements. This means greeting people warmly but self-confidently; they
are, after all, mere equal human beings, as fabulous and as flawed as we are. I don't
care if they're the President, and by the way even if they are, unless they are narcissists,
they're sick to death of people being nervous and unnatural around them. It's also our
opportunity to state our case – who we are, why we're here and what we have for them. If
we choose however to stay firmly in the OPEN section in our working relationships or linger
too long, the outcome is stagnation. Nothing changes, and while we might believe we are
protecting a seemingly successful status quo, atrophy has already set it.

Hidden

The HIDDEN section is where we've chosen not to disclose things to others. These are
likely to be things that for some reason we are ashamed of or embarrassed about, or
private things that we don't yet feel comfortable in revealing for fear of making ourselves
vulnerable. But it will also include skills and competencies, achievements, and things we
are proud of, but which to share would feel like showing off. The HIDDEN section is
where we start to give and earn trust, and this has two elements to it. The first of these is
vulnerability. If I am not prepared to show vulnerability to you, how will you learn to trust
me? And if I am above you in the hierarchy, making you go first could feel abusive, since
to demur risks displeasing a person with power over you. So as a leader and manager
you *have* to go first. The second critical element of trust is clarity. People trust firm boundaries, clarity of expectation and consistency of message, and most of all in this regard,
they trust people who do what they say. So as a leader and manager you have to be clear
with people on expectations and the rules of engagement. To so many modern managers
this feels like behaving like an autocrat and using the power they've been given, and so
they shy away from directness and from clarity. But when you have power over another
human being, trying to pretend that you don't is neither effective nor caring. The trick is
to demonstrate that you are utterly trustworthy with the power you hold and that you will
never, ever abuse it. And the best way to do that is to give it away to the very people you
have power over, but more of that later. People feel safe when they know the expectations
and the boundaries. They feel unsafe when they don't and an unwillingness to be direct
is not noble, it is cowardly.

As we see trust growing, we can of course start inviting the other person to disclose more to us through our coaching and our genuine care for them. Remember, people need huge amounts of encouragement, licence and permission to disclose what they feel to be weaknesses. And every time they reveal something to us that was previously hidden, we demonstrate our trustworthiness in the way we accept them. In the therapeutic relationship this is called Unconditional Positive Regard and as leaders and managers we have to bring this fundamental state of mind and our profound belief in the goodness and potential of every human being into our relationships. It is in this section that we get our first glimpses of the extraordinary talents in people, and where we start the journey with them whereby they grow their confidence in their work and in themselves. In the process we teach them that genuine care for others does not mean rescuing, but inspiring.

Blind

Okay, so we've come through the emotional connection piece. We're trusted and we've started to experience the joy of developing meaningful relationships with other people committed to pursuing a common cause. But now we come to the tricky part – the part where we will say to ourselves, 'oh why can't it all just be plain sailing? Why do people have to have flaws?!' The reality is human beings are flawed – yes they are *brilliant, gorgeous, talented and fabulous*' (Williamson 1992) but they are also weak, messy and imperfect. The flaws they are aware of will come out in the Hidden section, and we can either choose to accept them as part of who they are, or we can choose to work with them to modify or even eradicate those flaws. But what about the flaws that people seem stubbornly to ignore; that they are not even aware that they have; that are in fact Blind to them. Who is going to tell them, since someone must if they are to progress? Well that would be us – their leader, their manager, their coach – so it's a good job we've earned their trust. Giving someone feedback on a behaviour, habit or trait that they are unaware of is a great gift, even though they might well reject it when first offered. This type of feedback must be given as an observation first, ie not as a judgement, but it can then be followed up with advice if appropriate, or indeed if requested. A great way to show people the potential consequences of their flaw is, rather than being threatening, to express your worry for them if they do not address the issue.

Giving tough feedback is hard and it is so tempting to avoid it, but it is neither caring nor respectful to do so. I have flirted many times with retreating to the comfort of not going through with feedback, but I believe that one of the prime characteristics that has made me successful as a leader is my willingness to push through this discomfort and deliver the feedback with the greatest amount of love and respect I can muster. Many times I've had someone say to me, in deep gratitude, that no one has ever given them such profoundly valuable feedback before. My late, great friend Aidan Halligan, to my astonishment called the feedback I gave him the greatest act of kindness anyone had showed him in four years at the Department of Health. I had told him very bluntly that he was wearing his 'Maverick' reputation as a badge of honour rather than taking responsibility for the fact it was causing his peers and colleagues to side-line him and ignore him. I told him he was getting in his own way and allowing his greatness and thus his effectiveness to be neutered. I felt awful giving him the feedback, but he was right in one thing – it was indeed an act of love.

I've majored on flaws so far in the Blind section, but people also have amazing latent talents. The talents they wish to acknowledge will have come out in the Hidden section, but those they are genuinely unaware of, or that have been battered and buried by critical parents or by fear-based workplaces, will be unknown to them. They may have come to believe that they do not have any talents other than their employed specialism, and that is not just depressing but profoundly wasteful. So as we develop a meaningful relationship with another human being, surely one of our greatest responsibilities to them is to look for, spot and then comment upon the talents we see in them. Surely the greatest gift is to believe in someone, to a greater level than they believe in themselves. As a leader and manager, how much of your time and energy and focus do you put into this with each one of your team?

They may have come to believe that they do not have any talents other than their employed specialism, and that is not just depressing but profoundly wasteful.

Unknown

And so we finally arrive at the most sublime place imaginable – the Holy Grail of every organisation, let alone our most profound personal relationships. Unknown is a truly magical place where we uncover our potential, our creativity, our unique brilliance, maybe even our unique purpose, not in isolation but in community, as we journey together in a common enterprise. But notice how offensive Unknown is to some managers – how unacceptable it is in most corporate cultures to say 'I don't know'. The state of not knowing scares many managers to death.

We enter Unknown through a simple gateway – trying things out. The most inspiring leaders frequently exhort their followers to 'go try'. They have of course first built a solid foundation of psychological safety, since people will only experiment if they know they're safe to fail. And it is in Unknown that our coaching really comes into its own, constantly and carefully nurturing an environment for people to take personal responsibility, setting their own goals, monitoring their own performance and correcting their own methods and strategies. All we have to do is to keep believing in them, not passively but actively, with encouragement, challenge, feedback, coaching and recognition. In Unknown, we can really start to have fun with each other, as we explore the myriad ways of being creative – rehearsal, role play, modelling, even involving our stakeholders in our games. Customers adore playing, as do shareholders.

With human beings, there's always more to come, Not in terms of effort, but in terms of creativity and ingenuity. The lazy manager simply drives people harder. The caring manager is on constant watch to coach. Which is your predominant mode?

Notes

Goleman, D (1996) *Emotional Intelligence: Why It can Matter more than IQ.* London: Bloomsbury Publishing.

Biopsychosocial Model The biopsychosocial model attributes disease outcome to the intricate, variable interaction of biological factors (genetic, biochemical, etc), psychological factors (mood, personality, behaviour, etc) and social factors (cultural, familial, socioeconomic, medical, etc).

Johari Window The Johari window was created by psychologists Joseph Luft and Harrington Ingham in 1955. Luft and Ingham called their Johari Window model 'Johari' after combining their first names, Joe and Harrington. The Johari window is a technique that helps people better understand their relationship with themselves and others. It is used primarily in self-help groups and corporate settings as a heuristic exercise.

Dale Carnegie Dale Carnegie was an American writer and lecturer and the developer of famous courses in self-improvement, salesmanship, corporate training, public speaking, and interpersonal skills. He was the author of *How to win Friends and Influence People*, a bestseller that was voted 'Business book of the Twentieth Century'.

Carl Rogers Carl Rogers was an American psychologist, widely considered to be one of the founding fathers of psychotherapy research. He was honoured for his pioneering research with the Award for Distinguished Scientific Contributions by the American Psychological Association in 1956. Rogers coined the term 'unconditional positive regard' in the context of the relationship between therapist and client.

Marianne Williamson 'Our Deepest Fear' is a 1992 poem from *A Return to Love: Reflections on the Principles of a Course in Miracles,* Harper Thorsons; Thorsons Classics edition (31 December 2015).

Aidan Halligan Referenced in Chapter 1.

Additional Acknowledgement

While I've not quoted directly from the following book, the contents were useful in helping me shape and synthesise my thinking on the links between EQ and CEQ.

Caruso, D and Salovey, P (2004) *The Emotionally Intelligent Manager: How to Develop and Use the Four Key Emotional Skills of Leadership.* New York: John Wiley & Sons.

Chapter 10

Pillar 1

Awareness of Our Unconscious Controlling Habits – OUCH!

We know we're not Brilliant, but we Think we're OK

The biggest single obstacle to our changing anything about how we behave at work is our complete lack of awareness of our controlling habits. Why would we change if we already think we're doing the right things? When I ask managers how good a Coach they are, the typical answer will go something like this.

How good a Coach am I? Well, I could be better, and I'm sure I don't coach enough, and maybe don't coach when I should be coaching, but I do coach my guys. Don't get me wrong, I really do want to learn how to be a better Coach, but I think I'm doing OK . . .

It sounds like an honest self-assessment; we might even say that it signals a high level of self-awareness. The problem is twofold. First, it's hardly a state of expediency to change – no burning platform there, and so the development of coaching skills gets filed in the 'good thing to do when things have settled down a bit' section of our diary planning. Even when our boss or our HRBP organises coaching training for us, we're still quite likely to try to duck out on the day if 'real life' is simply too busy or important or pressured for us. Unless the development of coaching skills is seen as essential, why would anyone invest precious time in training?

But the second aspect of the problem is even more serious, because it is highly likely that the part of the response that says 'I do coach my guys' is actually not true. It's not that the person is wilfully lying, it's that they are conveniently deluded. The reality is that when they believe they are coaching, they are either in fact teaching or they are manipulating their team member into coming to the 'right' solution.

It's not hyperbole to say that most managers who go through my Coaching Excellence training programme, having held the typical belief about themselves as Coaches prior to the training, realise that they've probably never coached anyone, no matter how many years they've been managing people.

The bizarre thing is that we know what coaching is and we know how to do it. Whenever I ask a group of managers what the purpose of coaching is, they always respond with slight variations on '*developing people, bringing out people's potential, raising performance etc*'. And whenever I ask what the prime skills we need to be good Coaches are, they always come up with listening and asking great questions. So we know what coaching is and we know how to do it. The problem is we're not doing it, but we think we are. This is the fundamental re-calibration we need before anything significant can change.

By the way, teaching people things is a valid and essential activity for a manager to engage in. I simply urge managers to know the difference, and if they are consciously choosing to drop into 'teacher' mode, to do it clearly, proudly and gloriously. But teaching is not coaching. Teaching is teaching. The real culprit is manipulation – we kid ourselves that we're coaching, when we are actually manipulating the other person to come to our solution. This has become a great skill in the millions strong cohort of managers across the world.

So we have to 'feel' ourselves dropping into these manipulative habits in order for us to have the opportunity to change our behaviour. We have to experience an OUCH! Welcome to Our Unconscious Controlling Habits.

We know our bad Habits

The merest tweak of our amygdala makes us feel out of control. Every fibre in our body that is involved in the goal to survive is focussed on getting back in control, either of ourselves, since we are suddenly demonstrating insecurity, which we abhor and will do anything to mask, or of the other person if they are either the reason the 'threat' situation has arisen or the obstacle in our way (or both). Since our fear has projected certain catastrophe unless we take action, we don't care if we abuse or hurt or threaten the other person in that moment. In fact a small part of us says they 'deserve' to be punished, and will not learn unless they are.

We know our bad habits, but we don't know the cure. On commencing a coaching training programme, with delegates still fresh into the room and still with that air of *'what's this going to be about?, don't they know how busy I am?, couldn't this have waited for a few*

'what is your worst habit as a Manager when you are under pressure?'.

months?' around them, I ask them to be open and honest about a habit they have as a manager that they are not proud of or that they dislike about themselves and that they would therefore like to cure. I ask them the question 'what is your worst habit as a Manager when you are under pressure?'.

What would your answer be?

And out pours the honesty. I write them up on a flipchart and these then stay with us through the programme to keep us both focussed and honest. Of the many hundreds I've collected over the years, here are a small sample. I have not chosen these because they are the worst, but because of the sheer poetry and self-knowledge of their expression.

'I get frustrated when things go wrong, going from standstill to red hot in the blink of an eye an eye.'

'I expect my team to be mindreaders, then I get frustrated when it's clear they've not grasped the situation.'

'I let people off the hook then I use wit/sarcasm when things get in a pickle.'

'I look for data as the answer to everything; people around me are idiots for not seeing it.'

'I pass pressure to go faster; then get angry and annoyed and swear.'

'I do my 5-step dance – Judge/ Close Mind/ Dictate/ Patronise/ Resent – I become a
  Pompous/ Super Hero/ Dictator.'

'I go dictatorial and just tell people the answer; I won't listen to inputs and then I see
  people closing down around me.'

'I can be a poisonous monkey when no one can do a thing right; I make people duck.'

'When I'm mad I go quiet and I'm the only person I need; I do it myself.'

'I become focussed and selfish; I involve lots of people and ignore their workloads.'

See how well people know themselves? The honesty is always stunning.

What we Notice when we're Paying Attention

At the end of the exercise I ask people what they noticed as their colleagues were fessing
up to their worst habits. They usually notice the following.

- There was a lot of laughter through the discussion.

- People knew their bad habits really, really well.

- There were lots of similarities and common themes.

- People actually started to exhibit the very habits they were recalling, even as they
  spoke about them.

- There were some very interesting hand gestures.

- They wanted to 'fix' each other by suggesting what they should do.

- They wanted to make each other feel better by justifying the bad habits.

- They knew what they *should* do instead.

- They were well aware of the negative impact on their team members.

So people notice a lot, although they invariably miss two important dynamics, which I
always have to point out to them (and even then they struggle to identify them as actually
having been present) and which I will explain below.

Let's explore each of these in a little detail.

Laughter Through the Discussion

Why on earth does discussing something so bad make people laugh, when really if anything it should make them cry? First of all there's the immediate identification. It's the first
rule of stand-up comedy – give your audience something to identify with. It's the knowing
smile that says 'I do that too; that happens to me'. Secondly if we really did engage with
the emotions that are evoked as we fess up, we'd end up feeling depressed, and corporate cultures cannot handle 'negative' and 'unhelpful' emotions. Depressed people are

not effective! So much more comfortable if we can salve our consciences by colluding with each other to find it amusing rather than abhorrent.

People know Their bad Habits Really, Really well

No one struggles with this question. While we may never give conscious consideration to what our worst habits are, for fear that we'd really *have* to change then, the fact is that we know. We know because we're doing it all the time, and having to suppress, deny even, the emotions that come up for us as we are acting out our worst habits. So while it's not uncommon for the first answer to the question to be less than the whole of the truth (people often send a little 'scout' answer out first, just to check the lay of the land and assess whether it's safe to confess the worst), it's not hard to dig for the truth. These things are our constant companions; we live with them every day. Of course we know what our worst habits are. Interestingly, once the 'scouts' have been recalled, people enter into the discussion with alacrity, confessing to their worst excesses often with a competitively zealous *'you think that's bad, you wait until you hear what I do to people!'* I often have to intervene in a discussion and remind them that the object of the exercise is not to find *the* worst.

There are lots of Similarities and Common Themes

Fundamentally, under pressure, managers will either be over aggressive or over passive.

Fundamentally, under pressure, managers will either be over aggressive or over passive. After all, they're in 'fight or flight' – 'fight' means aggression, and 'flight' means withdrawal. 'Fight' says *'you haven't done what you should have done; I am not going to do it for you; you will now do what you should have done before, and you will do it now!'* or words and nonverbals to that effect. However much we try and mask our impatience, our irritation and our frustration, it will be felt as an attack, which of course it is. The aggressive energy will be received. I am your threat and, surprise surprise, you are now in 'fight or flight' too. Your primal instinct will weigh up the odds in a split second, judge 'fight' to end in near certain death, so 'flight' kicks in (or 'freeze' as we've seen in earlier chapters). What is the easiest way to activate 'flight'? Just comply. It's all the manager wants at that moment. Blind compliance. Just say yes, get the threat situation with over as quickly as possible, and then worry about how you're going to deliver what you've just committed, even if you know it is not possible. How many times have you said yes to something knowing you can't deliver, instantly regretting your weakness, and asking yourself why you continue to do it? Actually of course what you will immediately do is use all your creative energy on coming up with incredibly plausible reasons (excuses) as to why you've been unable to do what you committed to do, and here is the damage and sheer inefficiency we create in a nutshell.

'Flight' says *'you haven't done what you should have done; now give it to me, go away, leave me alone, I'll do it myself'*. Once again I am your threat and I put you into 'fight or flight' but at least the threat passes quickly and you don't end up having to make commitments you can't keep. You are in fact completely off the hook. It's a shitty feeling of course, and leaves you metaphorically twiddling your thumbs until I deign to come back to you with the solution beautifully gift wrapped.

It's horrible working for a manager who allows their over-aggression to get the better of them, but it's equally horrible working for the opposite type. Under a serial over-aggressor, I will learn to become invisible, and if I am caught out, to pass the aggression onto others, through picking on people below me in the food chain, and I will learn to work out well in advance who I can blame if I come under attack, so that I can deflect that attack onto others. I will learn that I have to be a bully myself.

Under a serial over-pacifist, I will learn to get my manager to do the critical (whatever 'critical' means to my manager) parts of the work early in the process, and I will learn to check everything with them to ensure they are completely happy at every stage. I will learn that I am stupid and cannot do anything on my own initiative.

Notice that although our choice of which mode to invoke is mostly situational, we do have preferences, driven by our psychometric profile. For example, I am a natural over-aggressor. I'm a high Red personality type, and ENTJ, and so my natural instinct is to fight; in fact I quite enjoy having an excuse to have one. It just feels wrong in my body to withdraw – against my instincts. '*Let me tell you what you need to do . . .*' is the exhortation of the over-aggressor.

Some of us, on the other hand, are naturally over-passive. That does not mean cowardice or abdicating responsibility, it simply means we'll withdraw rather than confront. '*Leave it with me*' is the lament of the over-pacifist. So the high Blue or Green personality type, or the ISFP type, is more naturally inclined to do the work themselves, since that more naturally constitutes control for them. If I do it myself, I know it's done, and what's more I know it's done to the exact quality and standard required. Over-pacifists are not natural delegators!

People Exhibit the very Habits they are Recalling, even as they Speak about them

As we've seen earlier, our brains cannot really distinguish between types of threat. Yesteryear's threat of death or mortal wounding from a predator; today's threat of judgement from someone above us in the food chain at work – it's all the same to our simpleton of a brain. Adrenaline and cortisol are not precious, only deigning to be released if it's worth their while – if only our brains had so evolved. We've not developed an instant arbiter, since it would just be too risky; even a second of delayed reaction might mean death, or so our primitive brain judges, so let's react first and ask questions later. We might look stupid but at least we'll be alive. Worst case of course is that someone else is damaged, and that's unfortunate, but what's a mere mortal in survival mode meant to do? After all it's a dog eat dog world, and the survival of the fittest and all that, and so they should have been looking out for themselves better. Our corporate gene pool is the stronger without them . . .

Our brains can so easily be fooled into believing a threat is abroad. In fact all we have to do is relive a stressful experience, and our amygdala is tweaked. So even as our colleagues were merely talking about their worst habit, their amygdalas were activated, the circuit breaker to their neocortex was switched off, adrenaline and cortisol were released, and suddenly the whole physiological change pitches up right in front of our eyes. We see our colleagues flush and maybe even sweat, we see the veins in their neck or temples stand proud, we hear their voice tone change, we see their hands fly about or wrap themselves up. The person who not two minutes ago was exuding calmness and self-control, is a mess. And it is quite beautiful to observe because it is so authentic.

It is the very dynamic of the brain being so easily fooled that makes this exercise so powerful for people, because even though they're in a classroom, it is suddenly feels so real. All training should simulate the pressure of real life situations, and this is one way to contribute to building that environment.

People use very Interesting hand Gestures

Because people literally re-live the physiological experience of how they behave under pressure, their nonverbal communication goes into overdrive. The over aggressors' hands fly about the place, with demented karate chopping, finger pointing and clicking, and desk hitting. There may even be self-abuse, since they can't strike you. They are in fight mode, remember, with just enough blood left in their pre-frontal cortex to tell themselves that they cannot strike or shout at people. But while they can just about control their mouths, their bodies will betray them. The brain says *'since I can't strike you, I'll strike myself by slapping my hands together, or I'll strike an object'*. Even in those over aggressors who've worked hard to 'hide' their impatience, irritation and frustration, the little taps of their fingers will betray their restrained aggression. I've seen some over aggressors work so well to control their hand movements, only for their heads and necks to do the metaphorical striking. When I see this I'm always reminded of the *Not the Nine O'Clock News* team's punk parody 'Headbanger', which has a wonderful line: *'I'm a headbanger, headbanger yeah, I like to bang my head; and one day when my head falls off, I'll bang my neck instead'*.

And since they cannot shout, their clicking of their fingers will scream at you to go faster. Or their tone of voice will change, adding both decibels and percussion. I know I'm de-scribing these behaviours as rather cartoon-like, but if that helps you to be more obser-vant ... all this rich information is right there in front of our eyes, but we have become blind to it.

The over-pacifists on the other hand will do something entirely different with their hands. They might put the flat of their hand up with palm towards you in a defensive gesture. They might cuddle themselves. They will certainly withdraw their eye contact, and their atten-tion. Everything about their nonverbal communication screams 'go away, leave me alone'. They won't be saying much, if anything at all, because they are deep in thought, almost as if they've gone into a trance. If they do speak it will more likely be aimed at themselves and not you (most confusing). The fact is they've already mentally withdrawn, and they may even appear surprised that you're still there when they finally 'come round'.

People want to 'fix' People

Although I exhort people to stick to the question, specifically asking them not to go into solutions, it seems physically impossible for people to resist fixing. After all it is what we do every day. We are serial problem solvers, and so, when presented with a problem, our natural instinct is to fix it. Since our brains get a big hit of dopamine from solving a puzzle, or anything that yields a sense of achievement, it's no wonder we become addicted to it. Dopamine is a neurotransmitter that helps control the brain's reward and pleasure centres. It also enables us not only to see rewards, but to take action to move towards them. Adrenaline is addictive because it gives us such a rush, making us feel superhuman, but dopamine is the real killer addiction. Adrenaline may be our alcohol, but dopamine is pure crack cocaine. So when I point out to people that they've slipped into fixing mode, they smile at me, because they hadn't noticed. Two minutes later I'll be having to point it out to them again, and they'll smile some more. They think they can humour me, poor things.

It's our addiction to dopamine that causes us to problem solve rather than coach. It's the dopamine that makes us immediately ask the closed question to get immediately to the solution, like we're involved in some private competition to see how fast we can crack the puzzle that is eluding our poor unfortunate subordinates. There's a lovely scene in the very first series of *Prime Suspect*, where the DI (not Jane Tennyson of course) does everything in his power to break the station's record of time elapsed between a body being found and a murder suspect being charged – he gets it down to 14 hours, and there are high fives all round followed by some drinking of beer. (Of course the team have got the wrong man, but who cares?)

It's not that we need to wean ourselves off dopamine – I'm not advocating that we all become monks or humanitarian aid workers or pig farmers or tree surgeons. It's that we need to get our dopamine from a different source – we need organic dopamine from the Farm Food Shop (an ethical purpose and respect for each other), not the dopamine from the Organised Crime Dealer (hitting short-term arbitrary targets and abusing each other in the process).

People want to make People feel Better

If I feel completely safe to expose my flaws, my darkest and most shameful habits, then I am less likely to slip back into self-justification. But my defence mechanisms and my bullet proof denial may seduce me without my noticing. My defence will start gently with a *'of course I'm only talking about rare exceptions, I certainly don't do this very often . . .'.* But the defence of infrequency still leaves me open to being found guilty, so now I need to move into full blown justification, which will sound something like this:

Of course, the issue is that if I don't demonstrate a bit of urgency, the job doesn't get done, and no one benefits from that, and besides I believe people learn valuable lessons from tough situations, so realistically I need to behave in this way on occasions, after all if I try and be Mother Teresa at all times, no one would either believe me or respect me, and frankly we'd all be up shit creek!

Notice how eloquently I can move into total, impermeable justifiability. Why would I ever take a risk in changing, if I can convince myself and everyone around me that I have to behave in this way to be a good and effective manager? And by the way, be honest and tell me that I had started to convince even you, dear reader, as you got further along that sentence, it is so powerfully plausible.

> *Notice how eloquently I can move into total, impermeable justifiability.*

And as I slip into defence and justification, my colleagues notice that we're all starting to feel better – nodding sagely to each other like some modern-day Statler and Waldorf. A few seconds ago a chasm was opening up as we were all about to agree that we really did have to change the way we behave. But thankfully one of us has brought us to our senses. Phew, that was close.

And even if as an individual I am able to control myself and stay with my own flaws and frailties, in all their rich and authentic honesty, it will prove too much for someone in the group, and they will step in, uninvited of course, to tell me why I am justified in my behaviour. This is not for my benefit of course, although it is presented as such, to the extent where I notice some sense of gratitude to them. No, it is entirely self-serving, since their own fear and insecurity will not allow the group to go off in any 'enlightened' (naive in their book) direction. This isn't a therapy session (actually it is of course) – we're in a dog eat dog world and it's the survival of the fittest, and if we employ wimps who can't take the merest hint of urgency and accountability, then we're better off without them. And it is sooooooooo tempting to side with them, for then we could stop this and go back under our warm, safe duvet of denial. Yet it doesn't feel right to agree with them. So we don't. But neither do we disagree – ah, Edmund Burke's good men and women doing nothing.

People know what they Should do Instead

Rarely, having confessed, are people left bereft of alternative strategies. They will tell themselves and each other precisely what they should do in those moments of bridled adrenaline. They will tell each other willingly and without a trace of clumsiness that they should stay calm, ask some open questions, really listen to people's inputs, value them, maybe give them some clear feedback and re-direction . . . basically respect them and treat them like the beautiful, flawed geniuses that they are. They should Coach them.

They know this, and yet they don't do it. So clearly this is not an intellectual battle. We know what we *should* do, but in the moment of pressure the calm strategies for coaching are simply unavailable to us. They've disappeared from the tool kit.

> *Our problem is that we have an unshakeable belief that coaching takes longer; far longer; too long.*

Our problem is that we have an unshakeable belief that coaching takes longer; *far* longer; *too* long. Coaching is only therefore relevant when we have lots of time and when things are not urgent. Oh, and when would that be then?

Knowing what we should do is simply not enough to motivate us to make any change at all, and since we are surviving, maybe even high-achieving, despite (or, denial here, *because of*)

our worst habits, then change would be too risky anyway. So let's plough on as we are, gently (and not dishonestly) striving to make some small behavioural changes along the way. After all we can't return to our team and be radically different, since they'd all think we've gone mad, or they'd lose respect for us since clearly we've picked up some new-fangled ideas from a book, or a course, or a so-called guru who's never run a business. Besides we never got around to telling them we're on a training course. Training courses are for wimps!

People are well Aware of the Negative Impact on Their team Members

When asked to (for 'asked' read facilitated, encouraged, forced, pushed, given permission to, given licence to) consider their worst habits, the inevitable question arises after some reflection: so what? So we raise our voice a bit, get a bit angsty, a bit stressy, and maybe we do go into problem-solving mode too quickly, and become a bit of a pain-in-the-backside checker – so what? No one died, no one is even complaining, plus this is business, we're not a charity, and we pay people well, oh and we're getting the job done. Powerful voices of well-practised denial. But the truth is we are well aware of the negative impact on people, but we just cannot allow ourselves to engage with that awareness. It's the dynamic that allows a caring nurse to walk past a patient in distress. We are well aware that we cause people to freeze like rabbits in the headlights, that we confuse people, that they often have to guess what we want, that we take over, leaving them feeling mistrusted, anxious, nervous, on-edge, scared even; frustrated, exasperated, angry even. And we are all too aware that we cause them to become guarded in their actions, unwilling to really use their initiative or experiment or take risks, even to tell us things for fear of our reaction. We do know what we reap. But we have to play it down, and in order to play it down, we have to blame them for not being good enough. If they just learned to do what they should have done in the first place, none of this would have to happen.

And this is the potentially hopeless dynamic at the heart of so much corporate woe. Good people knowing that what they are doing is wrong, knowing what they should do instead, but genuinely feeling incapable or just too fearful of doing it.

We know that at the very moment of greatest opportunity for us to have a team member grow in front of us, our behaviours cause them to shrink. Just when we need people to be at their most creative, courageous and fabulous, our behaviour causes them to be defensive, tentative and completely ordinary. In a situation where we most need their extraordinary latent potential to be unleashed on the world, our behaviour causes them to bring out only tried and trusted strategies. In a moment of greatest learning potential, when they could be learning the wonderfully positive lesson of how best to raise their performance, with all the added bo-

> *Just when we need people to be at their most creative, courageous and fabulous, our behaviour causes them to be defensive, tentative and completely ordinary.*

nuses of reinforcing that learning for future accessing, our behaviour cements the negative learning of simply how to survive. Instead of leaving them learning that they *are* the solution, we leave them learning that they are, in fact, the problem.

How dare we.

The two Unconscious Habits no one ever Notices

And so to the two dynamics that groups never notice from the worst habits discussion:

First the habitual misuse of the personal pronoun – people frequently use the word 'you' in their descriptions rather than the word 'I'. So (remembering that they are answering the question 'what is your worst habit as a manager when you are under pressure?') for example I'll hear someone say *'you get impatient and then you find yourself not listening and you take over and either do it yourself or you just tell the other person what to do'*. They're clearly talking about themselves yet studiously avoiding using the correct personal pronoun. It's as if they're speaking on our collective behalf. Frequently, and I always think a little comically, I often hear people's colleagues punctuate their 'vestra culpa' remarks with *'yes, you do, don't you . . .'*-style approbations.

The misuse of the personal pronoun has become one of the most common habits – it's a classic dissociation from a state of discomfort. When I describe my faults in the second or third person, I am emotionally safeguarded from feeling the ensuing guilt or shame; and since the people I'm talking to are empathising with me, actually tacitly confessing that they are equally guilty, no one notices that I am avoiding taking personality responsibility, because it *sounds* as though I am.

If that person used the correct personal pronoun 'I', notice how it would now sound and feel the difference: *'I get impatient and then I find myself not listening and I take over and either do it myself or I just tell the other person what to do'*. How powerful it is, when people truly own their own stuff, and how much harder to avoid taking responsibility. If I use 'you' then I anaesthetise myself from feeling what I need to feel in order to make a change. The moment I switch and use 'I', my emotions can do their work. My actively changing something is of course not guaranteed, but it's sure never going to happen if I'm not owning it. Notice by the way that not *one* of the examples listed above uses the incorrect personal pronoun, which is partly why they are so beautiful to read.

This is the very same reason by the way that we ask questions using the pronoun 'we' when we really mean 'you'. When we ask, 'so what are *we* going to do about that?' we actually mean 'what are *you* going to do about that', but it feels too direct, so we soften it. No wonder people end up confused.

The second dynamic people never notice is how we habitually soften the otherwise stark nature of our faults. Let's say the truth is this:

My worst habit as a manager when I am under pressure is that I get impatient, I stop listening to people and I just tell them what to do.

Beautiful – clear, honest, authentic. Here's how it might sound if I were softening:

My worst habit as a manager when I am under pressure is that I almost get a bit impatient, not that I show it of course, and then it's not like I stop listening, but I guess I'm not taking everything they're saying in, and then I sort of tell them what to do, well it's more of

a suggestion probably, but it's almost as if I'm giving them orders, not that I'm aggressive or anything . . .

Oh well, that's clear then, no problem really. The number of times I hear people say that they 'almost, probably, sort of' do things is amazing. Again, notice that if I express my faults in the latter format, what I'm really doing is excusing myself and giving myself licence to carry on.

If we know our bad Habits, why don't we just stop?

Our defence mechanisms against having to change these habits are very powerful. First, we believe that we need a huge amount of *time* to change. Second, we fool ourselves into thinking that we will *get* that time when the world settles down a bit. In the meantime, our people get used to our ways and seem to forgive us for them, thus reducing the imperative for us to change.

The biggest problem, however, is that we simply do not know how to change our behaviour when we are feeling pressured and *still* get the job done. And since experience has taught us not to try new 'enlightened' methods when things are too critical for any element of experimentation, and it's easy to see that we are locked into a world of unchanging behaviours. So we tell ourselves that all we can do is work harder and longer, trying to control more things, and this therefore becomes completely cultural. The vicious downward spiral continues – we get more frustrated and so do our people. We blame them and they blame us, and when they can't blame us, they blame others outside of their control. And in that dynamic, *no one* is going to change.

The good news for managers is that the sort of habits listed above are not the problem. In fact, while I would never encourage anyone to be proud of such behaviours, I also exhort people not to be scared of them, since they are symptoms of their environment and their conditioned unconscious learning. Habits they may be, but they can be quickly unlearned. And they are arguably authentic, since they are only invoked due to the frustration that comes from wanting things to be right. Why would I want to neuter the fundamental passion behind the mission, or to have people become clones of some spurious perfect manager? As we've seen in Chapter 2, so much of modern leadership development is about seeking to change these behaviours without giving managers the fundamental psychological understanding of what is causing them. And thus all the training really does is help managers manufacture inauthentic strategies. Oh, and feel more guilty.

Our Unconscious Controlling Habits – OUCH!

I think perhaps the most profound personal learning from my time in the corporate world is my 'discovery' of our unconscious controlling habits – the things we do to wrest back control from situations of 'threat', when that threat remember is not real, but a product of the corporate environment.

And here are the *real* culprits – Our Unconscious Controlling Habits – OUCH:

We ask closed questions.
  (like machine gun fire!)
We fill silences.
  (anything over a few nanoseconds with so much cortisol banging around)
We answer our own questions.
  (if we waited for them *for goodness sake . . .)*
We let people answer a different question.
  (we can't be rude, and besides we probably didn't notice anyway)
We make statements.
  (since they are clearly lacking motivation, our words will inspire them)
We give multiple inputs.
  (it's quicker to dump out a stream of consciousness, it being so valuable)
We use 'we' instead of 'you'.
  (we want to be inclusive and we are scared of being direct)
We issue instructions.
  (tell me, explain to me, take me through your thinking . . .)
We interrupt and talk over people.
  (only if what they're saying is nonsense of course . . .)
We finish people's sentences for them.
  (well we knew what they were saying, but they were taking forever . . .)

On the surface these might seem completely innocuous. So we interrupt people, or talk over them or finish their sentences. This may seem like a small thing, but it is abusive. When we're doing it, it doesn't feel like an act of abuse and it certainly is not intended to be disrespectful. And yet it is both. We act in that way solely to gain control of the moment; to gain dominion over the other person and thus over the situation; to have the other person comply with our energy and our direction. If the other person is acting in a way that makes us feel that they are not under our control, our fight or flight really kicks in. Flight says shut down, withdraw and then do it yourself. We don't interrupt someone if we're in flight mode – we'll simply stop engaging. Fight says batter them into submission. We'll definitely interrupt, and we'll talk over them with increasing volume if we're in fight mode. If you still don't believe that interrupting someone is abusive and disrespectful, see how you feel the next time someone does it to you.

These are the habits that actually get in our way, and that cause us to behave in ways that create that downward spiral.

These habits are unconscious – we have become unaware that we are doing it. And habits are universal – I've met thousands of managers across the entire globe, and I haven't met one yet that doesn't suffer from these when they're under pressure. It doesn't matter what language, culture, faith, values, childhood upbringing or any other variable – put a manager from anywhere in the world under pressure and out will spill these unconscious controlling habits. They are utterly predictable; and my experience is that managers adopt them within minutes of taking up their responsibilities, firstly because they've had such consistent role models, and secondly because frankly what's the point of being a manager if you can't exercise power and authority over others?

And these habits are all about control – the instant we experience the merest sensation of being out of control, our basic neuroscience takes over, exacerbated as it's been through a poundingly repetitive conditioning, and we drop into one, or all, of the habits listed above.

Who taught us to behave in these ways? When in your management career did someone take you to one side and teach you to ask so many closed questions? These habits are inevitable and predictable, arising solely from our threat responses. They are tolerated and therefore nurtured, due to a lack of feedback from those we are managing, or at least a lack of feedback that actually has an impact upon us. And they are tolerated and nurtured because they work, and that's always going to win the Darwinian argument. Well, they work in that they give us an immediate sense of being back in control, and in the sense that they get the job done – the immediate task anyway. So why wouldn't we simply carry on? We get immediate relief (positive feedback to keep doing it) and the task is completed, when it was in severe danger of not being so. These are powerful reasons to keep doing what we're doing. So we get enormous amounts of practice, and so we get really, really good at them!

And then some new-age 'expert', who's never actually had to run a business, comes along with their 'enlightened' ideas, and exhorts us to change our ways for the better. And of course we understand the ways of enlightenment, for who can argue that they sound so plausible and moral and even intellectually credible. But we are firm in our absolute knowledge that they don't work. Or they don't work in isolation. Or they might well work, but we don't have time to put the world on hold while we 'coach' mediocre solutions out of people who now believe that we've gone soft on them, so they'll probably get lazier. Truly the forces against profound change are immensely powerful.

This is why the self-awareness piece has to be truly gut wrenching.

Our bad habits are not the cause, they are the symptom, and the more we try and control them, the more frustrated we become. However, when shown the underlying habits of our behaviour under pressure, things we were simply unaware we were doing, the light goes on. We become aware, and with awareness come true choice. Now we can put *new* habits in their place; things as simple as asking open questions one at a time, allowing people a few seconds to think and respond, asking a question again if the person does not answer first time around and not accepting that they 'don't know' the answer.

Simplifying it down further, the three main Unconscious Controlling Habits are:

1. **closed questions;**

2. **filling silences;**

3. **giving multiple inputs.**

Closed Questions

So we ask lots of closed questions. What's the problem with that? Well the problem is that closed questions have become our prime controlling tool. Notice how rarely you are asked a closed question without the other person telegraphing what the right answer is through their tone of voice. Closed questions feign curiosity, but they are not curious – we don't ask '*are you going to talk to X?*' because we're curious, we ask because we think that's the solution, and our question betrays that. The person we are asking will know what we think, will feel controlled and will most likely give a defensive answer (since they are under attack).

Closed questions have become our prime controlling tool.

Even when we are asking from curiosity, the closed question contains a controlling energy. We ask because we're checking up. This time the question will come out as '*have you spoken to X?*' My brain has come up with a solution, and immediately needs to check – not for your benefit, but so that my brain knows where to go next in the flowchart approach it's adopted to solving *your* problem. Just listen to the insanity of this question – here we have in front of us a beautiful flawed genius of a person, with huge untapped potential, who owns this problem (both getting paid to solve it and wanting to enjoy the satisfaction of solving it) and who has had this problem for a while, therefore is highly likely to have tried all the obvious things. And then we come along, consider the problem for 20 seconds and come out with a lazy and fatuous closed question, like '*have you spoken to X?*' Is that really the best we've got? Oh how I wish people would be brutally honest in their responses, because if they were it would likely sound like this – (angry voice) '*have I spoken to X? What do you think I've been doing? How stupid do you think I am? Of course I've spoken to X!*' But we're never really presented with the consequences of our laziness, so we never learn. But, again, a defensive answer will be initiated even if the other person is skilled at hiding their defensiveness – which they are of course because they get a lot of practice!

And finally, closed questions layer on guilt and shame. We've become experts at delivering both solutions and feedback all in one. Brilliant! In this example, the closed question would come out as '*do you think you need to speak to X?*' or if we're feeling in a particular mood to punish, '*don't you think you need to speak to X?*'

Again, notice how innocuous these sound without the dynamics of the 'threat' situation, with no adrenaline or cortisol running. With no 'fight or flight' in place, being asked '*do you think you need to speak to X?*' might even feel helpful and supportive, although even then it could be delivered so much more supportively and respectfully as a piece of advice, if that is our intention. But as we've seen, we completely deny, or at best seriously underestimate the power dynamic and the degree to which people's defences are triggered by the merest whiff of threat, even just our presence since we are above them in the hierarchy. So we have to work hard and diligently to eradicate any unconscious control from our armoury.

What *should* we do? If we want the person to take an action and we are not prepared to bend on that, then we should not be scared to issue a directive. We can still be polite and respectful about it, maybe as simply as 'Please go and talk to X before you do anything else'. If we don't feel that strongly about it, we may offer a piece of advice. Something like 'my advice would be to talk to X before you do anything else'.

By the way, conscious control I believe is OK, since anything we do consciously we stand a chance of doing well and of having our motivation trusted, even if we're clumsy in our execution. We just need to exercise conscious control very sparingly and only in exceptional circumstances.

Closed questions fall into three controlling categories:

1. **checking questions (micro-management);**
   Have you, did you, could you, are you, is there, has she, will he, can they?
2. **planting questions (giving you my solution);**
   Do you think, do you feel?
3. **judgemental questions;**
   Don't you think, don't you feel?

The bottom line is that closed questions don't work. We get the feeling of control that we want, but it is merely an illusion. In fact, it's not just that they don't work, closed questions do damage. We can get anyone to say yes to us, if we have authority over them, but they're saying yes is absolutely no guarantee that they'll do what they say. Even as the word 'yes' is reluctantly forced from their lips, they are plotting their excuses and defence for when they fail to deliver. Notice how people invariably give a long answer to a closed question, since giving a straight 'yes' or 'no' passes complete dominion and gives no hiding place for future obfuscation or procrastination.

And not only do they not work, they actually make matters worse, because they build a culture of defensiveness and a systemic lack of initiative, courage and creativity.

So what's the correct use of a closed question?

First, we should only use them when we are completely sure that the environment is safe for the other person, when we are trusted. If there is the merest hint of threat in the air, if the other person is clearly running some adrenaline and cortisol, we need to exercise supreme care, including avoiding closed questions like the plague. Secondly if we do use them it should be like a scalpel, not a battering ram. We should insist on a clear 'yes' or 'no' response, since if we wanted a long or equivocal answer we would have asked an open question. When coaching people and having carefully selected the scalpel, I frequently have to add *'Yes or No'* as a suffix, when I see the other person about to give me a long answer. This is frequently followed by the classic *'It's not as simple as that'*, to which my response is to either leave a silence, or to offer the observation that their complicating the issue is what is holding them back. I remember losing a client in this way – I'd done a piece of consultancy at a chocolate factory in Halifax, part of a global consumer brands business, and I was presenting back to the UK Board of Directors in London. After hearing my clear recommendations, one of the Directors commented *'it's not as simple as you've made out'* and I responded, *'and if your Halifax factory colleagues were here now, they would say that that is the problem with their Directors – everything is complicated and nothing gets decided'*. I was not asked back to do any more work after that.

But if we've built a safe environment, we can use closed questions in one of the following ways:

As a Teacher – asking genuinely curious yes or no questions in order to establish where the other person is in their process or their learning, so that we can overtly teach them the next step or guide them through another iteration of steps that we are patiently teaching them as they learn how to do the job. Notice, teaching them *what* to do in terms of processes that they are lacking knowledge of, and *how* to do in terms of the skills they need to practice and master.

As a Coach – to 'force' the other person off the fence and into action. We don't care what they do, we just care that they act. We are not attached to whatever solution they put in place, but we cannot sit idly by and see them procrastinate any longer. So the closed question needs to go to the core of their beliefs, rather than be about their methods or even their skills. A good way to start one of these questions would be 'do you believe . . . ?'

'Do you believe you have the time available to . . . ?'

'Do you believe X is going to make it?'

'Do you believe the customer is being completely honest with you?'

The beauty of these questions is that once the other person has come off the fence, firmly on one side or the other, then all their positive energy and best strategies can come into play to ensure a great outcome. That can't happen while they're procrastinating, being equivocal or hesitating. It's OK to have a doubt as to whether someone is going to make it, but the longer we hold the doubt the more we conspire to contribute to their failure. The moment we are forced to reaffirm, reinvigorate even, our belief in them, their rehabilitation can commence. Our belief and support does not of itself guarantee their success – these are humans not machines. But withholding or being equivocal in our support sure as hell condemns them to almost zero chance.

As a Coach I am interested only in what people feel passionate and excited about, and in what they will therefore confidently commit to. It is their energy that gives me evidence of commitment and accountability, not them saying 'yes' to me.

A quick word on open questions here, although more later.

We don't have to be taught open questions. We may need a reminder or refresher, but we do know what they are and we do know how to use them well. They actually come completely naturally to us, apart from when we work under corporatism. I am often implored by hard-pressed managers with newly found self-awareness, to help them make coaching become more 'natural' for them. My response is simply to urge them to practise, since all

I'm really doing is re-introducing them to an old friend; a friend that has served them well in their life; a friend that facilitates their curiosity, learning and journey of discovery; but a friend they left in the entrance lobby the moment they arrived at work.

And I prove this to people by asking the following question:

'What age were you when you were at your very finest as an asker of open questions?'

What age were you when you were at your very finest as an asker of open questions?

And back come the knowing responses – when we were about three years old! Three-year-olds ask stunning open questions, but more than that – they are completely ruthless with us if we try and fob them off. A three-year-old can ask a question, the answer to which really demands a knowledge of the laws of thermodynamics, and can still tell when we're winging it. How do they know? This really tells us something about our innate human ability to read nonverbal communication.

Why do three-year-olds ask open questions? Simple – because they want to learn. After all, when you're that age, it's your survival mechanism. You're trying to survive in an environment that is large, complex and full of wonder and danger in just about equal measure. And since Mum and Dad are the ones in our lives who seem to know everything, and the ones to whom we can be most irritating and get away with it, we bombard them – our appetite for learning is utterly insatiable. Good job we come in attractive, wide-eyed, cute little packages; and certainly a good job that we have absolutely no shame in not knowing what we ask. No one needed to teach us open questions, we worked it out as part of our mastering complex language. It's actually really simple.

Three years old! Voraciously drinking in every bit of knowledge we can grab with an unquenchable thirst and asking open questions unashamedly and gloriously. And here we are 20, 30, 40, 50 years later and we struggle to ask even a single open question? What happened to us in the intervening years?

Simple, first of all we started to learn about control and manipulation and started to introduce closed questions into our lexicon. 'Can I have a biscuit, Dad?' 'Are we going to the park today, Mum?' 'Do I have to go to school tomorrow, Grandma?' 'Should you be smoking that, Grandad?'

And then we went to school and started to navigate SATS and tests and exams. Oh and competitiveness – in ability, appearance, wealth, strength, and courage. And then we went to university, and in between the distractions, started to specialise our knowledge (power) base. And then we went to work, where closed questions are seemingly pretty much all we hear, in fact what we learn when we go to work is that we have to fathom everything for ourselves, that we have to be clairvoyant, and that we have to 'fake it til we make it'. The induction and training we receive before being let loose on the actual work is probably lacklustre so we learn the tasks admittedly quite quickly, but we also learn that it's not OK to use initiative or be curious or to believe that things can be done better.

As for having to be clairvoyant, we learn this very quickly, firstly because our manager seems to be afraid to be clear, explicit and direct in letting us know what's expected of us, and then because they keep asking me questions that start with 'do you feel...?' or 'do you think...?' Ah I get it, the game here is not to be genuinely curious and ask the obvious question 'what do you think?' or 'how do you feel?' – that would be far too simple and obvious. No, clearly the game is to try and guess how the other person is feeling or what they are thinking. It frankly seems a bit stupid, but since everyone is joining in, who am I to put my hand up and say 'I think there's a better way...'

And then this whole 'fake it before you make it' culture. Again it seems a bit weird, but since everyone is doing it... the game is you use your energy and skill to always appear positive, confident, in control, pacy, knowing all details, virtuous, compliant and creative. So even though there are times, maybe even almost all the time, when the reality is that we are anxious, pressured, struggling and hesitant, we are not to show it. And since our manager never asks the question 'what are you struggling with?' we are never given the licence or permission to admit that we are all those things. Which is really sad, since we've been given stretching objectives, short timescales and scant resource, so we are bound to struggle. And because we're bright and creative and full of the most amazing untapped potential, we are motivated by struggle, since why would we want to work on things that were easy for us to achieve? If only it was OK to struggle at work; if only it were positively celebrated.

The truth is that we've all but eradicated open questions from our armoury at work because fundamentally we don't want to learn; fundamentally we want control. Even if we start to form an open question, our brain intervenes and overrides instantly. It tells us that asking an open question will likely produce a hugely inconvenient answer, so don't give any leeway, just close things down. If I ask you how you feel, I could be still here in ten minutes time, with you having convinced yourself that you're not feeling in the right state to make progress.

> *We've all but eradicated open questions from our armoury at work because fundamentally we don't want to learn; fundamentally we want control.*

And I can't have that. So I won't take the risk. I'll just ignore the human niceties and go straight to solving the problem because I deliberately want to send the message that it doesn't matter how you feel, I expect progress.

But how do I do this if I need to show I'm a caring boss? If it would actually be too overtly rude not to ask. What are my options? Well I could simply tell you how you are feeling with one of those ridiculous closed questions such as 'So, are you feeling super confident today?' Or if that's a bit too naff even for me, then I could do it by answering my own question, with a 'How are you feeling today? Are you OK?' Yes, that's the one... I've asked the open question, demonstrating that I care, but I've still ensured you are going to make progress.

I wonder what would happen if I really did try to be open. Maybe what I really need is the ability to ask an open question, but in such a way that the other person can only really give me the positive response. So here goes. I'll put on a huge smile first of all, and then I'll bound in with a Tigger like energy about me. Even if they're feeling a bit shit, my very presence will perk them up. Then I'll ask the *'how are you?'* question with as much positivity as I can muster, adding a faintly theatrical melodic soundtrack, as if we were in some cheesy West End musical, metaphorically slapping each other on the back and all being incredibly cheery and positive. That'll work. And of course it does . . . but at what cost?

And so we become indoctrinated, very quickly, into the powerfully persuasive corporate culture where we learn almost immediately that it's just easier to play the game. It's not inherently satisfying of course, since it's not honest; but we can learn to enjoy the rewards, even if we are denied the intrinsic rewards of striving and learning and developing and mastering and achieving – the intrinsic rewards of performing. Good job we entered that Faustian Pact. Good job we have the daily fix of status and power and control, and good job that we can earn more money than from doing anything else, so we can then have the life we really want outside work. What a fatuous contract.

But open questions don't just work because they are inherently more honest or even because of curiosity. They work because of neuroscience.

When we were three years old, we could knock out an open question without even thinking. Although they came as a product of our development and increasing mastery of complex language from about two years old onwards, the driver to ask them was initiated in our limbic system. At two years old our brains were working perfectly as organs of learning. We would try something out, and if we got positive feedback we'd do it again. And again and again. And if it didn't work, we'd eventually learn to stop. We may bump our heads on the furniture several times, but eventually we'll get it. Our emotional brain learns skills (and habits) through a constant drip feed diet of iteration and repetition. This learning, this knowing, is then passed into our unconscious so that we can do these things without having to think, without having to focus conscious attention.

That was fine when we were two or three, but here we are now as fully developed human beings, with advanced cognitive functioning and much greater potential to act consciously, but with a limbic system that has learned closed questions and statements.

So this is what happens in my brain when I consciously choose to ask an open question. First my limbic system activates and I start to form closed questions and statements. The other person receives this energetic communication and goes into threat mode, ready to defend themselves. But I catch myself and exercise a split second of self-control. I literally stop myself from speaking. Instantly the other person perceives a change of energy. The care I am taking over myself is communicated as me exercising care over them. Already their threat state is downgraded. In order to form my open question, I need to put some blood back into my pre-frontal cortex, since it is that part of my brain that I require to come up with a well-structured question. The engagement of my pre-frontal cortex, and my system's requirement therefore for some blood to power it back up, has the effect of lowering my adrenaline levels. As mine drop, so do yours, powered by hundreds of thousands of years of evolutionary collective consciousness. If you are around me and I start to run adrenaline, you will sense this and go into threat state, even if you cannot see the danger that you are reacting to. Conversely if we are in a threat state and then my adrenaline levels drop, clearly the threat has passed.

We communicate energetically, with a sensitivity and calibration that we don't just underestimate, we actually deny! And now you are in a state where I am trusted by you sufficiently to receive my open question as genuine, even if it is clumsily delivered, and even if it is as trite as 'what do you think?' or 'how do you feel'. Since every molecule within you yearns to be honest, to be witnessed, to be validated, to be understood and to be accepted, you meet my act of care in due spirit. One tiny act of self-regulation. One open question. Fifteen seconds into an interaction, and we've changed the course of the future. Hyperbole? Maybe, but try it . . . I make no apology for banging on and on about closed questions. They have become our prime controlling tool and we are completely unaware of this. What hope do we have? When I run my Coaching Excellence programmes I say to participants that if I could give them one gift and one gift only, it would be that they never hear a close question the same way ever again. If we can gain control of this habit, everything is possible. If we cannot, then we are doomed. I really do believe it is as simple as that.

> *One tiny act of self-regulation. One open question. Fifteen seconds into an interaction, and we've changed the course of the future.*

Filling Silences

I'll ask a group of managers a question on this subject – 'how long can we last with a silence?'. Even those who determine that they'll play a game with me in response, find it almost excruciating to ensure even ten seconds of silence. Someone always breaks, rarely with as much as ten seconds having elapsed. Every time I do this I experience discomfort if the group last longer than about five seconds, but I'm never the first to break.

Under threat our adrenal glands release adrenaline and cortisol. The adrenaline induces dramatic changes in blood flow, while the cortisol floods our brain inducing dramatic changes in our ability to focus. I am convinced, although I've never found anything written about this, that cortisol speeds up the frequency at which our eyes view the world. Our eyes typically view the world at about 60 frames per second. This is simplistic, of course, as there are many conditional factors, but it will do for the purpose of my argument here.

Our brains are like an old-fashioned projectionist, stitching together reels without the audience noticing. Our brains collect the 60 frames per second of reality sent to it and weave them into one apparently seamless whole. So we see a movie. But under threat, 60 frames per second won't cut it – it's simply not slowing the world down enough for us to react as quickly as we need to, to avoid that spear or that car. If you've ever heard anyone describe the moment of impact of a road traffic accident, you'll hear them say that it was as if time slowed right down. They can describe, in rich technicolour, the details of every millisecond. They describe an event that lasted maybe five seconds, as if it had lasted ten times that long. I had a wonderful example of this happen to me just recently. I was driving through some country lanes in broad daylight with no other traffic around, when a very large deer ran out of the undergrowth on the right-hand side of the road straight towards my car. How we didn't collide is beyond me, but it veered away at the very last second, narrowly missing my door mirror. The whole episode was over in under five seconds. And yet I can describe both the colour and the texture of the deer's hide. I can still see it, as if in freeze frame, through my side window, literally inches from me. The colour was a rich and glossy dark reddish brown, just a beautiful colour that only nature can create. But what is more remarkable is that I can describe the texture of its hide. While the overall appearance was of a smooth and glossy velvet coat, I could see the detail of its fur, quite close knit, about half a centimetre in length and lying with the nap going down the animal's flank. It was breathtakingly beautiful.

So here's what happens to us as we try and manage someone – we immediately see the problem at hand, and we pretty near immediately see the solution. We go into our heightened state, running adrenaline and cortisol. But we know that we need to at least try and coach our team member, so we ask an open question. Silence – not because they don't want to answer, or that they can't answer, but because our question actually made them think, and they not unreasonably need a few seconds to consider their response. But the cortisol in our brains makes this few seconds feel like a lifetime, and our impatience is a powerful initiator of impulsive action.

Our brain says,

For God's sake it wasn't a hard question, I sent you an email about this three weeks ago and you should have been further ahead or even completed the task by now anyway, so I'm only really being polite in asking you one of those soft and fluffy open questions, but if you can't even muster the gumption to answer it, then clearly I need to step in and take control.

All of that in three seconds (thanks cortisol) during which time our team member senses our impatience, spiking their own adrenaline and cortisol levels and putting them into freeze. Now they're their brain says to them.

I've sort of got an answer, but it's not perfect or even fully formed, and I'm in such a state of anxiety now that even if I can get some words out, I'll probably stumble or dry up, and oh there goes that flushing round my neck that I get when I'm flustered, and oh shit perhaps I'll just resign now . . .

In that frame of mind not only are we highly likely to break the very silence we ourselves created, but our team member will actually feel relieved when we do! After all they're now off the hook – well, they've survived a tricky moment of threat, and that's all that matters right now.

But how to break the silence? Well, we have a choice. We can either answer our own question (when we're in control mode we never ask a question to which we don't already know the answer – it's too risky) or we can make a statement designed to motivate them to answer. An example of the first would be something like – *how are you progressing with client X?'* . . . silence . . . *'have you met with their CMO yet?'* What a beautiful question we asked first up. If we had more patience, even just a few more seconds, our team member would then be giving us (more importantly telling themselves) where they are in their progress, and would probably go on, unprompted, to tell themselves what they need to do next. One of the amazing things about coaching, when we're under good self-regulation, is that people coach themselves!

> *One of the amazing things about coaching, when we're under good self-regulation, is that people coach themselves!*

But now, since we've indulged our inner controller with the closed question, they have to defend themselves. If they've not met with the CMO yet, they'll feel foolish and judged, even if they have met with them, they'll immediately leap to being judged again when we ask them how it is then that they've not made the progress they should have done. Another sliding doors moment – the difference is binary, massive, transformational.

Our other choice is to stay in 'coaching mode', or so we kid ourselves, and resisting the temptation to give them the answer, we instead try and motivate them to answer it for themselves. Our brain makes a quick judgement that what they are lacking is not knowledge or competency, but urgency, drive and an appreciation of just how critical things are. So if we can transmit this to them, if we can pump some urgency and drive into them; if we can have them instantly appreciate the criticality of the situation, then not only will they answer our question, but they'll be in the right frame of mind, and we can then be more confident of a) having helped them and b) that they'll bring home the bacon. Here's a few examples of a statements we might make (please read in an oratorical tone of voice, as if you were delivering the opening lines of a speech designed to inspire). *'I can't stress enough to you just how urgent the situation is'* or *'I'm not sure you really appreciate just how critical it is for the company that you bring in this order'* or *'let me remind you that it's absolutely essential that you raise your game if you're going to stand any chance of success with this client'* or . . . well, you get the picture.

Our propensity to sabotage ourselves is immense. I've listened to thousands of coaching conversations, and before coaches are aware that these unconscious habits even exist, I'll hear this filling silence habit a lot. The most entertaining part is when Coaches are made aware of the habit and are practicing its elimination from their armoury. I watch them physically wrestle with themselves, it is such an ingrained habit. Some people literally have to put their hand over their mouth to stop themselves talking.

Giving Multiple Inputs

Finally of the Big Three, we have our habit of giving multiple inputs – asking several questions in a row, most likely gabbled into one rambling diatribe, that might also contain some statements as well. We do this because we are solving the problem out loud, and so our brains launch a stream of consciousness through articulation (speech), and our fear is that if we stop speaking, we'll stop processing and we'll lose all the good stuff that's coming out.

So notice nowhere in this dynamic is curiosity or listening, and no sense of any belief that the other person can solve their own problem – certainly not a breath of coaching going on. So what's it like for our team member to be on the end of one of these streams of consciousness? Well first of all they're going to start running adrenaline and cortisol because they're literally under attack, or that is how it will feel. They'll wait in a state of freeze for their turn to speak, since it's not only disrespectful to interrupt, but far too risky. It's a frustrating experience for them, since we are sparking so many thoughts but not giving them the space to respond or even to add or embellish the ideas tumbling out. But the end comes and now is their chance to grab back control. Since we've given them a multitude of inputs, they can now choose which ones to respond to.

Which one would you respond to? The risk, and it's near guaranteed, is that our team member selects the 'easiest' input to respond to. What is their criteria for determining 'easiest'? Simple – the one where they can most please us and therefore lower the threat levels to enable this potentially uncomfortable interaction to come to an end. The last thing they're going to do is bring us back to the most haunting and challenging question we asked.

Why is them selecting the 'easiest' input so damaging? Because we're now discussing something that's going really well, that our team member is completely comfortable in and where there is no likelihood of further significant or ground-breaking progress. Not only are we missing a massive and potentially one-off opportunity to help our team member with what they are struggling with, but worse than that, we create conditions where our team member colludes with us to believe that things are going far better than they are; that things have a much greater chance of success than is the case. This is the stuff of unrealistic forecasts and future inevitable and utterly predictable 'surprises'.

Do People Learn they are the Solution, or that they are the Problem?

When we allow our unconscious controlling habits to rule, our team members quite understandably and justifiably use all of their well-practised defence strategies to survive the moment of threat – this conversation, this 1:1, this meeting. True sliding doors moments when the world can literally go one way or the other.

At the very instant we require people to step forward in all of their brilliance and fabulousness, our unconscious controlling habits make them play safe and small. Our lack of awareness neuters our ability to calmly coach people, and we end up creating the very opposite of what we set out to achieve, and of course since we do lack self-awareness, we will blame our team member, which only increases the mutual frustration, and is the foundation stone of the belief that says we don't have the right quality of people in place. WE DO!

And worse than the impact of the specific interaction is the learning it creates, for what is our team member supposed to learn? Instead of creating the positive learning, where our team member learns that they are the solution, our crass and lazy habits teach them that they are the problem. And I call that abuse.

Notes

Insights Discovery and MBTI   Referenced in Chapter 8.

BBC TV Not the 9 O'Clock News   'Headbanger' from series 1 in 1979 www.bing.com /videos/search?q=headbanger+not+the+nine+oclock+news&view=detail&mid=6 D818A66B0ACEA4A58806D818A66B0ACEA4A5880&FORM=VIRE   (accessed   25 May 2018).

ITV Production *Prime Suspect*   Written by Lynda la Plante, and aired on ITV (7 April 1991).

The Muppet Show   A television series produced by puppeteer Jim Henson that lasted for five series consisting of 120 episodes, first broadcast in the UK on ATV (5 September 1976 to 15 March 1981). The characters *Statler* and *Waldorf* were two cantankerous old men who consistently jeered the entirety of the cast from their balcony seats, nodding sagely in agreement with each other's withering heckling.

Chapter 11

Pillar 2

Promoting Positive Learning

How we Learn

The reason we are so successful as a species is that over the last 200,000 years we've developed an incredible system for learning. There is the conditioned learning that goes on in the Limbic system, where with sufficiently repeated stimuli, a specific input or event can trigger an automatic instinctive response. The work of Ivan Pavlov is the most widely known in this area, where he was able to trigger conditioned responses in animals by them repeatedly associating an outcome with an input – the most famous experiment was where he could get his dogs to salivate at the sound of a bell, by giving them a number of repetitions of the bell being linked to the arrival of food. Pavlov's work on 'classical conditioning' set the groundwork for present-day behaviour modification practices.

But we humans have developed a much more sophisticated method of learning skills and of taking advantage of the incredible manual dexterity we possess.

Our neocortex is separated into – being incredibly simplistic – front and back. Our frontal lobe, or more precisely our pre-frontal cortex, is where we can consciously take in infor-mation from all our senses, think about it, chew over it, maybe discuss it with others, com-pare it to other data including what's in our memory banks, strategise over it, prioritise it, and decide to take an action. This is the part of the brain that makes us human, and it is a conscious process or function that no other animal on the planet possesses.

And then through a process of repetition and iteration, the emotional part of our brain, our limbic system takes over, and we move the motor processes into our muscle memory – our bodies take over and the skill is now available to us without thinking. I say skill and of course it is, but actually what it has become is habit.

Let me take you back to the very first time you sat in a car to learn to drive. How does any-one do this? It's unbelievably hard. But because we're so committed; we want it so much, we persevere, and through practice we learn – and here we are now in a position where we can drive a car while thinking about something else. And for those gamers among you, how do you 'learn' how to advance to the next stage of the game? Yes, you die countless times, and each time you die you learn something that helps you make at first big and then ever more refined adjustments to your skills. When we are learning positively, our good friend dopamine rewards our efforts. We learn through feedback, or consequences, and so that feedback has to have a purity and an unsanitised honesty. We learn because the consequences of our mistakes are painful to us and we do not wish to repeat the dis-comfort. Or we learn because we try something and magically it works and so we calibrate our actions and behaviours accordingly.

> *We learn through feedback, or consequences, and so that feedback has to have a purity and an unsanitised honesty.*

We learn through watching great role models and seeking to emulate them, by doing, from feedback, from working things out for ourselves (planning, strategising, experimenting) – but we also learn by being taught. I frequently use the term 'teacher' to encompass every corporate role I've ever had, since I've spent so much of my time fundamentally being an educator.

We teach by informing, by coaching (helping people structure their own thought processes), by role modelling, by observing and giving feedback, and sometimes by simply directing (do this and I promise you it will work!) How much time are you spending teaching people things? What do your people need educating in?

You can see people learn – the evidence is right there in front of us if we're paying attention. We have the human relationship skill of knowing whether someone is learning negatively or positively. We can see if someone is scared, pressured, running adrenaline and cortisol, and therefore in the mode of learning negatively. And we can see if someone is open, trusting, excited to take an experimental step or try something new. We can see it and we can feel the difference. So we have no excuse for presiding over negative learning and pretending we didn't know what we were doing. When we see negative learning we need to change our state, re-build trust, ask some questions, give some encouragement and start the positive learning loop.

We're Always Learning

We talk about learning as something that we choose to do consciously, as if on all other occasions we're simply maintaining a benign state of readiness for when we can move forward again. But the rather inconvenient truth is that we are always learning. Our brains, our neurons, are constantly and incessantly firing and wiring. We are either learning 'negatively' through our increasingly conditioned responses to threat, or we are learning 'positively' through conscious consideration, deliberate action and immediate feedback in the form of consequences. Of course learning through conditioned responses is very valuable for our survival, but frankly once we've gone beyond the point where we are so young, naive and unaware as to be a danger to ourselves and others if we are let out on our own, it should pretty much all be about the positives. What stage of development in our lives can we be reasonably certain of not requiring further conditioned learning? Probably just beyond adolescence which means that by the time we arrive in the workplace, we should be predominantly fed positive learning experiences. Wow, all those skills we can develop as we insatiably consume knowledge and learn through constant experimentation, rehearsal and performance on the job. And with all the amazing feedback we get, both immediately, in terms of 'natural' consequences when things we try just don't work, and from our colleagues and especially our manager, we're surely on the path to growth, uncovering and unleashing our massive potential in service of this wonderful enterprise we've joined.

This is not mere idealistic fantasy on my part. This is completely within our dominion if only we had the sense to organise our workplaces accordingly. After all it happens gloriously in sport and the arts, so as humans we are most definitely capable. And I urge you to be very watchful of any scepticism that might wash over you at this point, since positive learning is not a 'nice to have' – it is a complete essential. If we do not create the environment and the cultural conditions for positive learning, it's not just that we'll suffer the frustrations of unrealised potential, it's that we'll actively do harm. There is no neutral state - you are either actively fostering a positive learning environment or you are a steward of negative learning.

If we do not create the environment and the cultural conditions for positive learning, it's not just that we'll suffer the frustrations of unrealised potential, it's that we'll actively do harm.

Human beings look solid, secure and reliable with any change happening quite gradually, almost imperceptibly. At least they look like this at work, since they've learned so to appear. In our natural state, free of threat, nothing could be further from the truth. Human beings are organisms in constant change, a mass of vibrating molecules in a dynamic state of flux. We can learn to appear solid and unchanging, but give us the freedom to be ourselves, and we are dynamic, active, clumsy, messy and completely beautiful. I use a descriptor in my training courses – we are all beautiful, flawed geniuses. Unfortunately, at work we've become so petrified of the flaws and the messiness, that we've crushed the human spirit in so many of our organisations, trading it for conformity, compliance and 'just enough' growth. Whereas we should be giving positive learning total priority in our working environments, in my experience corporatism is appalling at this, focussing as it does almost all learning energy on controlling or even seeking to eradicate the inconvenience of human beings.

The learnings that are critical for our creative growth and development in the corporate world are things like:

- be better prepared;

- talk to people in advance;

- prioritise differently;

- be more courageous;

- find new ways;

- rehearse;

- experiment;

- be more creative;

- involve others;

- give ideas away;

- be open and transparent;
- consider potential alternative outcomes and have contingency plans;
- trust your colleagues;
- be tolerant of human failings;
- be aware of possible unintended consequences;
- celebrate difference;
- take calculated risks;
- hold clear boundaries;
- give honest feedback.

These all sound so sensible that it's easy for any of us to argue, even believe, that we foster and encourage these things. We may even be able to point to the evidence of how we have communicated that these are the things that we want and expect from people. But it's not our words that people follow, it's our actions, our behaviours, our responses. Our fine and noble words are found out in how we behave under pressure.

And so often the reality is that our behaviours teach people the following:

- Don't make me cross.
- Don't let people down.
- Don't miss deadlines.
- Don't say 'no'.
- Over commit.
- Have an excuse ready in case anything goes wrong.
- Don't take risks.
- Give sugar coated feedback (don't hurt people's feelings).
- Don't express emotions.
- Work long hours.
- Give instant responses.
- Don't say what you really think.
- Play safe.
- Hide your beliefs.
- Agree with those who have power over you, better still do things to please them.

Leaders are often exasperated that they've exhorted people to do the right things, and yet those people still appear to be afraid to do so. Or worse, those people use their initiative and patently do silly things. Infuriating! But at least if all the employees have signed the Health and Safety policy, then clearly it cannot be the fault of management when one of them gets their arm caught in the machine. And so the bottom line is revealed for many hard-pressed managers – in the absence of the elusive and probably mythical profit/ethics/sustainability trinity, I can live with average or even mediocre results as long as I can survive by blaming others. Surely all we have to do is employ the right people and be relatively decent to them and they'll do the rest won't they? If we provide good salaries (well, market rate anyway), good benefits (well, in line with other employers in our industry), free tea and coffee etc; if we tell them that we want them to use their initiative and that's it's OK for them to make mistakes (especially if our Values say this); and if we're reasonably good at moving bullies out of management roles, then surely people have everything they need to flourish, don't they? It's this underlying belief, borne out of some frustration, that leads to the oft-quoted 'if only we had the right people . . .'. Whenever I hear that (or a more sanitised management speak version which sounds less inhumane) I simply retort 'you've *got* the right people, they are in fact amazing, but they're just waiting to be led'.

It's not that 'positive' learnings are by their very nature more elusive, it's more that the 'negative' learnings are so dominant. Remember how we are wired – our brains are five times more sensitive to negative feedback than positive, so we have to work five times harder on nurturing the positive learning. And this is exhausting for leaders, mainly because they have 'day jobs' themselves – they simply don't feel they have the time to be constantly walking the floor encouraging everyone. They are leaders, not pastors. So being pragmatic, the question becomes how leaders can genuinely 'walk the talk', ensuring that fine words are completely matched by their responses and subsequent behaviours under pressure.

Consequences are the Ultimate Feedback

In real life, do something stupid or reckless and there will be dramatic consequences. Your partner will leave you, you'll be arrested, you'll lose a limb, you'll cause an accident. Furthermore, apart from business, in pretty much all other areas of human endeavour and performance there are consequences to our behaviours and actions. We play a howler and get dropped from the team, we choke at the audition and we don't get the part, we write a crap book and no one buys it, we play a 'bum' note and everyone hears it, we injure ourselves and so miss the final. These consequences are frequently 'unfair' and often seem wholly arbitrary. Yet they are final. It doesn't matter whether it's fair, we did something and there was a consequence. We got the ultimate feedback.

In areas concerning health, death, injury, risk etc, we've systematically built feedback and learning systems that take each dramatic consequence and ensure that lessons are learned. Consider aviation safety as an example – simply the safest form of travel, because every accident, every death has been analysed for cause, and steps have then been taken to reduce or even eradicate future risks.

But with corporatism this law of thermodynamics seems to be suspended, particularly for managers. Managers seem able to carry on behaving in ineffective and even threatening ways, and there are no consequences. They don't get fired (they've learned to stay within the 'acceptable' tolerances) and even when they preside over poor results (feedback) they seem able to argue zero culpability. Of course one problem is that corporatism is a rather weird aberration to nature, in that short-term results can be produced by poor management behaviours, and many managers get rewarded for this very dynamic.

> *It's simple – if we wish people to behave in certain ways, then there have to be consequences (feedback) when they do not.*

But let's focus for a moment on consequences of behaviours. It's simple – if we wish people to behave in certain ways, then there have to be consequences (feedback) when they do not. If there are no consequences to poor or undesired behaviours, then why would anyone change? If we want people to turn up on time to meetings, then we need to establish a clear consequence when if they habitually come late, such as not allowing them into the meeting. That might feel like treating a grown adult as a child, but their refusal to respect their colleagues is childish behaviour. Corporatism does not shy away from the harshest of consequences in the marketplace, it cannot, since customers are free to be promiscuous, but it sucks at internal consequences, relying instead on verbal feedback, or in some cases, passive-aggressive mutterings.

So managers certainly have to give constant feedback, creating cultures whereby feedback is sought and given respectfully, and remembering that the absence of feedback will always be interpreted as a 'carry on' message. But they also have to have some clear non-negotiable boundaries, and those boundaries need to be backed up with clearly communicated consequences. This is a great piece of work for any new team to do, since the leader can of course position themselves as Head Teacher, but the more effective positioning is as facilitator of agreed group rules.

And managers have to bring the consequences of the market inside the company. It's too easy for 'internal' people to lose sight of the realities of the front line with customers. Give poor service and the customers complain and then they walk. But give poor internal service and there can often be no consequences at all.

Change is Different from Learning

While all successful change processes involve a high degree of learning, especially if the

> *So if we want things to change, we need to implement change management processes that tackle conditioned habits and then encourage new learning.*

change is to be embedded and sustained, as strategies we need to be able to manage them as separate and discrete. Although we are learning all the time, as we've seen this does not automatically lead to change, in fact more often than not it leads to a cementing of ever more ingrained habits through conditioning. So if we want things to change, we need to implement change management processes that tackle conditioned habits *and* then encourage new learning. We simply cannot blur the two and expect people to get it right.

Change starts from a survival instinct – and fear is the driver for survival strategies. But they come to life and are then sustained through our collective thriving, and safety is pre-requisite for any human being to engage in thriving. Fear = survive; safety = thrive. This is why any change strategy, programme or initiative has to have people feeling the heat, before it can get people seeing the light. People will only engage in change when they are more scared of staying where they are than they are of embarking on the journey.

Psychological Safety

This phrase has become a bit of a brand now for the modern corporate. It was first coined by William A Kahn in 1990 and he defined it as *'being able to show and employ oneself without fear of negative consequences of self image, status or career'*.

In the future I believe a proven lack of psychological safety may be grounds for lawsuits, especially when CTSD gets recognised as a specific and separate anxiety disorder.

Do I now have your attention?

Leaders talk psychological safety but I've not really seen hard evidence that they mean it. It's not focussed on, rewarded, measured or even actually wanted. I've dug into this question with many senior leaders and underneath the fine and noble words is a fear that safety means the risk of complacency. The harsh reality is that leaders don't really want their people to feel safe. Under pressure, the value of positive learning that only comes when people feel safe is not honoured or promoted because it is fundamentally not accepted as valuable. And so negative learning is the name of the game. Rather than learning 'TO' lessons, employees learn 'NOT TO' lessons.

So much of what employees do is driven because they are fearful, desperately trying to ensure that a feared outcome is avoided. And much of what managers do unconsciously creates or exacerbates fear in others. Fear of failure; fear of rejection. Fear of being poorly rated by superiors; fear of being poorly rated by peers; fear of being poorly rated by direct reports – trapped in a Cat's Cradle of anxiety. Fear infects and erodes our core beliefs.

Safety *can* create complacency, but only in a vacuum. People who feel safe may well take the opportunity to rest, and that's surely legitimate at times, but it's the vacuum of poor leadership, facilitation and coaching that we have to avoid.

Leaders talk about psychological safety, and promote employee well-being in their rhe-toric, but then betray the opposite in their focus and actions, and mostly in their inactions. This creates a disturbing dissonance. Here's a simple example: with the time difference between the US and Europe, many Video Conferences have to be done in the evening by employees in Europe. It is quite usual therefore for them to be working at home in their evenings. This cannot be described as a genuine choice, since if they did not make themselves available, they simply could not stay in their roles. Their US bosses will of course say that their direct reports have absolute autonomy to work flexible hours but '*I don't want my people to feel like they have to . . .*' is not the same as '*I don't want people to . . .*' It's the same convenient language that allows people to appear to be apologising when they are not – the thoroughly slippery '*I'm really sorry you feel that way*' method. The former is an abdication that conveniently allows fear to rule the day. The latter would be a stronger leadership statement that could be genuinely promoted for cultural well-being – it just wouldn't be true.

The truth is we *do* want people to . . . the argument being of course that employees are superbly looked after and therefore much is demanded of them, and anyway no one is ever sanctioned for prioritising family, well not overtly anyway. The threats that employees perceive may indeed be spectres, but that does not stop those spectral threats from driving unhealthy behaviours. Leaders who hide behind their exhortations are actually negligent in their duty of care.

Carrot and Stick has Morphed into Bribery and Coercion

When does a carrot become a bribe? Stick has always been openly coercive, but has often been substituted in definition with consequences, allowing leaders to 'legitimise' coercive behaviours. The more modern form of stick is much more subtle – the hinted potential of a reduced performance rating, the expression of disappointment, the raised eyebrow of judgement, the closed question implying the desired action. Because of the fear in the system, the corporate pathology, and because of the power in the hands of the person above us in the hierarchy, we're already receiving a controlling communication, before our manager has even opened their mouth. We anticipate it, so we feel it. We anticipate it, so it becomes manifest. We are coerced without even knowing it.

> *The more modern form of stick is much more subtle – the hinted potential of a reduced performance rating, the expression of disappointment, the raised eyebrow of judgement.*

In the good old days of Henry Ford, Frederick Taylor and maybe even of Jack Welch, all managers really had to do was to maintain some balance between carrot and stick. Employees knew where they stood with the consequences of their behaviours, and entered what was a fairly honest contract, with sufficient carrot to keep them relatively satisfied.

But in the twenty-first century corporate our employees are more demanding, and since we've educated a whole generation of leaders through our business schools and our Authentic Leadership Programmes not to use stick (and therefore actually to be more manipulative in the process) the corporate world is now a place of greater coercion than ever. It's just far more subtle and sophisticated. So to compensate, we've developed what we feel to be way more sophisticated carrots.

We've developed sophisticated meritocratic reward systems, with an often really complex matrix of factors such as performance rating, feedback scores, promotions or grade or level advancements, let alone the financial rewards of salary, bonus and equity awards. In my experience these have stopped being effective rewards in the manner of what Dan Pink would call 'now that' rewards – in other words genuine rewards for exceptional achievement, and they have morphed into bribes – what Pink calls 'if then' rewards. Given the costs in pressure and anxiety to employees in achieving ever more arbitrary and unrealistic expectations, the rewards have in fact turned into negatives, with employees fearing the non-achievement of the rewards as a punishment for not being a perfect employee. When does a carrot become a bribe? When the fear of its withholding outweighs the incentive value of its potential achievement.

The modern corporate looks after the hygiene needs of its employees in ways that were unthinkable 20 years ago, with free restaurant-style food, self-direction, autonomy, health and well-being support, diversity, parental leave, sabbaticals even. This is starting to create an alarmingly high level of dependency. I was talking recently to a 12-year tenure Tech company employee about to go on Mat Leave for her first child. When she told me that one of her biggest anxieties in facing childbirth was that she was going to have to learn to cook, I thought at first she was joking. She wasn't.

So the final question on carrots is, when does a bunch of carrots become a pair of handcuffs? Contemplating leaving a company is hard enough when considering the impact on your CV, but to leave the food? OMG, unthinkable!

Integrity is Paramount

Integrity is when actions match words. When I do what I say, I have integrity. When my actions are clearly in line with my stated principles or values, I have integrity. Integrity creates trust and trust creates safety. So many Leaders are not doing what they say. Their published intentions are fine and noble and even inspiring. But then they leave it to chance, and since their focus and their actions do not match their words, they cannot be trusted. This is I believe the biggest single issue of leadership in the early part of the twenty-first century – that leaders are not committed to ruthlessly ensuring that they mean what they say and are true to their word. They believe that it is enough to issue the fine and noble words and have their followers accede to them. Given the rewards they give unconditionally (in their view) and given the additional rewards on offer for exceptional performance, leaders seem to expect compliance to principles without having to do anything to ensure it happens; without having to manage accordingly. And since leaders seem to believe that their role is not actually to create an environment, a culture, but to solve the complex issues that are beyond their followers, they inevitably unconsciously role model the very behaviours they say they eschew in others. Integrity goes with positive learning because it relies on a clarity of intentions and on a fundamental awareness and control of conscious behaviours.

Notes

Ivan Pavlov   1849–1936 was a Russian physiologist known primarily for his work in classical conditioning, winning the Nobel Prize for Physiology or Medicine in 1904. Pavlov was one of the first scientists to demonstrate the relationship between environmental stimuli and behavioural responses.

Kahn, W   (1990) Psychological Conditions of Personal Engagement and Disengagement at Work. *Academy of Management Journal*, 33: 692–724.

Henry Ford   (1863–1947) was an American business magnate, founder of the Ford Motor Company, and the sponsor of the development of the assembly-line technique of mass production. He is credited with 'Fordism': mass production of inexpensive goods coupled with high wages for workers. His intense commitment to systematically lowering costs resulted in many technical and business innovations.

Frederick Taylor   (1856–1915) was an American mechanical engineer who sought to improve industrial efficiency. One of the first management consultants, his ideas were highly influential in the Progressive Era (1890s–1920s). Taylor summed up his efficiency techniques in his 1911 book *The Principles of Scientific Management*. His pioneering work in applying engineering principles to the work done on the factory floor was a huge influence on Henry Ford and many subsequent industrialists.

Jack Welch   was chairman and CEO of General Electric between 1981 and 2001. During his tenure at GE, the company's value rose 4000 per cent. He had a reputation for being very tough, perhaps even brutal, but he was a passionate supporter of genuine employee engagement, introducing a problem–confrontation/change–acceleration process called 'workout' that calls a 'time out' from typical bureaucratic practices and behaviours and substitutes continuous focus, efficient decision making and accelerated implementation.

Pink, D   (2011) *Drive: The Surprising Truth About What Motivates Us.* Edinburgh: Canongate.

Chapter 12

Pillar 3

Transparency and Vulnerability

Why Transparency must Conquer Secrecy

As we've seen, secrecy is the facilitator of fear and control, and the disease attacking organisational health. Add to that our seemingly total unwillingness to show normal human emotions at work, and we have a recipe for the worst excesses of corporatism to thrive. How are we supposed to trust our corporate lords and masters, when it's perfectly clear that they keep things from us, that they are dishonest and manipulative, and when they so utterly disapprove of anything that smacks of emotion or weakness? Even when the corporate values espouse openness and honesty (or some wordsmithed variation), the manifestation of these words is that we are only trusted with information our masters deign to believe we'll understand, and only with information that won't cause problems should it get into the public domain. Truly we are both thick and untrustworthy.

I don't know about you, but treat me as if I'm thick and untrustworthy, and I'll react pretty badly. I'll probably prove you right! You certainly will not gain my unquestioning loyalty, nor will you bring out my creativity in pursuit of the mission you are leading. Many, many secrets are kept in the name of competitive forces and commercial confidentiality. I haven't come across that many in reality that would really hurt our mission should they become public knowledge. We can, after all, legally protect patents, intellectual property and brand names, and everything else is intangible. We run scared of people leaving us with their proverbial rolodex – scared of ideas and strategies falling into the hands of competitors; we are spooked by the rumour-mongering that is around every corporate sector or industry, believing somehow in our increasing paranoia that our competitors have nothing better to do than focus all their attention on us, scheming and plotting our downfall as their greatest priority.

My experience is that we give way too much weight and credence to all of these things, as we do to all fears in corporate life. They belong to that endless list of things we are scared of that are simply never going to happen. And even if they did, we still do far more damage in not trusting our people than we could ever do by allowing a competitor to steal our strategy. I am protective of my intellectual property, after all I have spent a corporate lifetime designing it, honing it, refining it, polishing it, to the point where it works reliably, predictably and effectively. But I am only really protective of it so that I can earn a proper and reasonable return for my skills and my effort, and my fees understood and accepted by clients. If a competitor decided to steal my IP, first of all I probably would never know, secondly I'm sufficiently arrogant to believe they would not do that well with it (if you want to short cut yourself to glory by stealing my IP, you've probably not got the sound foundation to make it come alive), and finally I'm pragmatic enough to know that actually the pond is big enough for us all to swim in.

Transparency is the single most powerful factor in protecting against unethical behaviour, so let's have everything out in the open.

Transparency is the single most powerful factor in protecting against unethical behaviour, so let's have everything out in the open. Competition despises transparency since it relies on things being kept secret. How frequently I've seen companies put their salespeople through negotiation training, only really to have those people emerge as more professional liars and manipulators even as they supposedly pursue a win–win situation.

Collaboration works on openness, trust and a willingness to subordinate personal glory or advancement (Ego) for the sake of the cause. So we have to have observation built into the system, with feedback and learning happening positively so people go about joyfully mastering skills.

I abhor the dynamic whereby senior managers leave the room so that their people can talk honestly about them. This merely colludes with the secrecy and the setting up of shame. How dare they assume on behalf of their people that they are too scared to be honest. The issue is that if feedback is overly sanitised then it won't hurt enough to spur leaders into changing – they will politely say they've listened and heard but nothing fundamental will change. Of course we should use anonymised feedback surveys in our overall cultural stewardship, but leaders need to be wary of setting themselves up as different, special, not to be trusted and certainly not to be upset. No – go in with your people and demonstrate that you are trustworthy and really want to know their truth. Reward those who have the courage. I've facilitated countless feedback sessions and all you have to do is ask the right questions and then show acceptance when you hear the truth. People are desperate to tell the truth, but they need massive encouragement and safety so to do. They will not do it on their own, it is simply too risky.

One of the most powerful examples was when I was leading an employee engagement process for a large UK food manufacturing and processing business. The Engagement Champions were continually being frustrated by their company Directors, who were well meaning, but had abdicated their own leadership responsibility, expecting the Champions and the Employees to 'get engaged'. It was as if the Directors simply did not appreciate or understand what daily life was really like on the factory floor. So I called a meeting between the two 'sides' and I carefully constructed a means of bringing out the issues for resolution. I deliberately lined the two 'sides' up facing each other. They were in conflict and needed to acknowledge this, so sitting round a board room table was not going to set the right environment. I instructed the Directors, in front of the Champions, that they were going to hear some things they would not like and some things that they were likely to take issue with, that the Champions might not be right in all cases, but felt strongly about things, and that they, the Directors, were to listen and not respond until the Champions had said what they needed to say. I carefully crafted a small number of questions for the Champions to address, and I wrote them up on a flipchart placed behind the Directors, so that the Champions could see the questions while maintaining eye contact with the Directors. These physical devices were crucial to the success of the meeting.

And these are the questions I crafted for the Champions.

1. **Why do I love this company?**

2. **Why did I volunteer to be an Engagement Champion?**

3. **What aspects of the problems we face in our daily work do you, the Directors, seem not to know, or frankly even seem to care about?**

4. **What are the actions you, the Directors, must take in order to make this company great again?**

Notice the rhythm of the questions – with the first two deliberately focussing on positives to help the Directors realise just how passionate and committed the Champions were, and to reassure them that the criticisms that were surely coming were based on sound mutual principles and were positively motivated. The third question was the one I put most skill into crafting. That question contained

> *The first two deliberately focussing on positives to help the Directors realise just how passionate and committed the Champions were.*

all my experience. It allowed the Champions to be brutally honest in expressing their frustration, exasperation even, with the Directors, while being appropriately respectful. Knowing they were not going to be interrupted was a huge safety factor, and the question then gave the licence and permission to give it to the Directors straight. How else would it have been possible for the Champions to say to the Directors *'you don't care'*. That session ended up being completely pivotal to the company's turnaround. Within 12 months, interestingly with three of the Directors who'd been in that room having been removed pretty soon after, the company had gone from very serious loss, to very satisfactory profit. The Champions knew what was needed, they simply lacked a voice that was being listened to.

Human Emotions are a very good Thing

Human beings are naturally messy, emotional, clumsy, imperfect. Corporatism desperately tries to condition these unhelpful and inconvenient dynamics out of its employees. But human beings are also fabulously talented, creative, extraordinary and resourceful, and Corporatism loses most of this amazing potential in the process. I believe you can't have the positives unless you are prepared to acknowledge and then live with the 'negatives'. This for me is actually the basis of diversity, not just the aspects concerned with race, gender, sexual orientation or disability, although these are of course crucial. A diverse working culture first of all embraces humanity in all its richness of human genius and human flaws. We are truly all beautiful, flawed geniuses. So leaders have to create and then nurture a working environment that allows people to be human. We have to talk about emotions. We have to ask people about their feelings. We have to notice when they themselves avoid the discomfort of doing so. We have to demonstrate that we are trustworthy and that we care. Trust is essential, so that people know they are free to be messy and clumsy and unsure and hesitant and down and tired; free to make mistakes and generally not be perfect. And when a working culture embraces these aspects, not just allowing them but celebrating them, that's when people start to unleash the good stuff – the stuff that's always been there and latently on offer, but which has been withheld because we as leaders have not earned the right to expect body *and* soul.

Again, this is not a 'nice to have' – it is essential. If we don't let people feel their emotions at work, then we reap a heavy penalty. First people learn, through that dreaded negative conditioned learning, that they must not feel their emotions, and that if they do they are weak. (We of course don't mind if they feel shame or guilt because that will make them work harder!) We teach people to dissociate from their emotions, and this is the start of the dehumanising process – the process that ends with a nurse walking past an elderly patient who's been left unattended for so long on a trolley in a corridor that they've soiled themselves, and are quietly whimpering in distress. It's also how corporate citizens come to be traumatised by the repetition of seemingly low levels of abuse from the unconscious controlling habits. Since they are not allowed to feel nor express their emotions at work, that emotional energy gets trapped in the body, and the sheer frequency and volume of repetitions adds an inexorable layering. This is how CTSD is contracted.

> *We teach people to dissociate from their emotions, and this is the start of the dehumanising process – the process that ends with a nurse walking past an elderly patient.*

The second damaging aspect of corporatism's abhorrence of human emotion is that if people cannot feel their own emotions, they invariably act out onto others, either projecting that anger, disgust or fear onto those around them, victimising themselves in the process, or becoming serially passive aggressive. If the corporate workplace were under the microscope of a psychiatric regulator studying levels of mental health safety, I suspect many companies would be shut down as blatantly unsafe. My goal for CTSD to be accepted as a recognised condition could be the catalyst for the worst companies and leaders to be identified and held to account.

Many psychologists now prefer the term 'emotional competence' to 'emotional intelligence'. Certainly, emotion recognition is a crucial human skill. In a report by Linda Geddes (2016), Marc Brackett, Director of the Yale Center for Emotional Intelligence, says

None of us are born knowing the difference between feeling over-whelmed and worried, elated and ecstatic. It's a language that has to be taught. When you take a physical change in your body and understand it as an emotion, you learn to make meaning out of that change.

Linda Geddes, 2016

In the mid-2000s, Brackett helped create a programme called RULER, now used in some 10,000 US schools, to teach children and young adults to interpret the physiological changes in their bodies linked to emotions, label them, and learn strategies to regulate them. Not only do competence levels rise after such training, but there is strong evidence that it improves the relationships between students and teachers.

Since gestures and movements are essential to the language of emotional expression, the more skilled we are as not just as listeners, but as 'noticers', the greater our opportunity to give people the space they need to make an honest connection with their emotions. Geddes continues,

Some of us of course learn ineffective strategies for emotional regulation, such as avoiding emotionally charged situations, or simply trying to shut down our emotions completely. Research shows that people who address emotional situations directly rather than avoiding them, have higher levels of wellbeing and are better able to cope with stress.

Linda Geddes, 2016

Checking up on People – Just what was Wrong with 'Time and Motion'?

In the 1959 Boulting Brothers film *I'm All Right Jack*, a company employ a 'time and motion' researcher with the inevitable consequence of the militant shop steward Fred Kite (played by Peter Sellers) calling his members out on strike. Although the workers refuse to cooperate, the time and motion study man tricks a new employee into showing him how much more quickly he can do his job than other more experienced employees. The film depicts trades unions, workers and bosses as equally manipulative and incompetent, and frankly deserving of each other!

Time and motion studies have thankfully gone the way of other outmoded management practices, since they were based upon a profound lack of trust in people and were used as a very blunt instrument by managers who simply wanted to exercise ever greater control over their 'human resources'. Very Frederick Taylor. Very 1950s.

And yet how are we to improve things if we don't measure efficiency? How are we to know that everything is as it should be if we don't check up on people? The mantra 'I trusted my people to do the job right' is not going to save any manager from the chop in the face of catastrophic failure. The problem, of course, is that we often shy away from checking up on people, for fear of them playing the 'you don't trust me' card at us. And aren't we supposed to be modern, inclusive, delegating leaders these days? Surely double checking and being a pain in the arse is 'old school' management?

> *The mantra 'I trusted my people to do the job right' is not going to save any manager from the chop in the face of catastrophic failure.*

One of my very first bosses, the late Michael Munn, had a mantra: '*in management, you never get what you expect, you only get what you inspect*' and while as a natural truster of people part of me railed against this as being a pretty negative view of people at work, I have to say I have had occasion to rue the day I didn't heed Michael's words.

And so I set out to establish processes that both trust people and check up on them – to establish performance management processes that both motivate and control. The key lies in the word 'performance'. I believe my success as a CEO and as a Chairman is primarily down to the skill I developed in checking that things are as they should be, while making people feel trusted and believed in in the process.

Checking up on people in their job performance, through spot checks or audits or simply by making them show you the evidence of their process or results, can of course make people feel like they are not trusted, leading in turn to a workforce who refuse to take risks and do the right thing unless specifically authorised or instructed by a manager. People's experience of being checked up on is negative – maybe they have been criticised in the past and maybe their bosses have used the process to beat them up.

And yet the experience of giving a performance in front of an audience is craved by many – and why wouldn't you want people to see just how brilliant you are if you are a great performer? What is there to fear? Lack of preparation and professionalism on your part, maybe and if that is the case then be afraid, but if you've put the work in, then bring on the audience. Of course it will be nerve racking. Of course we Brits in particular are not ones to show off. But performance builds confidence. A great performer loves a supportive audience, it's only the caustic and crabby critics that they hate. How did we turn ourselves from outrageous show offs at the age of seven, shouting '*look at me, Mum, look at me*' to the fearful and suspicious adults we are now?

So how do we create a 'performance' culture whereby employees actively want to be checked up on? Where they trust that transparency in their personal growth, with all its struggles and clumsiness, will be the thing we actually reward. We need to ask ourselves:

What is our fundamental motivation for needing to know?

First, we have to be clear in our own motivation for doing the checking. Of course there is an element of 'making sure' – of giving ourselves reassurance as managers, particularly if our arse is on the line if things go wrong. It's OK to be a Control Freak (like we could stop ourselves!). But if as a manager your greater purpose in checking up on people is genuinely to raise their standards, assist their personal growth and be part of them striving for ever greater levels of performance within this meaningful, purposeful and inspiring common enterprise, then check-on. When a community of individuals is so committed to the purpose, so committed to achieving the goals, then of course we all need to check on each other – or in a different parlance, to have each other's backs. Maybe it's just the language we use that needs to change.

As Chairman of a public institution a few years back, I was informed that, horror of horrors and disaster of disasters, we were to be subject to audit by government inspectors. When I expressed pleasure that we were to be audited, I was accused of naivety and offered a £50,000 budget from above, to make sure we 'got through' the audit with an acceptable rating. I declined. I was angry at the ease with which we could be offered such funds when budgets for service users were so miserly, but most of all I was proud of what we were doing. I also fundamentally believed that the Inspectors were motivated to do their job by the desire to make things better. Naivety in the extreme clearly!

The Inspectors duly came and saw us as we were. They were impressed by the things we did that were impressive. Where we fell short, their recommendations were genuinely helpful. All in all it was a hugely positive process, and all the employees were galvanised and excited by the whole affair. They were proud of themselves for the things they were praised for, and they took the more critical feedback as a spur to improve in the future. How much more positive than wasting £50,000 on stressing the staff, fooling the auditors and obtaining a correspondingly useless report.

As a consultant I have often recommended 'mystery shopping' (the use of people pretending to be prospective customers in retail outlets to check the quality of the customer experience) and have seen the very worst and best examples. In the worst examples, retail staff are genuinely afraid of being 'mystery shopped' and spend their time trying to 'suss out' a mystery shopper in advance in order to score the highest rating, and thus survive.

In the best examples, retail staff can't wait to be mystery shopped so that their bosses can actually see just how good they are. The difference – the motivation behind the schemes and the way they are organised. If people are fearful they will find ways round schemes. If they welcome it they will be proud to show you their performance.

A performance culture is not always comfortable; but watch how much it means for people on the Saturday night reality shows whether singing, ballroom dancing or ice skating, and see the quite phenomenal growth they accomplish in their technical and artistic performances. They are under the closest scrutiny, and they feel fear as a palpable and physically ever-present companion from their 'judges'. And yet they stand there and weep at the end of their performances – the experience has meant so much to them. And have you noticed that the only judge whose opinion the contestants really care about is the judge who is blunt, direct and maybe even at times unpleasant. Why? Because the fact that he or she is prepared to be disliked means that they are totally trusted as serving the performer.

What is the point in getting good at anything if there is no one to see it? What is the point in stretching ourselves to grow and learn, if no one is going to encourage us in our struggle? If you call it 'checking up on people' then it will surely fail. But if you are genuinely motivated to coach people and be a catalyst in their growth, then you are on a magically emotional journey and your people will not only follow you to the end of the Earth, but they will produce extraordinary performances along the way.

What's the Answer?

So we need to establish a very clear contract with our people. They have to understand how we will behave with them and that it will not always be comfortable, but that we are acting as we do in order to help them excel. We will be a pain in the arse, and we will not apologise or back off from this. And they have to understand that this is all in the

> *We cannot have our motives misunderstood or misinterpreted, for this is the cause of so many corporate woes.*

relentless and uncompromising pursuit of the goal we have all signed up to – that inspiring purpose that is bigger than all of us. We cannot have our motives misunderstood or misinterpreted, for this is the cause of so many corporate woes. As Jack Welch said:

Trust is crucial. When a leader is trying to promote a major initiative or lead through a crisis, people cannot be embroiled in a debate about their sincerity. People may disagree on the merits of the plan, but never on their motives.

Secondly, we need to build a culture of high self-esteem and self-confidence within our workforce, for people who feel good about themselves and their cause *love* being checked up on. They get it. This means actively investing in relationships of trust, removing fear from the workplace, being aware of our own controlling behaviours (and consciously reining them in) and rewarding others for the behaviours we desire, as opposed to punishing the behaviours we do not. A coaching culture is a fundamental requirement.

The mantra *'focus on results and nothing will change; focus on change and the results will come'* is intellectually accepted by many leaders; however, trusting this philosophy when the pressure is on is really hard. We have to have the supreme self-awareness as leaders that pressure is a result of expectation and that pressure causes us to want to focus on what's *not* happening. We need to recognise this for the ruthless tyrant it is and manage the pressure and the anxiety that goes along with it. Staying calm and serene in the face of judgemental and perhaps even maniacal challenges from bosses or stakeholders is one of the toughest things we have to navigate as leaders, but we simply don't have the luxury of caving in. If we truly trust that people growth = business growth, then we have to stay true to ourselves and our beliefs. We need a clear contract with our people for them to understand our behaviour under pressure. When considering how we deal with our own pressure from above, we can see that we also need a clear contract with our bosses. They have to understand what they are signing up for when they take us on as leaders.

As with all discussions and debates on leadership, this all sounds great in theory, but the acid test is how we are when the pressure is on. The trick is not necessarily to seek to change the way we behave under pressure, although maintaining a high self-awareness is important, but to seek to minimise the incidents and the incidence of pressure. So I advise my senior clients to adopt a very simple leadership technique called ACRC. It goes like this:

Awarenesss – be aware of the crucial moments and events in people's performances at work, when they are displaying courage or consciously taking a risk, for example when they are about to give a key presentation, attend a training course, carry out a performance appraisal they are fretting about, stand in front of the Board for the first time, or generally do something that they've never done before or that takes them way out of their comfort zone. Who helps you with this, by the way? Your PA maybe, but so should all of your managers.

Checking – being aware that one of these crucial performances is about to happen, go and check with them. Smile. Be excited for them. Ask them how they are feeling. Ask them what they need. The simple act of asking them will communicate so much – the very fact that you KNOW and cared enough to take five minutes out of your busy day or take 30 seconds to drop them an email will touch their hearts. And since we are busy, it doesn't always have to be in advance of the performance – it is also powerful to check after the event in a sort of *'didn't you make that critical presentation last week? – how did it go'* type of way.

Recognition – having checked, we now have to recognise and reward the behaviours we desire – people being courageous, confronting fears, going into difficult situations, using their initiative, being proactive. And a smile, an encouragement, a genuine 'well done' or 'good luck' is all that's needed. All people want is to be acknowledged for their courage.

Challenge – having recognised them and rewarded them, we can then challenge them to raise their performance even further. We can coach them to use their experience and what they've learned from tackling that courageous performance, to stretch them further. And they will respond, because they are finally learning that we are not trying to catch them out, we are simply desperate for them to achieve their potential. And in our desperation we will not compromise, and we will not shy away from being a pain in the arse!

If leaders consistently followed these simple steps as the foundation for their leadership activities, then the instances of extreme pressure would evaporate.

I do wish I'd been able to come up with an appropriate noun beginning with the letter 'D' for step 3 (ACDC rolls off the tongue so much better) but there simply isn't a 'D' word alternative for 'Recognition'. Or is there . . .

Observation

The critical interactions between managers and employees are simply not being observed. Of all the companies I've worked for as a consultant, this is the area that has been toughest to persuade leaders to systemise. Leaders get the theory, but so frequently fail in the execution. They seem simply so wedded to the practices they've grown up with and become comfortable with. Introducing a culture of observation feels too big to take on, with the fear of it consuming massive amounts of management time and then it not delivering tangible positive results. We are truly creatures of habit and our years of honing our problem-solving skills just cannot be set aside on some whimsical new faddy idea! Of course the underlying resistance is a visceral fear related to our self-worth. I know how to add value by solving problems. I don't know how to add value by 'merely' observing and then coaching. And even if I get good at it and it tangibly improves the performance of my people, the end result is they won't need me anymore.

> *Observation is essential. Observation is critical to the changes, the internal revolution I am espousing in these pages. Without it, good intentions will always be beaten by controlling habits.*

Observation is essential. Observation is critical to the changes, the internal revolution I am espousing in these pages. Without it, good intentions will always be beaten by controlling habits.

The reality is that it doesn't take much. I say to a manager, give me 10 per cent of your time to allocate to observation (ie stop some current activity) and I'll help you transform the culture of your business within three months. If a manager can spend five hours per week formally observing their people performing and giving them feedback, the manager's coaching skills will dramatically improve, the performance of the individual employees will make breakthroughs and the culture will be changed.

Managers interact with their employees in one of three situations. Ad hoc, formal 1:1 and in teams. We'll see later on how simple it is to have a calm and effective rhythm linking and balancing these three interactions, but for now I'll simply focus on the 1:1. If managers are not observed as they conduct 1:1s, it is highly likely in my experience that their 1:1s are woefully ineffective. They may be great update sessions (mainly for the manager to acquire details), and employees may even be finding them quite 'helpful' (receiving tips, advice and solutions), but they're only deemed to be 'helpful' by employees because the controlling habits of their managers have created conditioned habits of followership in them. If you've never really been coached, all you may know is the 'update/try this' version of a 1:1. When you don't know anything else, you might even give your manager a high rating for coaching!

When managers 'get' observing, facilitating and coaching, it's a rather beautiful thing. It's like watching a child discover a kitten for the first time. Enlightenment. The world not only looks different, but people look different too. The world is suddenly richer, deeper in potential, more vibrant – and so are people. People they manage and whom they judged as lacking competence and potential yesterday, have just astonished them today. The scales fall from the managers eyes in a sublime 'OMG' moment, and they're away. Now just let them play with their new toy.

Enlightenment is a beautiful thing and a joy to behold for all parties. But the thing that turns beauty into profit is that once seen in technicolour, the world can never go back to black and white. All parties now know something they did not know yesterday, and there is now no un-knowing it. All parties are changed.

Observation is not a nice-to-have, it's an essential. Spend five hours a week in that activity and you'll wonder how you ever managed without it.

Video Observation

'This call may be monitored for training purposes'. How many times have you heard that phrase when calling a customer service helpline? On hearing it, how many times have you

been affronted and immediately put the phone down? Exactly – none. It's become accepted practice so we think nothing of it, in fact our reaction is often positive in that we accept that people need training and we rather like the fact that the person we're about to speak to may feel that little edge of fear to be at their absolute best, just in case they're being listened in on. The introduction of taping and then videoing of police interviews with suspects under caution dramatically improved standards. The advancement of technology in wearable video devices now means that front-line emergency service and military personnel are now routinely presented with truthful feedback, valuable for both training and personal development, and for personal accountability and performance management.

Yes, in Parliament it may have unwittingly encouraged poor behaviour, people grandstanding or showboating, but that's only because it's not being facilitated properly, because the culture of the Commons is adversarial and theatrical, not grown up and collaborative.

But how frequently have you come across managers being videoed as they coach their people? The most crucial interaction affecting people's motivation and well-being at work – and we keep them secret. And don't buy the 'data protection' or 'employee rights' argument against the idea – usually brought out by a somewhat paranoid HR or Legal professional. That is a completely spurious defence, masking abject fear of what might be uncovered or the mass discomfort they anticipate being unleashed. If alleged offenders can be videoed being interviewed under caution; if soldiers under fire in the most desperate humanitarian aid and conflict situations can film every second of their mission, then managers can be filmed undertaking the somewhat more prosaic job of helping their employees perform better in their role.

I've used video whenever and wherever possible over the past 20 years, after I first saw the power of it in the late 1990s with the invention of the first wearable microcameras, and then used them to transform the 'mystery shopping' programme effectiveness in retail situations.

In the last two years I've initiated the filming of manager coaching sessions within a global tech business to great success. The initial scepticism (fear) was predictable – people won't agree, employees will feel put off so the 1:1 won't be natural, there are legal implications, who will store the videos and who will have access to them after the event, could they be called on by employees in the event of employment claims etc. But since the leader was up for the 'experiment', we went ahead and now it's in the culture, to the point where managers won't stop sending me videos so that I can give them feedback and where they are queueing up to have their videos 'used for training purposes'.

People love to perform, and they love to show off – they just need licence and permission to do so. They of course need to work in a culture of trust where the motivation for the filming is 100 per cent supportive of personal development. Since surely close to 100 per cent of employees now work in corporate cultures where McGregor's Theory X (people are untrustworthy so use coercion) has long been superseded by his Theory Y (people want to shine so use empowerment), once managers start to see how the videos are actually used, the take up explodes and the culture is changed. New managers are inducted into 'the way we do things around here', and while they might find being filmed a novel approach, it does not strike them as overly bizarre or scary.

I made an assertion in that last paragraph – that close to 100 per cent of employees now work in corporate cultures where McGregor's Theory X has long been superseded by his Theory Y, and I just want to expand upon that for a moment. I should more accurately make the following assertion – that close to 100 per cent of employees now work in corporate cultures where it is the conscious and publicly stated intention of the leaders, that Theory Y has superseded Theory X. That I believe to be true; but as we've seen, the biggest issue is leaders saying one thing and doing another – leaders who not only believe in Theory Y but believe they are managing in such a way that employees will be empowered and will thus shine. And in so many cases this is just not happening, thanks to our unconscious controlling habits. I have seen countless examples of managers becoming exasperated because they really feel they have 'empowered' their people, and yet their people have not taken it up and become empowered. If only we could get the right people . . .

The wonderful thing about the use of video with managers is that it completely exposes the unconscious habits and gives the immediate physiological re-calibration managers need to correct their habits and to start genuinely coaching (and thus genuinely empowering). Bingo – Theory Y blossoms.

The exposure of the unconscious controlling habits is matched by the exposure of pretty woeful observation, facilitation and feedback skills. But the poor level of skills in these areas are not down to a fundamental lack of competence, it's merely that the skills have never been used at work. People have these human relationship skills, and frequently demonstrate them with passion and alacrity outside work, yet they are not practised at bringing them to their role as a manager. Once the re-calibration is achieved, they're away; there's no stopping them. Most leaders have profoundly honest and ethical intentions, they've just been groping in the dark. Shine the light through eliminating the secrecy and the mystique of the 'dark art' of being a tough manager, and people flourish in their management and coaching skills.

So how do we observe? What are we looking for? Managers' unconscious habits are to focus on the problem being discussed on film and therefore coach people to be better problem solvers. What they actually need to develop are observational skills in spotting the opportunities for people to learn and for people to do think differently – to notice their state, their anxieties, their complacencies, their courage, their hesitancy, their blind spots, their perceived obstacles, and their potential breakthrough moments. More on this later.

Licence and Permission

This is why it's so critical for corporate leaders to develop skills in coaching and facilitation, bordering even on counselling and psychotherapy. How sad, that the common corporate employment experience is that actually it's not OK to be truly human at work.

We have to be something else – superhuman perhaps? What a tyranny to ask that of people every minute of their working life. No wonder there's no respite. Leaders must give a massive and conscious prioritising (my US clients would say over-indexing) on creating psychologically safe spaces for employees to be human. Leaders need to develop coaching and facilitation skills to give the monumental amounts of licence and permission that people need to be able to trust that they are safe to be the messy, fabulous geniuses that they are.

People fundamentally love to perform. I know some people are more reticent than others, some are perhaps even painfully shy, but I truly believe that people have an innate human drive to master skills and to be recognised for that increasing mastery. Perhaps their reticence and shyness is more of a learned protection from past negative experiences. The reticent and the shy certainly need more care, more patience, more sensitivity, less brashness, less gung ho challenging, more encouragement, more licence to show off, more permission to be fabulous.

People need immense amounts of licence and permission in order to perform in front of people – even me, and I am not known for my reticence and shyness. In fact I love to show off, but I also hate show offs, so I've learned over the years to temper my urges and wait for permission to release my inner Shirley Temple. I experienced a wonderful example of this just a few months ago when on a trip to Cuba with some leaders from around the world. On the final afternoon we were given one hour to work privately and individually to create a piece of art that represented our experience of the week. I am no artist. I spent 15 minutes despairing of what I could produce, while sneaking some looks at the glorious works unfolding before my eyes in the various parts of the grounds throughout which my peers had dispersed to create their masterpieces.

And then it came to me – I had been talking a lot that week about music and what it meant to me. I'd spent time with Cuba's leading hip-hop artist and with one of Cuba's oldest and most revered writer and performer of traditional Cuban music. So I wrote a song – a combination (I think the musical term might be a 'mash-up') of a rap and a salsa rhythmed song. The lyrics just wrote themselves in a few minutes, and I then spent the majority of my remaining ten minutes getting the melody and rhythm into my memory.

And so to the reveal. We revealed in small groups of four. I was incredibly reticent about performing my piece, because I felt exposed and I knew that to do it justice I had to throw my head back and launch in at the top of my voice. Given the other groups were only a few yards away, and were earnestly but quietly in conversation, I felt my performing would draw attention to myself and I would be negatively judged. I was both desperate to perform and would have given anything to not have to. The ultimate exquisite dilemma.

My fellow leaders in my small group noticed all this in me and helped me perform my piece. They organised themselves to provide a bit of a shield from the other groups and I was able to perform to an acceptable level. That was not enough for my colleagues though. Late that night, on the bus back to our hotel following our final meal together as one large group, they announced that the group would be receiving one final performance and then 'pushed' me to perform my piece from the front of the bus to the 25 happy and noisy passengers. One of them knelt in front of me holding up the flipchart sheet upon which I had written my lyrics, and he beamed at me as a threw my head back and launched into song. Not only did my fellow travellers enjoy my performance, they even sang along to the rather catchy hook (though I say it myself) of the chorus. I was showing off gloriously and loving every second. Left to my own devices I would never have done that. I needed the push; I needed to not be given a choice; I needed to not be believed when I said I was not at all bothered about performing it.

Who in your team is desperate to perform, but would deny it?

Transparency is the True Vulnerability

Vulnerability is quite a modern phenomenon in business. It is increasingly being pro-moted as a good thing for leaders to demonstrate, and many enlightened leaders have embraced at least the concept of showing vulnerability in front of their employees. But I've seen too many examples of leaders devising manufactured strategies for showing vulnerability, which sort of misses the point. The self-talk goes '*I know I need to show vulnerability, but I need to do so in a way that I can control and that actually makes me look strong and not weak*'. But telling your followers about your family is not displaying vulnerability, it's just being a courteous human being. In the US the ultimate example of this is how leaders can now wear their most horrendous mistakes as badges of honour, because unless you can show that you've founded and run companies that have then gone bust, you are clearly not a proper entrepreneur. It's weakness as strength, rather than weakness as human.

If you really want to demonstrate vulnerability as a leader, do two things habitually. First say 'I don't know' or 'I'm not sure' more frequently (or in many cases that exhortation should probably say '*start* saying . . .'). Second, share information that makes you feel un-comfortable, out of control, awkward and vulnerable to criticism from commentators. The leader that truly embodies vulnerability is the one that truly trusts the whole community to do what's best – and notice if you are going to do that, how much you should focus on creating the environment for all stakeholders to understand and embrace the purpose, the values and the plan.

Notes

Linda Geddes   'Control Yourself – Understand the Language of Emotions and We can Manage Them more Skilfully', *New Scientist*, 12 January 2016.

I'm All Right Jack   Released by Charter Film Productions in August 1959, this film is a satire of labour versus management and union negotiations starring Peter Sellers, Richard Attenborough and Ian Carmichael.

Frederick Taylor   Referenced in Chapter 11.

Michael Munn   A businessman who gave me my first MD role when I was 32. He was a tough chairman and could frequently be 'difficult', but he taught me a great deal. He died a few years ago.

Jack Welch   Referenced in Chapter 11.

Douglas McGregor   Douglas McGregor was a management professor at the MIT Sloan School of Management. His 1960 book *The Human Side of Enterprise* had a profound influence on education practices. In it he introduced his theories of human work motivation and management which he called Theory X and Theory Y. The two theories describe contrasting models of workforce motivation, with Theory X explaining the importance of heightened supervision, external rewards, and penalties, while Theory Y highlights the motivating role of job satisfaction and encourages workers to approach tasks without direct supervision.

Chapter 13

Pillar 4

A grip on Reality

What gets in the way of Being Ethical?

In the opening section we looked at the psychological and neurological factors affecting human behaviour at work, in particular the effects of fear, power and control and the ensuing anxiety and depression that can be created. We looked at the neurological factors of adrenaline, cortisol, dopamine etc, and the effect of these chemicals on our unconscious behaviours. And we looked at the psychotherapeutic dynamics of shame, projection, transference, identification, distraction, collusion, deflection, denial and code-pendency, which are also hugely critical factors affecting the way people behave.

The reality is that whereas outside work, with family and friends, it is more usual for human beings to be in integrity, doing what they say and basically remaining true to their values, inside work the opposite is more likely – that people are not doing what they say they will do, not meeting and honouring agreements, not being honest, and fundamentally operating (albeit unconsciously) from a place of survival. This is why so many corporate exhortations are completely unspecific and utterly meaningless.

In this environment, when people are predominantly inauthentic, the ground is ripe for other dynamics to take over. If we are not going to commune with each other honestly and straightforwardly and confidently, then we have to have another way of being; we have to develop a whole new world of nonsense and lunacy. And so we create the rich breeding ground for those most damaging and yet most human frailties and flaws – the everyday dynamics of basic human nature: gossip, melodrama, comfort, procrastination, boredom, complacency, blame, 'tribes' (silos), 'us and them' etc. Our place of work is our daily drama, and our leaders are often the protagonists in our very own soap opera. Of course we cannot do this too openly, so we have all developed fantastic strategies for making these behaviours look rational and sensible. We use management speak, we create needless bureaucracy, we hide in meetings, we always make sure we are looking a bit stressed and a bit put upon, we in fact throw the kitchen sink of obfuscation at hiding the reality. And we become so good at this, that it becomes our pathology – our corporapathology – it becomes our reality. Unconscious, all consuming, all distracting. Nonsense and lunacy indeed. But since we are all invested in maintaining it, who's going to blow the whistle? Who's going to point out that the Emperor has no clothes on?

And many leaders have become so deluded that when they stand in front of us and give speeches on issues of principles or values or behaviours, they genuinely believe what they are saying; they exhort values from their core, from every fibre of their being, with passion and complete belief. And so we believe them, because we trust their core, and we feel the honesty of their words, their passion and their principles. We trust them. Until their words are put to the test. Until we witness and endure the classic gaps between what they say and what they do; where they habitually and almost disarmingly say one thing and then go and do something entirely different.

Unrealistic Expectations

When Chairman of a Plc some years ago, our CEO made a wonderful speech at a Christmas dinner. He told a story of how he'd been helping his young daughter rehearse a violin piece in preparation for her school's Christmas concert, when she burst into tears. He'd asked her what was wrong, and she pointed at a section of the music with the word *prestissimo* above the stave. He asked her what that meant and she said 'play as fast as you can'. He started to sympathise, saying that he understood that playing as fast as you can was challenging. She glared at him, with the withering stare that indicated that he (as usual) was completely missing the point, and then pointed at the word above the stave some 12 bars further on in the music – *accelerando* – that, she said, meant 'play faster'. '*How can I play faster when I'm already playing as fast as I can!?*' she fumed through her choking tears of frustration. The CEO drew the comparison to what we ask of people at work.

> **Often what we ask of people is completely unrealistic – just plain unachievable. Leaders will frequently do this as a quite deliberate strategy, believing that it is the way to guarantee the maximisation of the potential results.**

Often what we ask of people is completely unrealistic – just plain unachievable. Leaders will frequently do this as a quite deliberate strategy, believing that it is the way to guarantee the maximisation of the potential results. 'Shoot for the stars and you might just land on the Moon', translates as 'if we want to land on the Moon, it's too risky to set that as the target. Push people to go further; to aim higher'. I call that manipulative. Defenders of this as a strategy will often point to 'evidence' that it works; they'll even say that people don't know what they're capable of until they are stretched, until they are 'forced' to find hidden resources and previously unknown capabilities and talents within themselves. There is of course some truth in this; fear does indeed create exceptional, even superhuman performances. Under threat, people find an extreme physical strength, a resilience, and a dexterity they never knew they were capable of. When we need to survive, fear is unquestionably the best motivator for us – the proper and appropriate tapping into our primeval survival instincts. But it cannot be our predominant tool. We're simply not designed for such an onslaught of perpetual pressure. We become traumatised.

When we need to thrive, *safety* is the required motivator. Fear will absolutely not get me to innovate. Only safety will give me the conditions for that. When we need to collaborate, we need the trust that can only come from safety.

Fear sets up the competitive win–lose, survival of the fittest dynamic, with individuals solely focussed on themselves. Meritocratic performance rating and reward systems simply exacerbate individualistic and competitive cultures. Corporate cultures are all too often guilty of using fear as the predominant, sometimes the only, motivator. And that is madness. Life does not work like that. We are not under threat every minute of every day, in fact in our corporate bubbles, we are not under threat at all! Our corporate roles are *so* cool. We're likely paid well above the average wage, and we don't have to shovel shit. Even if our work involves some physical effort, we get breaks and refreshment, and some satisfaction from mastering crafts and skills. More likely we are 'professionals' that sit at desks, use computers and meet with other people. The reality is that any pressure we feel is an artificial construct – very real to our brains of course and thus to our bodies, but artificial nevertheless. The stress and anxiety we cause people by 'forcing' them into unrealistic expectations is at best counterproductive at worst abusive.

But the 'binary' win–lose dynamic is endemic within corporations, as share prices are shored up artificially through growth curves and re-rated price/earnings (PE) multiples, so execs simply cannot afford not to hit stretching growth targets, quarter after quarter after quarter. Then potential mergers and acquisitions (M&A) deals are struck on valuations not based on actual results but based on the promises of results to come, in order to secure higher prices. I've seen so many prospective deals that were clearly never going to happen because the price was predicated on a future unrealistic profit target. All these factors place undue if not abusive pressure on the employees as fear of failure takes a grip and drives behaviours.

Targets, specifically the inexorable demand for continual growth, have created a binary win–lose dynamic. Thus fear rules, because the survival instinct inevitably kicks in. 'Fear to Survive' – yes. But we have to move to an organic creative dynamic of 'Safety to Thrive'.

In pursuit of a win–lose goal, not accepting a slackening in pace, for example, is understandable. But the same cannot be applied to forecasting, otherwise we set up a culture where people will not tell the truth or call out problems.

In their defence, leaders would say no one is 'forced' to do anything; that people are absolutely free to speak up, to challenge, to 'push back'. In fact it would be welcomed. And so we're back to our words-versus-actions dilemma, with leaders genuinely believing they are encouraging challenge because they openly state that challenge is welcome. But how do they behave when challenged? Do they reward the challenger with smiles, openness, validation for the act of challenge? Or do they patronisingly explain why the challenge (and therefore the challenger) is stupid or naive? More critically perhaps, how do leaders behave when they are *not* challenged? Do they actively seek it out, providing a safe forum for people to express their genuine worries and concerns, and then meet those concerns with compassion and understanding (which is usually all it takes to enable people to move forward and get with the programme!). Or do they take absence of challenge as evidence that everyone is happy? That's very convenient but utterly delusional. It is of course defensible and maybe that's the prime motivation . . .

'Prestissimo, accelerando' is asking the impossible. It is madness. It's the same madness (and the same counterproductive result) as when we ask someone who's been working on a complex problem for some time *'have you tried X?'*. It's madness to believe

that we can come up with an option in five minutes that they've not considered in five months. But when we work in a system that is built on a founding belief in the alchemy of maximum rewards from minimal effort, it's no wonder that madness prevails. Corporate life is littered with moments of insanity – of unreality. Yet no one seems to notice, let alone call it out; our collective denial is simply too great. We must embrace struggle. I am all for setting people stretching objectives, but then please for God's sake make it safe for them to struggle, safe for them to fail, safe for them to learn and to grow and to keep uncovering their potential and their dreams. If we're about to die, to go under, to lose the bid, then fear can be helpful, necessary even. But that's probably 1 per cent of the time. We live in fear of Spectres – always fearful of something that *might* happen. How quickly that turns to paranoia.

> *I am all for setting people stretching objectives, but then please for God's sake make it safe for them to struggle, safe for them to fail, safe for them to learn.*

We have to start actively promoting 'Safety to Thrive'.

The Perfect Cocktail for Self-Inflicted Stress

While I remain firmly of the conviction that abusive behaviours are still rife in the corporate world, I am also acutely aware of just how many leaders are desperately trying not to be so. But we have another problem now, in that many modern businesses have created the perfect cocktail for self-inflicted employee stress.

We take highly talented people who are used to success and give them the three ingredients almost guaranteed to create fear – unboundaried autonomy, unreasonable expectations and inadequate coaching. High levels of adrenaline and cortisol are cultural, and employees experience these abnormal levels for extended periods of time – caused by the perceived threat levels from pace, expectation, volume of external stimuli and a transactional and distracting work rhythm. What are people learning, really? The positive conscious learning of how to be genuinely creative and collaborative, or the negative reinforced conditioned responses – playing safe, not taking real risks, deflecting, staying small?

When a culture is predominantly based on positive learning, metrics and targets are incredibly helpful, and demanding 100 per cent compliance to processes is seen as a helpful underpinning of creativity and collaboration; when a culture is predominantly based on negative learning, metrics and targets skew behaviours in a destructive manner and compliance is experienced as fear and coercion. We know what the difference between negative learning and positive learning looks like – but this demands that managers are paying attention to the person, and not overly focusing on the result or the business problem at hand.

Coaching within organisations is not really coaching. It's either teaching (showing people how to do what we're asking them to do – a very valid and necessary management activity, but it's not coaching) or it's manipulation, where the manager tries to look like they're coaching, but actually they are leading the person to come to a pre-conceived conclusion – to the Manager's idea of the solution. Hence the accent in my coaching training programmes on making managers aware of their unconscious controlling habits. I've seen little evidence in universal manager cohorts of genuine encouragement and the active giving of licence and permission to struggle, to be wrong, to be uncertain, to make mistakes – to be genuinely creative and collaborative.

Culturally there are still too many manifestations of 'undesirable' behaviours being valued – people being promoted for being visibly effective; the achievement of short-term numbers are being dominantly rewarded and the missing of targets is being unconsciously punished. Salespeople have a mortal fear of failure; they feel it as a wounding – a foreshadowing of ultimate rejection. Whereas Engineers welcome failure, celebrate it even, as a necessary and positive step towards exceptional achievement. This fear of rejection is driving undesirable behaviours – competitiveness, self-promotion, short-term results over long-term growth, an unhealthy obsession with achievement of targets.

Insecure over-achievers often get the senior leadership roles due to their 'drive' – probably the most prized executive attribute. These people are not easy to work for, mainly because their insecurity is so often triggered, since they've accepted ridiculous targets on behalf of their team. One of the most common dynamics I see in businesses is the insanity of sales teams being predictably and often seriously behind target at the end of Month 1 of a new year. It's the end of Month 1 and we already know that we'll never make the year's number in 11 months' time. There are two reasons for the pathetic predictability of this. First of all, we had to pull as much business as possible forward into Month 12 of last year, since we had to get to the highest possible number (having been behind all year but still forecasting that we could make it up somehow). So we started this year effectively in negative territory. Secondly, our leader does not have the courage to negotiate reasonable sales targets. Their ego will simply not allow them to 'fail'. And so here we go. Insane stress levels from Day 1, and all pathetically predictable.

> *Insecure over-achievers often get the senior leadership roles due to their 'drive' – probably the most prized executive attribute.*

Autonomy is a good thing, of course; a great thing. Dan Pink's work on motivation shows us that what people want in their work is autonomy, meaning and mastery. People want the freedom to choose how they work and the respect, dignity and space to work things out for themselves. People want to work on something that matters; that will genuinely make a difference to the world and to people's' lives. And people want to master things, to learn new things and develop and grow their skills. But most managers idea of giving autonomy is to abdicate responsibility, in the rather fatuous '*my door is always open, call me if you need me*' way. Except that most people don't call their boss when they're really struggling because their experience of doing that is not positive. And although this is often unfair on the manager (it's one of those Spectres where the fear of what *might* happen rules) that does not exonerate managers who substitute abdication for autonomy.

I could forgive the first two parts of the cocktail, if the standard, quality and consistency of management and coaching was decent. It does not need to be perfect or actually anywhere near perfect (in fact as we've seen, clumsy is great); it just has to be decent. Managers have to care enough to coach. Abdication says '*my door is open, call me if you need me*' – I make everything *your* responsibility. Autonomy with coaching says, '*how are you doing, where are you struggling, what do you need?*'.

A participant on a recent coaching training programme I ran asked a fabulous question. She said, '*why does it feel so incredibly valuable to be coached, yet feel so desperately unhelpful to coach?*'. And this question goes to the heart of the issue of what is real versus what we fear. The feeling of such immense value from being coached is absolutely real. The feeling of being unhelpful when coaching someone else is not real – it is one of our powerful Spectres.

We need to know what is real, and what is fear. So here's my general rule – most of what you think you know is fear, and not real. When in doubt, assume it is your fear filtering your perception of reality. And the solution?

You could commune with nature – go for a walk, listen to the birds, watch the clouds roll by. You could count your blessings – savour the beauty of your life, list what you have to be grateful for. Or you could do something doubly valuable – connect with another human being – ask someone how they are, listen to them, pay attention to them, show them some kindness.

In just a few minutes you will have re-connected with reality, and you'll know what to do next.

It's just a job

In 1987 Boris Becker, having won Wimbledon the year before at the tender age of 17, crashed out of the tournament in Round 1 – a real shock exit. I recall watching the post-match interview and him saying '*nobody died, I lost a tennis match*'. He must have been churning up inside, but he was right. It was, after all, just a tennis match.

How often I have concluded a tough coaching session with a senior client, having worked to help them navigate the often-extreme stresses and pressures of their role, with the words '*And remember it's just a job; it's a game; it's important, but it's not real life*'. And I say these words not to belittle the massive investment of personal time, energy and skill that the client has made, nor to downplay the difference the client's company is making to people's lives. I say it because the client is in danger of taking their responsibilities (or their inflated perception of them) *so* seriously, as to potentially damage themselves and their families.

I say '*it's just a job*' not to give anyone access to feeling better through not caring, but to give people the clarity and means to get a grip back on reality, and to stand up, speak up and do the right thing. Without a strong touchstone in reality, we simply won't have the humility we need to be trusted and to lead with real authenticity; and therein lies the road to hubris. If we believe we are indispensable, then we will surely be proven wrong sooner or later, but after a huge self-inflicted cost. So it doesn't work.

However, while I am of course concerned for the well-being of *all* clients, the open acceptance of the Faustian Pact means that at least the most senior ones are getting very well rewarded. My main concern therefore is the damage caused to those who have the misfortune to be led by the seemingly omnipotent ones. Our belief in our indispensability will cause those we lead to learn that they are lesser mortals, incapable of doing what we do, thinking like we think, moving as fast as we can move, caring as deeply as we care. And they will learn that they *are* dispensable, with all the fear that this creates for them. If indispensability is the gateway to hubris, then dispensability is the entrance to the abyss.

Corporate citizens in well paid, cerebral, clean, civilised roles can sit back from time to time and salve themselves by saying '*it's just a job*'. The vast majority of the population do not have that luxury. For most, a period of unemployment could genuinely mean hardship, loan sharks, bailiffs, kids going without. I understand the fear felt by employees and will work tirelessly for workplaces of safety and freedom from anxiety. I have less tolerance for the fears of the 'privileged' corporate citizens. I'm not denying the fear, indeed in some cases the abject terror, of being out of work while trying to pay a huge mortgage and private school fees, but that's about shame not hardship. So as you say whisper the mantra 'it's just a job' under your breath in self-therapy, and once you've restored yourself to normality, use that mantra to stand up, speak up and do the right thing. If '*it's just a job*' doesn't work for you, then simply try '*get over yourself!*'.

Leave, Endure or Overthrow

When I am coaching executives who bemoan their lot, I offer a choice of three simple strategies – Leave, Endure or Overthrow. If it is so bad that everything in your life is turning to shit; so bad that you can't sleep; so bad that you hate your work, then Leave. Quit, with no thought or intention to go with anything more than your contractual entitlement. Work out your notice, start looking for what's next, but do not endure anymore.

If it's bad but you simply cannot contemplate leaving; if your financial situation is such that you cannot afford to be without income for a period of time; if it's bad, but in reality no worse than any corporate role you've had in the past (and you survived *them*); bad, but you've moved around quite a bit and you really need some stability on your CV; bad, but actually you're learning lots and couldn't get this experience anywhere else at this time; bad, but actually the location and the freedom you have in the role mean you have breakfast everyday with the kids, and haven't missed a school play since you took the role, then Endure. Design some coping mechanisms and activities that will proactively assist you to survive in the role and keep your mental health. Sit it out for as long as the situation lasts while you do your very best to keep your integrity and do your work well.

Above all make a positive decision to stay, and then put mechanisms in place to cope with the worst aspects of the role, and count your blessings for the good bits.

If leaving or enduring still feel wrong to you, and if you have the stomach for it, then Overthrow. If it's the culture or situation that is the cause of your distress and unhappiness then come up with a plan of how it should be and how to change it, and communicate that plan to the people who have the power to change things, demanding that they act; if it's an individual who's the cause, then stop accepting the abusive behaviours or treatment; blow the whistle; 'out' the bully; plan to defeat them and out-live them. But whichever of the three strategies you choose, stop moaning and start taking positive action.

While I promote these as viable alternatives, it is a device on my part to get people out of Victim mode and into self-controlled mode. As their coach I need to get them into a place where they will start to take personal responsibility again: out of Victim mode, out of Child mode, and into Adult behaviours. Choosing one clear strategy from Leave, Endure or Overthrow means that the client takes positive action, leaving their depressive state behind almost instantly.

The Drama Triangle

But the problem with the Leave, Endure, Overthrow strategy suite is that it still plays squarely into the 'Drama Triangle' invented in the 1960s by Stephen Karpman. Karpman was a student of Eric Berne, adapting with his mentor's blessing and encouragement, Berne's pioneering development of Transactional Analysis in the field of family dynamics and psychotherapeutic diagnoses and interventions. Berne wrote what is arguably the very first 'pop psychology' book, *Games People Play*, in 1964, bringing his development of Transactional Analysis (TA) out of the therapy room and into the public consciousness. TA introduces the three states of Parent, Adult and Child, hence sometimes referred to as the PAC model.

Parent is our ingrained voice of authority, developed through conditioning from a young age in relation to authority figures. Parent is our 'Taught' concept of life. Our survival instinct tells us to get to Parent state as quickly as possible in order to have control and to have power over others. Parent behaviours come out positively as protective and nurturing, absolutely appropriate if people are being a true 'parent' to one of their own children. But so many 'parental' behaviours come out when we are simply seeking to impose authority over others outside our family, in which case even these positives can be received as patronising or even infantilising. Then of course there are the negative 'Parent' behaviours – angry, judgemental, critical and controlling.

Child is our pure, unfiltered emotional reaction to events. We can also choose Child state in relation to someone who is in Parent state. Child is our 'Felt' concept of life. Child negative behaviours include petulance, inappropriate humour, gossiping, tantrums, teasing, talking behind someone's back. In a workplace these negative behaviours are ugly and offensive. The positive Child behaviours are honesty, creativity, joyfulness, exuberance and playfulness. Child is arguably our most 'authentic' state – absolutely unfiltered, therefore in many ways completely trustworthy, and so incredibly valuable in the workplace, if only we knew how to facilitate all those inner children.

Adult is our ability to think and act for ourselves, based on our own core values and our objective sense of reality and the facts before us. Our Adult keeps our Parent and Child under control, allowing us to experience the positive aspects of those two states, but not be slaves to them. Adult is our 'Thought' concept of life. Adult behaviours, if genuine, are all positive – attentive, self-aware, non-threatening, listening to understand, noticing mood, caring. I said 'if genuine' – adult behaviours can be manufactured and as such are manipulative and certainly *not* authentic. If I pretend to care about you, I am really in Parent state seeking to manipulate your Child into trusting me. Genuine Adults know when to value Parent and Child in others, and are not scared of those states, however messily they might show up. We might not endorse Child behaviour, in fact we might well have to sanction it, laying down (Parent) strong boundaries (Adult). But Adults know the inevitability of and the value of the honesty of Child reaction.

Karpman took Berne's TA model and overlaid a 'Drama Triangle', developing his approach through his work with actors. He realised that in every 'drama' there were fundamentally three characters – *Victim, Persecutor* and *Rescuer* – and the drama and intrigue played out for the audience in the relationships between the characters, the identification of the audience with themselves in the characters and the roles they assumed, and in the characters' journeys between the roles. For example, the journey of a thoroughly unappealing Persecutor, gaining the sympathy of the audience when we see glimpses of the Victim within. This dynamic is absolutely at the heart of Stockholm Syndrome, and it is how Corporate Hostages come first to understand, then identify with, and then even perhaps adore their Corporapathic masters.

I reference TA and the Drama Triangle a lot in my work since I observe the 'game' and role playing so frequently – in so many situations and at the root of so many dysfunctional cultures and relationships. I observe the game of 'Heroes, Villains and Martyrs' frequently. The Hero rescues us from a crisis; the Villain is out to get us; the Martyr simply suffers.

The issue with Heroes is that they often unconsciously create a crisis to give themselves a reason to be heroic. No crisis? No requirement for Heroes. One of my first clients in my consulting life, a VP of Engineering at a global tech business, ruthlessly tried to eradicate what he called the 'culture of the diving catch'. His view was that if the processes were fit for purpose and people used them properly, there would be no need for anyone to ever perform a diving catch. He was always wary of lauding people for such acts, exhorting them instead to be better prepared and to use the process in future.

In a competitive marketplace it can be convenient to portray competitors as Villains – companies to be beaten, to be out-thought and out-marketed. Unfortunately the Villains are all too often within our own company – the classic, and hugely destructive, 'them and us' dynamic. How many departmental leaders are guilty of eye-rolling at the mere mentioning of another 'villainous' department. And so the drama is set up.

And then there are the Martyrs – endlessly suffering, enduring their torture stoically (though not privately) and at pains to ensure we all understand that their suffering is greater than anyone else's. No one is working harder than the Martyr, hence the visibly long hours in the office, and the ridiculing of anyone having the temerity to leave 'early'. My bully of a boss all those years ago basically ping-ponged between Martyr and Hero. The Martyr version would be on the phone to me most mornings around 6:30am and he'd start by telling me what he'd already done that day. He had to let me know that he'd been up earlier than me. It was as if his world would fall apart if even for one day I could best him on effort. Even as I write this now, I can feel the disgust and I could not help myself from joining in the drama – although I would not play the part that he wanted me to play. I recall one time being called to a meeting with him at Head Office, a drive of around two hours for me, for a 7:30am meeting. Knowing he arrived in the office just before 7am each day, I decided to have some fun by getting there earlier than him. I was in the car park at 6:15am to make sure of my plan. It could not have gone better; the bonus was that he was actually a few minutes late! Joy of joys! He arrived at 7:10am, clocked me sitting in my car, although the script demanded that he pretend he hadn't seen me. I gave it a few minutes, knowing that the receptionist would be arriving around 7:20am. When she arrived, on time, I went in and asked her to let my Boss know that I was here. I knew he would be fuming, and he then acted completely in line with past behaviour when thwarted. He made me wait. No acknowledgement of my presence; no acknowledgement of him running behind schedule. He wanted me to sweat; he wanted me to know who had the power. Imagine his chagrin when he eventually deigned to meet me, nearly 90 minutes after our schedule time, and I walked in calm as a cucumber, as if everything was completely as it should be. And then I got my Hero in first, telling him that having the additional time before our meeting had been incredibly valuable as I'd been able to rescue a situation. It was hugely enjoyable, and yet one of the saddest days in my corporate life. I quit not long after.

Often the mere raising of awareness of these psychological constructs is sufficient to allow clients to make breakthroughs in their confidence and thus in their strategies for handling tough situations.

Leave, Endure, Overthrow still plays the Drama Triangle. The client is the Victim and the Boss or the company are the Persecutor, and each of the three possible strategies effectively plays the Victim role. If the client Leaves, they allow them to 'win'. The client is still Victim although we shorten the timescale. Of course, the Client might then move into Rescuer mode by throwing a lifeline to others to come and join them on the outside. If the client Endures, they are Victim and remain so for as long as they choose that strategy. If the client Overthrows, the roles reverse, with the client becoming Persecutor.

So we have to move from the Leave, Survive, Overthrow strategy as quickly as possible. My intent in introducing it is simply to raise awareness and to effect in my client the taking of a confident step of personal responsibility, possibly the first Adult act the client may have taken in quite a while.

But move into what? 'Convert'? Can we actively seek to 'convert' our Boss or our company to a more enlightened way of thinking and being? Possibly, and 'Convert' might arguably be a more ethical form of Endure, but even this is still playing to an underlying belief that the Boss is knowingly and deliberately and intentionally acting towards us in a controlling or manipulative way. We endow our Boss or our company with Machiavellian motives, when maybe, just maybe, our Boss and our company (that's all the other human beings remember, not a machine) are just like us. Honestly trying to be decent and do right, but unaware, in denial or just plain scared to stand up.

So maybe our move is simply into 'Being Human'? Why can we not feel that being human is enough?

> *So maybe our move is simply into 'Being Human'? Why can we not feel that being human is enough?*

Being Human in a Corporate World

Being human, having humility, means we have to be super sensitive to exercising power and control over others. The best thing to do with power when you get it is to give it away as quickly as possible – just give it to the right people; the people whose motivation can be trusted; the people who genuinely want the enterprise to be successful and sustainable; the people who are not greedy, not out for themselves. Even when we think we're not exercising the power we have or that we could be exercising, we are by osmosis and by default. So we have to eschew the trappings of status and power, and we have to politely and sensitively reject subservience.

In my last CEO role, leading retail outlets all over the UK, I devised a crude but symbolic device in an effort to communicate that I was at the service of the employees and not the other way around. Since I had initiated a culture of openness and education on business performance across the company, personally attending several management accounts reviews every month, and insisting on employees being active participants in those reviews, I established a line on the management accounts for each outlet for the costs of me and my fellow Directors to be charged out. I took our salaries and those of our PAs, the costs of our cars and benefits, and the rental cost of our office space, divided the total by the number of outlets and then charged that amount into the outlets' accounts each month. That way I earned the right to be judged in two ways – firstly for an accurate estimation of our salaries, which were not outrageous, and secondly for the return on the outlets' investment in me and my fellow Directors as leaders. I've always supported total transparency in executive earnings. First, if executives are ashamed of what they earn then they are clearly overpaid in relation to their added value. Second, in my experience employees always over-estimate what their leader earns. I've never been ashamed of what I earn, but maybe that's because the maximum I've ever earned is around 12 times the lowest paid employee in the businesses I've led. I feel privileged and lucky and grateful to earn what I've earned in my career. Could I have earned more? Absolutely – I've turned down a number of offers of very highly paid roles, including one ludicrously highly paid one. Don't get me wrong, I'm no saint, and I'll take something for nothing if there's no catch, but frankly I've never wanted the pressure of the insane expectations that go along with being paid obscene amounts of money.

Being human is not about survival – we are not really human when we are in survival mode. We are animal – run by our survival operating system of fight or flight, and it's not edifying. Being human is feeling and relating. Smiling, being kind to people, being generous of heart and spirit, savouring the nourishment of emotional connections with others, accepting each other, trusting each other, loving each other, being grateful, humble, giving service, helping others, encouraging, believing in people, living life in all its richness of beauty and messiness; of sadness and joy.

I smile a lot. Channelling Major Marsden and John Pallin, I deliberately get myself into a 'happy' place in order to give tough feedback. I would say that most of the really challenging feedback and direction I've given others when I've been in a position of power over them, has been with a smile on my face. And not a manufactured smile, or the cold psychopathic smile of the assassin, but a genuine warmth of a caring leader; the smile that accompanies an act of love. We've come to believe that we take care of people by doing things for them, by protecting them from reality, by sparing their feelings, by giving them solutions, but these things merely infantilise. They are the well-meaning but ultimately patronising and disrespectful acts of people who are only really concerned with managing their own discomfort. There's a good reason that the airlines have learned to exhort us to 'Put your own oxygen mask on before seeking to help others with theirs'. We can best take care of others when we are taking care of ourselves first. I don't mean that we should indulge in 'screw you, I'm going to save myself' behaviours. Far from it. I mean that when we take care of ourselves by recognising our state, what's triggering us, what our feelings of anxiety are actually about; when we exercise conscious self-regulation, calming ourselves down and re-connecting emotionally with the people around us, then and only then can we truly care for others, and consciously choose our approach and our communication.

> *Finding joy in our work must be our ultimate goal, since there is no law of physics that says work has to be horrible*

Finding joy in our work must be our ultimate goal, since there is no law of physics that says work has to be horrible, and since a community of joyful people will always produce truly astonishing and wholly exceptional results, that no amount of control could even dream of.

Nature is real

I have always loved nature – it was one of my father's gifts to me. I was born in a brand new house on a modern (1957 version!) housing estate, yet we overlooked farmland. Behind us were thousands of houses, but in front of us was endless countryside. So I lived and played (ah the days before parental paranoia) in woods and fields. I developed a love of bird watching at that time, honing a skill that I could not have imagined would transfer and serve me well in business – the skill of spotting the slightest movement out of the corner of my eye. I truly believe my skills as a facilitator were born standing stock still in woods and fields, waiting for some obscure and shy bird to declare itself.

Nature has two wonderful aspects – first of all nature is real. It is unpredictable, uncontrollable, volatile, beautiful, grounding, constant, reliable, astonishing, ever changing, ever evolving; I could go on. Secondly nature gives pure feedback. No sanitising, no desire to manipulate or rescue.

I have stated earlier in this book that I believe all managers should receive some training on psychotherapeutic dynamics of projection, transference and codependency. I also believe that all managers would greatly benefit from exposure to nature and what it can teach us. Take horses for example. Horses are flight animals. They can fight, but frankly they suck at it, and so when adrenaline gets the better of them, they're off. The wind gets up, and they get spooked. A leaf falls off a tree, and they freak out. Every day horses require confirmation of safety. They constantly test their boundaries to check that they are safe. If one small detail changes, they are filled with dread. It's exhausting. The only reward a horse ever wants is an absence of threat – they don't want their ears waggled (they're not cocker spaniels), and although they do of course want food, it does not work as a reward.

When managers first work with horses, using all the control, manipulation, coercion and bribery that works on humans, it's hugely frustrating for them. They simply cannot get the horse to do what they want it to. And although horses are flight animals, they rarely feel threatened by the humans' antics, instead merely wandering off through a rather bemused boredom part way through the exercise. As the humans become more frustrated, so do their controlling behaviours get worse. And it does not work on horses. Horses give a purity of feedback that is at first exasperating, but given its purity, when things start to happen, the immediacy and the trustworthiness of the feedback is exhilarating. So how do 'things start to happen'? Well it's when the humans stop trying to get the horse to do what they want and start, instead, to build a relationship of trust and purely energetic communication. Horses read energy, and once that energy is trustworthy, a horse will follow a human anywhere, since the human now represents the absence of threat.

> *Horses give a purity of feedback that is at first exasperating, but given its purity, when things start to happen, the immediacy and the trustworthiness of the feedback is exhilarating.*

Every manager should have working with horses as part of their training. I've seen over-controlling managers humbled and changed by it, and I've seen timid managers gain confidence in setting and maintaining boundaries through it.

Well-Being

Our leader may well speak about work/life balance in the most ethical and humanly sensitive and compassionate way, exhorting us to take our full holiday entitlement, to always attend our children's nativity plays and sports days, to take our elderly relatives to the doctors when needed, to leave the office before 5 o'clock if we've been in since 7, to keep our weekends sacrosanct, to switch our laptops and mobiles off and ignore emails during 'family time', to take our full maternity leave, to not come into work the day after we've flown back from China etc – so that we genuinely believe them. They may even express that these things are not just acceptable, but almost necessary or even mandatory, with their exhortation accompanied by a homily on the subject of personal well-being, and how our families are more important than the company.

But our leaders then let us down – within seconds. First of all, they do not live by their own rules. They do not do many, if any, of the things they tell us to do. They send emails at all times of day and night. They seem always to make sure they are the first in and the last to leave. They work weekends. They work on holiday. They miss their kids' seminal school events. They not only eschew taking their full maternity leave, they work right up to the moment their waters break, or even worse they schedule a C section at the 'best' time for the company, and then work from home until they return full time after just a couple of weeks. They are the most appalling role models, and yet they can't see it. So in fact what they set up is one of the most powerful and unconscious platforms in creating a 'them and us' culture, where they set themselves up as superior beings, since clearly the only rational explanation for them exhorting us to have a work/life balance when they don't have one themselves, is because we are lesser mortals to be tolerated and patronised. We are in fact a necessary evil.

Secondly, they live very different lives to the rest of us, but judge us and manage us by the rules that apply in their world not ours. They assume that we would want to live their life if only we had the opportunity, and that therefore we think like they do and reference our personal decisions like they do. We're just not as fortunate as them (cue patting of heads). In reality their work is often more of a calling than ours. They are more likely to have autonomy and more likely to be engaged in work that truly plays to their strengths. They have nannies and drivers and cleaners and PAs that create an artificial world where things are generally easier for them than for us. They can travel business class, and since their kids may be at private school, they are free to work and travel deep into the evenings. Some of them will not have seen their aged parents in weeks, months may be, especially as they might well live hundreds or even thousands of miles away. What different lives they lead, and that's fine for them (clearly their Faustian Pact has a big payoff).

I had experience a couple of years ago of a wonderful (pejorative usage) example of just what I'm talking about here. A CEO was determined to 'reward' his team with time at a swanky hotel with partners. He communicated his desire for people to arrive at the hotel around 6pm for drinks, followed by dinner and dancing, an overnight stay and breakfast together, followed by a round of golf or a spa session, whichever people chose. He was very excited about his decision to reward his team in this way, telling them all how much it cost, and telling them all how much they had earned and deserved this wonderful treat. And then I watched him become a petulant child as his team did not respond as he had expected. Typically, they responded with reluctance, hesitancy and even a little dread, though of course they tried to hide this. Their lack of enthusiasm was down to a number of human and wholly predictable factors (well, predictable to any decent non-egotistical adult with a grain of EQ) – most of them travelled a great deal on business, and so the prospect of another night in a hotel was not appealing. The prospect of spending 'social' time, and a huge amount, with their colleagues did not fill them with glee. Worse still, the CEO's dream took absolutely no account of their family situation, organising of childcare overnight etc, and no account of the fact that partners might have a life that would be disrupted by this amazing plan. The prospect of playing golf induced suicidal feelings in some, and the spa session felt uncomfortably close to a 'bottle of sweet sherry for the ladies' gesture. The event got cancelled, and the team were suitably punished as the CEO adopted one of his favourite roles – the 'why do I bother when they are so ungrateful?' role.

Thirdly, and most perniciously of all, the reality is that our humanity is actually a massive inconvenience to our leaders. And so when the pressure is on (and when isn't it?) our adoption of their words irritates them. And they show it. When they said leave before 5 if you come in at 7am, they didn't mean on a day when the board report is needed. And what really irritates them is that you should know this and manage yourself accordingly, and this in turn makes them angry that they now have to point this out to you and risk being unpopular, and they deeply resent that you put them in this position. It is up to you to determine the context, situation and appropriateness of applying the principle, and since in this instance leaving before 5 was clearly (any idiot would have known this) inappropriate, you should have considered this and suspended the principle in these exceptional circumstances. When they said don't answer, don't even look at emails on holiday, they didn't mean you to do this while you've got a big deal on the boil, and they should be able to trust you to this. When they said attend your child's sports day, they didn't mean you to do this when your number 2 was doing the same on the same day – surely any idiot can work out that we can't have *both* of you out of the office at the same time!!! And so we believe them, we act accordingly and we are immediately punished with their patronising, their anger or their resentment, or a heady cocktail of all three. And we learn very fast, after just one instance, to NOT believe them, ever again.

Employee well-being is rightly now high on the agenda of companies, but what format does this 'concern' take? Many of the large tech businesses pioneered free food at work, and not just free food, but the highest quality bistro-style food in fabulous restaurant settings. This has spread rapidly to the professional services firms supporting them and beyond now into wider industry. The days of making employees pay for a cup of crappy coffee from a machine, or seeing them fight over the milk with their name on it in the communal fridge, are surely over for most? In addition many of these tech firms (and thus a growing wider constituency) offer free employee support services way beyond mere food – medical and therapeutic services, massage, gyms, community project support, internal peer support groups etc. These employee well-being services can easily add £'000s to the annual cost of employing one person. So these firms must feel that they get a return on that investment. And of course the benefits are huge: loyalty, meaning lower attrition rates and hiring costs; well-being, meaning lower absenteeism and higher productivity; collaboration and innovation, from the socialising aspect of employees taking proper breaks and eating together. It's interesting how 20 years ago we culturally dictated that people ate sandwiches at their desks; now we culturally dictate that people take a proper lunch break. But the unintended consequences also produce downsides – high loyalty means that people are more scared to leave when they are not enjoying their work, or worse when they are being mistreated or abused or asked to do unethical things; higher well-being often leads to people working longer hours and then using the 'support' services to enable this.

Thirty years ago I recall a BP executive telling me that the reason he had quit BP was when he found out that 'the office plants make more than I do'. BP had moved into a prestigious new purpose built corporate HQ, and this exec was outraged when he found out what was being spent in that environment. Of course his outrage was the relativity; the prioritisation – all he knew is that he was being over-worked and under-appreciated, and the money spent on plants was the last straw.

Large firms these days may well be spending £'000s per year per employee on 'well-being' and I for one won't argue against that in itself. But it's the relativity – I ask these companies how much they are investing per annum per employee on the most vital aspect of well-being: having a decent human being as a manager. I think some firms take the easy way out – the easy way is to provide the free food. The hard way is to consistently invest in, monitor and ensure employee psychological safety in the workplace, and the biggest single factor in this is the line manager. When modern businesses invest an equal amount per head in ensuring employees have a decent line manager, as they do in providing hygiene benefits, I'll buy that they mean it when they say 'employee well-being is an absolute priority'.

Resilience

Resilience is another modern cultural phenomenon. It's like vulnerability; something that it is good for leaders to think about, focus on and get better at. No one could deny that leaders need an element of toughness to be able to endure the battering they receive from all quarters. But again I ask you to be wary of manufacturing something rather than being truly authentic. Promoting increased resilience as the solution to handling workplace stress and pressure is like prescribing steroids for a persistent cold. It is the same thinking as we seem to collectively apply to pretty much all health conditions caused by the way we live – we prescribe antidepressants when people are feeling down, and antibiotics

> *Promoting increased resilience as the solution to handling workplace stress and pressure is like prescribing steroids for a persistent cold.*

when people are feeling sick. In pursuing this strategy, we've created a real problem for ourselves, since the pills and injections are not working anymore. We always fail to tackle the root cause.

So rather than helping your people become more resilient, how about working to reduce the pressure and stress they are feeling? Rather than abdicating your responsibility to the people in your charge, making them get tougher in their endurance of stress, how about working on the environment you are creating and fostering?

Believing in People – Pygmalion and Golem

One of my absolute advantages and assets as a leader is that I have an unshakeable faith in people – in their ability and their desire to learn, to grow, to develop, to take responsibility (for themselves and others), to act ethically, to do the right things, to subordinate themselves to the cause, to be tough when they need to and compassionate when they need to, to be fabulous. To me people are beautiful, flawed geniuses. My faith in human nature is my God. And it has never ever let me down. Individual people let us down occasionally, people disappoint us occasionally, but are we not allowed to be human? If that behaviour is serial then maybe we can't be in relationship (since I am clearly not right for you either, but someone will be . . .) – if this cause is not for you, that's fine, but you now need to go and find a cause that you can give yourself to.

Now I understand that this can all sound a bit cult-like and we certainly need to be aware that our egos can start taking things very seriously. Pomposity is neither pretty nor effective. But the only reason we would not be able to get people excited about our cause is if there is actually nothing to get excited about – if our company serves no real purpose or adds no real value. Leaving things like cigarettes and arms aside, there are not many products that I cannot see the value in. I may rail against the rampant consumerism of needless consumption and disposability which is fuelled by capitalism, but I don't for example have a problem per se with luxury cars even though my socialist bone marrow shouts for us all to be driving Fords. My wife Rachel taught me, in an echo of both Karl Marx and Janis Joplin, that real socialists don't want to get the rich out of their Mercedes and into Fords, real socialists believe everyone should have a Mercedes. Let's not dumb down to the lowest common denominator, let's lift everyone to the highest quality.

So if every company has a purpose, then every company can achieve a culture whereby every single employee is a passionate evangelist for the cause – for the products and services, for the customers, and for the future destiny of the business.

One of my favourite leadership quotes was written about Ernest Shackleton. And this is what I profoundly believe to be true:

At the core of Shackleton's gift for leadership in crisis was an adamantine conviction that quite ordinary individuals were capable of heroic feats if the circumstances required; the weak and the strong could and must survive together. The mystique that Shackleton acquired as a leader may be partly attributed to the fact that he elicited from his men strength and endurance they had never imagined they possessed. He ennobled them.

Caroline Alexander, 1998

You may have heard of the famous experiment done by Rosenthal and Jacobson in 1965 with a group of Teachers and Pupils. A number of teachers of equal ability were split into two groups. The first group were given a cohort of pupils who were above average intelligence and attitude, and the teachers were openly told this. They were tasked with taking the above average students to an even higher level of performance and it was made plain that the school had very high expectations of both the teachers and the pupils. The second group of teachers were given a cohort of pupils of below average intelligence and attitude, and again the teachers were openly told this. They were tasked with doing their very best with the pupils, but the school accepted that the outcomes would be limited.

Unsurprisingly, when tested at the end of the programme, the first cohort of pupils achieved great results. The teachers had taken them to new heights of performance, and in fact their feedback was that actually the task was not that hard, but they were very proud of themselves and had had a thoroughly enjoyable year. Everyone was really happy. Unsurprisingly the results with the second cohort of pupils were very different, with little if any real progress, and actually with many examples of pupils having regressed, especially in attitude. And the teachers fed back that they had had a somewhat dispiriting year themselves and had even started to doubt their competence as teachers.

All this sounds predictable and perhaps inevitable. And that might be true, if it were not for one critical factor. The school had lied to the teachers about the abilities of the pupils. The pupils were in fact of all the same level of intelligence and attitude. There was no difference in the ability of the two groups. The *only* difference was the expectation of the teachers.

This is also known as the Pygmalion Effect – the phenomenon whereby higher expectations lead to an increase in performance. A corollary of the Pygmalion effect is the Golem effect in which low expectations lead to a decrease in performance; both effects are forms of self-fulfilling prophesy. A leader's expectations of their employees are influenced by their perception of both the challenge at hand, and of the competence and attitude of the followers themselves. Perception and expectation are interestingly found in a similar part of the brain, making us unconscious slaves to our pre-judgements. It's why one of my main exhortations is to believe that people are capable of the most extraordinary achievements and accomplishments, given honest leadership and a decent opportunity.

Boss: *I thought you'd never get here.*

Employee: *That's what took me so long.*

Ethics are all we have and all we are

Where is morality in our corporate worlds? What is it to be moral? One of the reasons that immoral and unethical actions can be tolerated, ignored or accepted by corporate citizens is that with our emotions dulled, we've become immune to the madness. Reacting with disgust is first and foremost a primal emotion that keeps us from ingesting substances that would be poisonous to our system. Trying to eat something that would make us sick induces a gag reflex, but even before that, our disgust reaction might kick in even from smelling something noxious about the offending substance. '*Ugh, that's disgusting*' we may say, so it is certainly one emotion we can name and own very easily. But disgust has also evolved through into our 'higher' human emotions, as a negative reaction to immoral behaviours.

We *know* when we are witnessing unethical policies, strategies, decisions and behaviours. Our body tells us, even if our cognitive mind is too controlling for us to consciously acknowledge it. We *know* when we ourselves are the objects of unethical behaviour – when we are being manipulated, coerced, bribed, threatened. Our body tells us, even as our brain persuades us that it's all perfectly normal.

And what constitutes a 'moral' profit? What is the legitimate return for the value our company adds in the supply chain? Occasionally businesses hit a purple patch and produce 'excess profits', but these quickly become the norm in terms of the expectations of our owners and the agents that wind them up. If those excess profits are returned to shareholders in a special cash dividend, then there is some logic and equity in that, and it is a clear communication that such profits cannot be repeated. But 'expecting' returns outside the norm over the long run? Where's the morality in that? Drop the price to the consumer; raise the remuneration of the employees; put money back into the community that is providing the profits; fill the hole in the pension fund at the very least! Anything else is just stealing. That excess return does not legitimately belong to us, so let it flow through and do some good.

Morality in the corporate world is making a reasonable, sustainable return from a wholly legitimate place adding real value in the supply chain. And we have to believe in and actively promote morality, since regulation can be usurped and side-stepped by clever legal and accounting devices, and since the enforcement of the law merely manifests in fines that can be built into the 'cost of doing business'. Fines don't work.

> *Morality in the corporate world is making a reasonable, sustainable return from a wholly legitimate place adding real value in the supply chain.*

A Willingness to lead

So this is where it all lands, where it all manifests. What are we going to do? And who is brave enough to go first?

We have to have some faith to even initiate the starting of the process. We have to trust – if we could prove it, we wouldn't need to trust – trust is not in the outcome, trust is in the intention and commitment of the person taking the act.

Empowerment is not and cannot be a passive act in that we give something away and then have no control over what people do with it. We cannot simply trust that people will do the right things through some sort of telepathy. People need vast and consistent amounts of encouragement, licence and permission. Empowerment is not an act that we do *to* someone else – we cannot empower people, just as we can't happy them.

The real risk in all of this is that we fall into the trap of believing that one man, one woman cannot make a difference. But this is the convenient inertia that sustains the status quo. We have to believe, not that one man or one woman can change the world, but that we can change our piece of the world, right here, right now. And we have to be willing to go first – we have to be willing to lead.

The management 'guru' Peter Senge wrote this in his introduction to Joseph Jaworski's 1996 book *Synchronicity: The Inner Path of Leadership*:

In the West we tend to think of leadership as a quality that exists in certain people. This usual way of thinking has many traps. We search for special individuals with leadership potential, rather than developing the leadership potential in everyone. We are easily distracted by what this or that leader is doing, by the melodrama of people in power trying to maintain their power and others trying to wrest it from them. When things are going poorly, we blame the situation on incompetent leaders, thereby avoiding any personal responsibility. When things become desperate, we can easily find ourselves waiting for a great leader to rescue us. Through all of this, we totally miss the bigger question: what are we collectively, able to create?

I do of course promote and endorse the highest standards of leadership, accepting that single individuals will always be massively influential. Demonstrating courage, leading with true authenticity, a willingness to inspire, to be great without being arrogant, to identify the deeper, nobler cause – of course these things are important, but they can feel revolutionary, simply too big and scary to contemplate.

Right here, right now there is just you, and you can lead.

> **Leadership is an act, not a state. Speaking up is leading. Being curious and asking a question is leading. Saying 'I'm not sure' is leading.**

Leadership is an act, not a state. Speaking up is leading. Being curious and asking a question is leading. Saying 'I'm not sure' is leading. Giving people space, encouragement, licence and permission is leading. I am not denying nor seeking to downplay the courage that is required to take these simple acts. Yet they are simple acts.

Take one.

Notes

Pink, D (2011) *Drive: The Surprising Truth About What Motivates Us.* Edinburgh: Canongate.

Stephen Karpman The drama triangle is a social model that was conceived by Stephen Karpman, a student studying under Eric Berne, the father of transactional analysis. Berne encouraged Karpman to publish what Berne referred to as 'Karpman's triangle'.

Berne, E (2016) *Games People Play: The Psychology of Human Relationships.* London: Penguin Life. (First published 1964)

Rachel Young My wife, referenced in Chapter 6.

Alexander, C (1999) *The Endurance: Shackleton's Legendary Antarctic Expedition*, Sleeve Notes. London: Bloomsbury Publishing.

Rosenthal–Jacobson Study Rosenthal, R and Jacobson, L (1968) *Pygmalion in the Classroom: Teacher Expectation and Pupils' Intellectual Development.* New York: Holt Rinehart and Winston.

Pygmalion Effect The Pygmalion Effect, or Rosenthal Effect, is named after the Greek myth of Pygmalion, a sculptor who fell in love with a statue he had carved, or alternately, after the Rosenthal–Jacobson study (see above). By the Pygmalion effect, people internalise their positive labels, and those with positive labels succeed accordingly.

Golem Effect By the Golem Effect, low expectations cause a decrease in performance. The Golem was a clay creature from Jewish mythology, created to protect the Jews of Prague. However, over time, the Golem grew more and more corrupt and had to be destroyed. The effect of low expectations causing lower performance was named after the Golem legend in 1982 by Babad, Inbar, and Rosenthal as it represented the negative effects of self-fulfilling prophecies.

Peter Senge Peter Senge is an American systems scientist, senior lecturer at the MIT Sloan School of Management and Founder of the Society for Organizational Learning. His best-known work is *The Fifth Discipline: The Art and Practice of the Learning Organization*.

Jaworski, J (1996) *Synchronicity: The Inner Path of Leadership.* San Francisco: Berrett-Koehler.

INDEX

Scrooge crept towards it, trembling as he went; and following the finger, read upon the stone of the neglected grave his own name, EBENEZER SCROOGE. 'Spirit!' he cried, tight clutching at its robe, 'hear me. I am not the man I was. I will not be the man I must have been but for this intercourse. Why show me this, if I am past all hope?' Scrooge saw his own bedpost. The bed was his own, the room was his own. Best and happiest of all, the Time before him was his own, to make amends in!

Charles Dickens, *A Christmas Carol*

"And the Leader Is . . . . .Leading Transformatively with CEQ"

Gareth Chick's second book, *And the Leader Is . . . .* will be published by Critical Publishing in March 2019. It is a comprehensive and practical guide in how to lead effectively with heightened Corporate Emotional Intelligence (CEQ). Drawing on his 40 year experience of every aspect of the Corporate World, from CEO to Coach; from manager to trainer, Gareth Chick covers the fundamental management and leadership competencies of coaching, high performance teams, authentic leadership and transformational change.

In his first book *Corporate Emotional Intelligence*, Gareth provided a compelling analysis of Corporate Psychology; giving us a profound new understanding of how working in the Corporate World causes thoroughly decent human beings to behave in unnatural and inhuman ways. The book concluded by outlining the 4 Pillars of Corporate Emotional Intelligence (CEQ), equipping us with strategies to raise our personal leadership effectiveness. *And the Leader Is . . . .* completes Gareth's personal corporate life mission to give hard pressed modern leaders and managers the practical competencies to be more effective, more fulfilled and more sustainable.

Whilst each book stands on its own merits, the combination of the two forms arguably the most important work on corporate leadership since Dr Edwards Demings' writings of the late 20th Century. It is fitting therefore that the Foreword for *And the Leader Is . . . .* is written by Tony Barnes, the youngest, and the last surviving member of the Deming team that revolutionised Japanese business and manufacturing practices in the 1950s and 1960s.

You can order *And the Leader is . . . . .* by Gareth Chick at www.criticalpublishing.com

Other titles you might be interested in:

Non-directive Coaching: Attitudes, Approaches and Applications
Bob Thomson,
ISBN 978-1-909330-57-3   192pp   April 2013

Dial M for Mentor: Critical Reflections on Mentoring for Coaches, Educators and Trainers
Jonathan Gravells and Susan Wallace
ISBN 978-1-909330-00-9   152pp   September 2012

Titles are also available in a range of electronic formats. To order please go to our website www.criticalpublishing.com or contact our distributor NBN International, 10 Thornbury Road, Plymouth PL6 7PP, telephone 01752 202301 or email orders@nbninternational.com